Living American Documents

Selected and Edited by

ISIDORE STARR
Teacher of American History, New York, New York

LEWIS PAUL TODD
Editor, Social Education, Official Journal of
The National Council for the Social Studies

MERLE CURTI
Frederick Jackson Turner Professor
of American History, University of Wisconsin

HARCOURT, BRACE & WORLD, INC.
New York   Chicago   Atlanta   Dallas   Burlingame

Foreword

What do the editors of *Living American Documents* mean by the word *document?* Why do they include Magna Carta and other landmarks of English history in a collection of *American* documents? And by what stretch of imagination do they refer to a dry and dusty record of the past as a *living* document?

These are reasonable questions. We shall answer them in a moment. But there are two other questions it might be well to anticipate before we go any further: With the curriculum already bursting at the seams from the increasingly heavy load it must carry, why should a high school student be asked to devote part of his time to documents? And if he is on occasion required to examine a historic document, how can he get a maximum return from his effort?

The term *document* defies easy definition. *Webster's New International Dictionary* defines the term "in its most extended sense" as "any writing, book, or other instrument conveying information." In a way, then, this book is a document, and so is the single sheet of paper on which these words are now being written. But *Webster's* also offers the more restricted definition of a document as "an original or official paper relied upon as the basis, proof, or support of anything else." It is this more restricted definition that the editors had in mind when they prepared the present collection.

Each of the documents here included is an "original or official" statement which stands as a bench mark in the story of American progress and, in a larger sense, in mankind's upward march toward freedom. For this reason, the editors chose to present the documents in chronological order. The collection includes Magna Carta, The Petition of Right, The Habeas Corpus Act of the English Parliament, and The English Bill of Rights because these famous English documents contain ideas and ideals that helped to shape, and now lie at the heart of, what we call "the American way of life." These documents record decisive steps in the development of representative government and in man's ceaseless quest for individual liberty and for equal rights and opportunities under law. Time and again, Americans have turned to Magna Carta and other English documents for inspiration and guidance.

Now it is all well and good to speak of "inspiration and guidance." The fact remains that with certain exceptions, such as the Declaration of Independence, official papers are written in dull, legalistic language which proves to be anything but inspiring to most readers. This being the case, how do the editors justify the use of the adjective *living* to describe documents long since yellow with age and crumbling into dust?

There is no more "life" in a document as such than there is "sound" when a tree falls in a remote forest far from any human habitation. Although the falling tree creates vibrations in the air, there is nothing we call sound until these vibrations are recorded on an eardrum. Even then, the sound of a falling tree has little meaning unless the person who hears it can identify the sound and, through his imagination, supply a mental picture of what is actually taking place in the forest.

So it is with a document, with a dry and dusty record out of the past. The eye can scan the printed page, and the mind can comprehend the meaning of the words, but it remains for the imagination to put the document in its real setting and to surround it with the flesh-and-blood people who took an active part in an exciting and dramatic episode in history.

So far as possible, the editors of this collection have tried to assist the student in his main job of *reading* each document. In some cases, the complete document is given; in others, certain sections that are no longer relevant or were at best irrelevant to the central issues have been deleted. In every case, the spelling and punctuation have been modernized and difficult or obsolete terms have been defined in bracketed portions of the text or in footnotes. Finally, in the brief headnotes that preface each of the documents in this book, the editors have identified the documents in terms of time and place and have located them in the main stream of the nation's development.

Editing and headnotes can help to open the door of history, but it remains for the teacher and the student to fling the door wide by providing the historical background for the document in question. Only an informed imagination can picture the barons at Runnymede confronting their king with a list of minimum demands; the *May-*

flower with sails furled rolling on a leaden sea while the Pilgrim Fathers gather in the tiny ship's cabin to sign their now historic *Compact;* or the loyal remnants of Washington's army reading Thomas Paine's *The Crisis* as they huddle for warmth around their campfires on the snow-covered banks of the Delaware River. No one can supply for another the thing we call an informed imagination. Each student must do this for himself. And this he can do by relating each of the documents to the concrete events and the continuing narrative of American history.

There is, of course, more to be gained from the use of documents than the recapturing of significant moments from the history of free men. Documents also provide the opportunity to practice and develop skills essential to critical thinking. We refer to those skills the historian uses when he employs the historical method to distinguish between the true and the false, to separate fact from opinion, and to evaluate the evidence from which he in the end will draw conclusions. It is hardly necessary to point out that every individual is confronted with the need for exercising these skills every day of his life, in matters both large and small. To the extent that he handles them well, he becomes a reasonable and responsible person. The importance of these skills cannot be overemphasized in a world that is so desperately in need of the guiding hand of intelligence.

I. S.

L. P. T.

M. C.

Contents

PART TWO

The Nation Divided

PART THREE
The Nation Reunited

PART FOUR
The Nation As a World Leader

INTRODUCTION

The Colonial Period

On a winter day, in the year 1606, three small ships weighed anchor in London Harbor and moved with the ebbing tide down the Thames River and out upon the open sea. Aboard the vessels were the men, a mere handful, who would build at Jamestown, Virginia, the first permanent English settlement on the continent of North America.

These first settlers, and the thousands of others who followed them across the Atlantic, carried British ideals and traditions to the New World where, during the colonial period, they established the basic institutions of what we now call "the American way of life."

Magna Carta

"To none will we sell ... deny
... delay right or justice."

More than seven hundred years have passed since that dramatic moment in 1215 when a group of bold English barons, determined at any cost to limit the power of King John, forced him to sign the Magna Carta. This ancient document, brittle and yellow with age, has been preserved as a priceless treasure, cherished not only in England, not only in the Western World, but by all men everywhere who believe that only under law can men be truly free.

In the Great Charter, the king agreed to certain limitations on his powers. Although the document did not protect the common people, it did represent a milestone in the history of human rights, for it served as a precedent for the growth of constitutional government. Evidence of how greatly American thinking was influenced by this document can be found in an examination of its provisions for due process of law,° freedom of movement, and taxation only with the consent of the legislature.

June 15, 1215

John, by the grace of God, King of England, Lord of Ireland, Duke of Normandy and Aquitaine, and Earl of Anjou: to his archbishops, bishops, abbots, earls, barons, justiciaries [royal judiciary officers], foresters, sheriffs, governors, officers, and to all bailiffs [sheriff's deputies], and his faithful subjects—*Greeting*.

Know ye, that we, in the presence of God, ... have confirmed [given assurance], for us and our heirs forever:

° *due process of law:* in this case freedom from arbitrary arrest and unreasonable searches and seizures.

2

1. That the English Church shall be free, and shall have her whole rights and her liberties inviolable [safe from sudden change]; . . .

We have also granted to all the freemen of our kingdom, for us and our heirs forever, all the underwritten liberties, to be enjoyed and held by them and by their heirs, from us and from our heirs. . . .

12. No scutage [tax for military purposes] nor aid ° shall be imposed in our kingdom, unless by the common council of our kingdom; excepting to redeem [ransom] our person, to make our eldest son a knight, and once to marry our eldest daughter, and not for these unless a reasonable aid shall be demanded. . . .

14. And also to have the common council of the kingdom, we will cause to be summoned the archbishops, bishops, abbots, earls, and great barons, individually by our letters. . . .

38. No bailiff, for the future, shall put any man to his law upon his own simple affirmation, without credible witnesses produced for that purpose.°

39. No freeman shall be seized, imprisoned, dispossessed [deprived of his land], outlawed, or exiled, or in any way destroyed; nor will we proceed against or prosecute him except by the lawful judgment of his peers [equals], or by the law of the land.

40. To none will we sell, to none will we deny, to none will we delay right or justice.

41. All merchants shall have safety and security in coming into England, and going out of England, and in staying in and traveling through England, as well by land as by water to buy and sell, without any unjust exactions [demands], according to ancient and right customs, excepting in the time of war, and if they be of a country at war against us; and if such are found in our land at the beginning of a war, they shall be apprehended [arrested] without injury to their bodies and goods until it be known to us or to our Chief Justiciary how the merchants of our country are treated who are found in the country at war against us; and if ours be in safety there, the others shall be in safety in our land.

42. It shall be lawful to any person, for the future, to go out of our kingdom, and to return, safely and securely by land or by water, sav-

---

° *aid:* a tax or payment paid by a vassal to a feudal lord.

° *credible witnesses produced for that purpose:* No bailiff can arrest anyone on the basis of what he himself believes. He must have the testimony of reliable witnesses that the arrested person has committed an offense.

ing [preserving] his allegiance to us, unless it be in time of war, for some short space, for the common good of the kingdom: ...

60. Also all these customs and liberties aforesaid, which we have granted to be held in our kingdom, for so much of it as belongs to us, all our subjects, as well clergy as laity [nonclergy, or laymen], shall observe toward their tenants as far as concerns them. ...

63. Wherefore our will is, and we firmly command that the Church of England be free, and that the men in our kingdom have and hold the aforesaid liberties, rights, and concessions, well and in peace, freely and quietly, fully and entirely, to them and their heirs, of us and our heirs, in all things and places forever, as is aforesaid. It is also sworn, both on our part and on that of the barons, that all the aforesaid shall be observed in good faith and without any evil intention. ...

Given by our hand in the meadow which is called Runnymede, between Windsor and Staines, this 15th day of June, in the 17th year of our reign.

The Mayflower Compact

"... to enact ... just and equal laws ...
for the general good of the colony...."

On November 11, 1620, the storm-battered vessel bearing the Pilgrims to the lonely shores of the New World sailed in from the open sea and dropped anchor in the chill waters of what is now Provincetown Harbor. The Mayflower was far off its course, and the Pilgrims had no legal right to settle in New England or to establish a government. But they had no choice, for winter was close at hand, and the colony had to be started. Confronted by the need for action, the Pilgrim leaders drafted the Mayflower Compact. Later, the men gathered in the smoke-blackened cabin of the ship and, in the flickering light of a fish-oil lamp, signed their names to the now historic document.

The Mayflower Compact became an important landmark along the road leading to democracy. True, it did not extend the privilege of participating in government to others besides the Pilgrims themselves. True, it did not outline, or even attempt to outline, a plan of government. But—and this is the significant point—the Compact did commit the Pilgrims to the creation of a government based on the consent of the governed.

November 11, 1620

In the name of God, Amen. We whose names are underwritten, the loyal subjects of our dread [revered and feared] sovereign Lord King *James*, by the grace of God, of Great Britain, France, and Ireland, King, Defender of the Faith, etc., having undertaken, for the glory of God, and advancement of the Christian faith, and honor of our king and country, a voyage to plant the first colony in the northern parts of Virginia, do by these presents [this document] solemnly and mutually in the presence of God, and one of another, covenant [promise] and combine ourselves together into a civil body politic [group organized for government] for our better ordering and preservation and furtherance of the ends aforesaid; and by virtue [authority] hereof, to enact, constitute, and frame such just and equal laws, ordinances [regulations], acts, constitutions, and offices from time to time, as shall be thought most meet [fitting] and convenient for the general good of the colony unto which we promise all due submission and obedience.

In WITNESS whereof we have hereunto subscribed our names at Cape Cod, the eleventh of November, in the year of the reign of our sovereign Lord King James of England, France, and Ireland the eighteenth, and of Scotland the fifty-fourth. *Anno Domini*, 1620.

[Signed by forty-one men on the *Mayflower*.]

JOHN CARVER	ISAAC ALLERTON	FRANCIS EATON
WILLIAM BRADFORD	MILES STANDISH	JAMES CHILTON
EDWARD WINSLOW	JOHN ALDEN	JOHN CRAXTON
WILLIAM BREWSTER	JOHN TURNER	JOHN BILLINGTON

JOSES FLETCHER
JOHN GOODMAN
SAMUEL FULLER
CHRISTOPHER MARTIN
WILLIAM MULLINS
WILLIAM WHITE
RICHARD WARREN
JOHN HOWLAND
STEPHEN HOPKINS
DIGERY PRIEST

THOMAS WILLIAMS
GILBERT WINSLOW
EDMUND MARGESSON
PETER BROWN
RICHARD BITTERIDGE
GEORGE SOULE
EDWARD TILLY
JOHN TILLY
FRANCIS COOKE
THOMAS ROGERS

THOMAS TINKER
JOHN RIDGATE
EDWARD FULLER
RICHARD CLARK
RICHARD GARDINER
JOHN ALLERTON
THOMAS ENGLISH
EDWARD DOTEN
EDWARD LIESTER

The Petition of Right

*". . . no . . . tax . . . without common
consent by act of Parliament. . . ."*

The English kings of the 1600's either had poor memories or preferred to forget the royal promises of the past contained in Magna Carta. It was only a few years after the settlement of Jamestown, Virginia, that the conflict between the Stuart kings and Parliament over the rights of Englishmen bordered on violence.

The arbitrary actions of Charles I—illegal taxes, quartering of troops, and arbitrary arrests and imprisonment—led Parliament to draw up this famous statement of their grievances, which he accepted. This petition for the protection of civil liberties and for recognition of the principle of taxation only with the consent of the legislature influenced the thinking of many who settled in America.

The document throws light on what the colonists meant by the "rights of Englishmen," and it is not surprising that the right to petition was made a part of our Bill of Rights.

June 7, 1628

To the King's Most Excellent Majesty:

I. . . . WHEREAS, It is declared and enacted by a statute made in the time of the reign of King Edward the First . . . that no tallage ° or aid should be laid or levied by the king or his heirs in this realm without the goodwill and assent of the archbishops, bishops, earls, barons, knights, burgesses, and . . . the freemen of the commonalty [the common people] of this realm; and by authority of the Parliament . . . [in] the reign of King Edward III it is declared and enacted that from thenceforth no person . . . [shall] be compelled to make any loans to the king against his will,

II. Yet, nevertheless . . . your people have been . . . required to lend certain sums of money to your Majesty; . . .

III. AND WHEREAS ALSO, By the statute called the Great Charter of the Liberties of England, it is declared and enacted that no freeman may be taken or imprisoned, . . . or be outlawed or exiled or in any manner destroyed, but by the lawful judgment of his peers or by the law of the land.

IV. And in . . . the reign of King Edward III it was declared and enacted by authority of Parliament that no man . . . should be put out of his land . . . nor imprisoned, nor disinherited, nor put to death, without being brought to answer by due process of law.

V. Nevertheless . . . divers [several] of your subjects have of late been imprisoned without any cause showed; . . .

VI. AND WHEREAS . . . great companies of soldiers and mariners have been dispersed into divers counties of the realm, and the inhabitants against their wills have been compelled to receive them into their houses. . . .

VII. AND WHEREAS ALSO . . . it is declared and enacted that no man should be forejudged of life or limb against the form of the Great

° *tallage:* a tax levied by a feudal lord on a tenant, sometimes in place of required services.

Charter and the law of the land; ... nevertheless of late divers commissions ... have issued forth, by which certain persons have been assigned and appointed commissioners, with power and authority to proceed within the land according to the justice of martial law ° ...

VIII. By pretext whereof some of your Majesty's subjects have been by some of the said commissioners put to death. ...

IX. Upon pretense that the said offenders were punishable only by martial law ... which commissions ... are wholly and directly contrary to the said laws and statutes of this your realm:

X. They [your subjects] do therefore humbly pray your most excellent Majesty that no man hereafter be compelled to make or yield any gift, loan, benevolence,° tax, or such like charge without common consent by act of Parliament; and that none be called to make answer, or take such oath, or give attendance, or be confined, or otherwise molested ... concerning the same, or for refusal thereof; and that no freeman ... be imprisoned or detained; and that your Majesty would be pleased to remove the said soldiers and mariners; and that your people may not be burdened in time to come; and that the aforesaid commissions for proceeding by martial law may be revoked and annulled; and that hereafter no commissions of like nature may issue forth. ...

XI. ... and that your Majesty would be also graciously pleased, for the further comfort and safety of your people, to declare your royal will and pleasure that in the things aforesaid all your officers and ministers shall serve you according to the laws and statutes of this realm, as they tender the honor of your Majesty and the prosperity of this kingdom.

° *martial law:* rules of law which are carried out by the military authorities, not by the civil authorities.
°*benevolence:* a special tax which the English kings imposed for their own benefit.

The Fundamental Orders of Connecticut

*"... to maintain the peace ... there should
be an orderly ... government established...."*

The British people do not have a written constitution. They have an "unwritten" constitution composed of customs, traditions, and important documents such as their Magna Carta and their Bill of Rights (pages 2 and 21).

Some of the Englishmen who settled in the American colonies, including the men who founded the colony of Connecticut in 1636, did not have much faith in this approach to government. Unpleasant memories of recent authoritarian acts by England's rulers prompted the Connecticut settlers to put their plan of government into writing.

The Fundamental Orders of Connecticut was the first written constitution in America. Whereas the Mayflower Compact was a general statement in favor of majority rule and government in the interest of the common welfare, the Fundamental Orders set up a detailed scheme of government in which sovereign power rested with the freemen. No mention was made of the king.

This document was a step in the direction of present-day democracy in that it set the example of a written constitution as the basis of government—a constitution which could be read and understood by all and which could not be changed by the will of one man or a small group.

January 14, 1639

... we, the inhabitants and residents of Windsor, Hartford, and Wethersfield ... knowing where a people are gathered together the word of God requires that to maintain the peace and union of such a people there should be an orderly and decent government established according to God ... therefore associate ... ourselves to be as one public state or commonwealth; and do, for ourselves and our successors ... enter into combination and confederation [union] together, to maintain and preserve the liberty and purity of the gospel of our Lord, Jesus, which we now profess ... and also in our civil affairs to be guided and governed according to such laws, rules, orders, and decrees as shall be made, ordered, and decreed, as follows:

1. It is ordered ... that there shall be yearly two general assemblies or courts: The one the second Thursday in April, the other the second Thursday in September, following. The first shall be called the Court of Election, wherein shall be yearly chosen ... so many magistrates and other public officers as shall be found requisite whereof one to be chosen governor for the year ensuing and until another be chosen, and no other magistrate to be chosen for more than one year provided always there be six chosen besides the governor; which being chosen and sworn according to an oath recorded for that purpose shall have power to administer justice according to the laws here established, and for want thereof according to the rule of the word of God; which choice shall be made by all that are admitted freemen and have taken the oath of fidelity ° ... (having been admitted inhabitants by the major part of the town wherein they live) or the major part of such as shall be then present. ...

4. It is ordered ... that no person be chosen governor above [more than] once in two years, and that the governor be always a member of some approved congregation, and formerly of the magistracy within this jurisdiction; and all the magistrates freemen of this commonwealth; ...

5. It is ordered ... that to the aforesaid Court of Election the several towns shall send their deputies, and when the elections are ended they may proceed in any public service as at other courts. Also the other General Court in September shall be for making of laws, and other public occasion [business], which concerns the good of the commonwealth. ...

° *oath of fidelity:* an oath that called for strict adherence to the Trinity, or the Trinitarian doctrine.

7. It is ordered . . . that after there are warrants given out for any of the said general courts, the constable . . . of each town shall forthwith give notice distinctly to the inhabitants of the same . . . that at a place and time by him or them limited and set, they meet and assemble . . . to elect and choose certain deputies to be at the General Court then following to agitate [discuss in public] the affairs of the commonwealth; . . . deputies shall be chosen by all that are admitted inhabitants in the several towns and have taken the oath of fidelity; provided that none be chosen a deputy for any general court who is not a freeman of this commonwealth. . . .

8. It is ordered . . . that Windsor, Hartford, and Wethersfield shall have power, each town . . . to send four of their freemen as their deputies to every general court; and whatsoever other towns shall be hereafter added to this jurisdiction . . . shall send so many deputies as the court shall judge meet . . . which deputies shall have the power of the whole town to give their votes and allowance to all such laws and orders as may be for the public good, and unto which the said towns are to be bound.

9. It is ordered . . . that the deputies thus chosen shall have power and liberty to appoint a time and a place of meeting to gather before any general court to advise and consult of all such things as may concern the good of the public, as also to examine their own elections. . . .

10. It is ordered . . . that every general court . . . shall consist of the governor, or someone chosen to moderate [preside over] the court, and four other magistrates at least, with the major part of the deputies of the several towns legally chosen; and in case the freemen or major part of them, through neglect or refusal of the governor and major part of the magistrates, shall call a court, it shall consist of the major part of freemen that are present or their deputies, with a moderator chosen by them; in which said general courts shall consist [exist] the supreme power of the commonwealth, and they only shall have power to make laws or repeal them, to grant levies, to admit . . . freemen, dispose of lands undisposed of to several towns or persons, and . . . shall have power to call either court or magistrate or any other person whatsoever into question for any misdemeanor, and may for just causes displace [remove from office] or deal otherwise according to the nature of the offense; and . . . may deal . . . [with]

any other matter that concerns the good of this commonwealth, except election of magistrates, which shall be done by the whole body of freemen.

In which court the governor or moderator shall have power to order the court to give liberty of speech, and [to] silence ... disorderly speakings, to put all things to vote, and in case the vote be equal to have the casting voice [deciding vote]. But none of these courts shall be adjourned or dissolved without the consent of the major part of the court.

11. It is ordered ... that when any general court ... has agreed upon any ... sums of money to be levied upon the several towns within this jurisdiction ... a committee be chosen to set out and appoint what shall be the proportion of every town to pay of the said levy, provided the committees be made up of an equal number out of each town.

The Massachusetts School Laws

*"... that learning may not be buried ...
teach ... children ... to write and read...."*

① The first law dealing with education in the American colonies (1642) required all parents to teach their children a trade and how to read well enough to understand the Bible
② and the laws. Five years later, a second law was passed requiring every town of fifty householders to hire a teacher of reading and writing; and every town of one hundred householders was ordered to provide a college preparatory school.

Writing exactly two hundred years later, Horace Mann, the great educator, declared that "the Act of 1647 laid the foundation of our present system of free schools." Certainly this daring step has turned out to be one of the greatest advances in the fulfillment of the democratic dream.

April 14, 1642, and November 11, 1647

April 14, 1642

This Court, taking into consideration the great neglect of many parents and masters in training ... their children in learning and labor ... which may be profitable to the commonwealth, does hereupon order and decree, that in every town the chosen men appointed for managing the prudential [advisory] affairs of the same shall henceforth stand charged with the ... redress [setting right] of this evil ... and for this end they, or the greater number of them, shall have power to take account from time to time of all parents and masters, and of their children ... especially of their ability to read and understand the principles of religion and the capital laws of this country, and to impose fines upon such as shall refuse to render such accounts to them when they shall be required; and they shall have power, with consent of any court or the magistrate, to put forth [as] apprentices the children of such as they shall find not to be able and fit to employ and bring them up. . . .

November 11, 1647

It being one chief project of the old deluder [deceiver], Satan, to keep men from the knowledge of the Scriptures ... that learning may not be buried in the grave of our fathers in the church and commonwealth, the Lord assisting our endeavors,

It is therefore ordered that every township in this jurisdiction [sphere of authority], after the Lord has increased their number to fifty householders, shall then forthwith appoint one ... in their town to teach all such children as shall resort [go] to him to write and read; whose wages shall be paid either by their parents or masters of such children, or by the inhabitants in general; ... and it is further ordered that where any town shall increase to the number of one hundred families or householders, they shall set up a grammar school °

College Prep.

° **grammar school:** a college preparatory school where Latin and Greek were taught.

... to instruct youth so far as they shall be fitted for the <u>university</u>, provided that if any town neglect the performance hereof above one year, that every such town shall pay five pounds to the next school <u>till they shall perform this order.</u>

Roger Williams' "The Bloody Tenet of Persecution for Cause of Conscience"

"... God requires not a uniformity of religion ... the ... foundation of civil power lies in the people ..."

Roger Williams knew what it meant to be a nonconformist in a colony where the union of church and state dictated what men should believe and think. Possessed of the courage of his convictions, he spent his life in a crusade to protect the dignity and integrity of each individual from the tyranny of the majority.

Persecuted for his beliefs by the church-centered government of Massachusetts, he fled from the colony and in 1634 founded Rhode Island. There, in word and deed, he pursued his ideals.

Later, in 1644, while on a visit to England he wrote a treatise, The Bloody Tenet,° dealing with his favorite themes: separation of church and state, religious freedom for all, and government by consent of the governed. The language and manner of expression sound strange to twentieth-century ears, but the ideals Roger Williams proclaimed ring clear and true to all who believe in democracy.

° **tenet:** In the original document the word "tenent" is used, but this is now obsolete. *Tenet* means principle, belief, or dogma.

1644

PREFACE

First. That the blood of so many hundred thousand souls of Protestants and Papists, spilt in the wars of present and former ages, for their respective consciences, is not required nor accepted by Jesus Christ, the Prince of Peace.

Second. Pregnant [weighty] Scriptures and arguments are throughout the work proposed against the doctrine of persecution for the cause of conscience.

Third. Satisfactory answers are given to scriptures and objections produced by Mr. Calvin, Beza, Mr. Cotton, and the ministers of the New England churches and others former and later, tending to prove the doctrine of persecution for the cause of conscience.

Fourth. The doctrine of persecution for cause of conscience is proved guilty of all the blood of the souls crying for vengeance under the altar.

Fifth. All civil ° states with their officers of justice in their respective constitutions and administrations are proved essentially civil, and therefore not judges, governors, or defenders of the spiritual, or Christian, state and worship.

Sixth. It is the will and command of God that (since the coming of his Son, the Lord Jesus) a permission of the most pagan, Jewish, Turkish, or anti-Christian consciences and worships be granted to all men in all nations and countries: and they are only to be fought against with that sword which is only (in soul matters) able to conquer, to wit [that is] the sword of God's Spirit, the Word of God.

Seventh. The state of the land of Israel, the kings and people thereof in peace and war, is proved figurative and ceremonial [outwardly conventional] and no pattern nor precedent for any kingdom or civil state in the world to follow.

Eighth. God requires not a uniformity of religion to be enacted and enforced in any civil state; . . . [such] enforced uniformity (soone or later) is the greatest occasion [cause] of civil war, ravishing [forcible change] of conscience, persecution of Christ Jesus in his servants, and of the hypocrisy and destruction of millions of souls.

° *civil:* civic as distinguished from naval, military, or ecclesiastical.

16 BLOODY TENET OF PERSECUTION

Ninth. In holding an enforced uniformity of religion in a civil state, we must necessarily disclaim our desires and hopes of the Jew's conversion to Christ.

Tenth. An enforced uniformity of religion throughout a nation or civil state confounds [brings to nothing] the civil and religious, denies the principles of Christianity and civility [civilized conduct] and that Jesus Christ is come in the flesh.

Eleventh. The permission of other consciences and worships than a state professes only can (according to God) procure a firm and lasting peace (good assurance being taken according to the wisdom of the civil state for uniformity of civil obedience from all sorts).

Twelfth. Lastly, true civility and Christianity may both flourish in a state or kingdom, notwithstanding the permission of divers and contrary consciences, either of Jew or Gentile.

... I infer ... that the ... foundation of civil power lies in the people ... and if so, that a people may erect and establish what form of government seems to them most meet for their civil condition. It is evident that such governments as are by them erected and established, have no more power ... than the civil power or people consenting and agreeing shall entrust them with. This is clear not only in reason but in the experience of all commonwealths where the people are not deprived of their natural freedom by the power of tyrants....

And if so, that the magistrates receive their power of governing the church, from the people; undeniably it follows that a people, as a people, naturally considered ... have fundamentally and originally, as men, a power to govern the church, to see her do her duty, to correct her....

The Maryland Toleration Act

*"... no person ... within this province ... professing
to believe in Jesus Christ shall ... henceforth be any
ways troubled, molested, or discountenanced ..."*

The long road to freedom is marked by many impressive
monuments to victory over religious intolerance. One of the
earliest of these monuments is the Maryland Toleration Act.

Lord Baltimore, the Roman Catholic founder of the colony, planted his first settlement on the shores of Chesapeake
Bay in the year 1634. From the beginning, Protestants as well
as Catholics were welcome to settle in Maryland. Finally, in
1649, in order to forestall any possible trouble and to guarantee the continuation of his policy of toleration, Lord Baltimore authorized the legislature to pass a Toleration Act. Although this act spread the mantle of toleration only over
Christians, it was the first law in American history that required the people to permit the existence of religious beliefs
different from those held by the majority.

April 21, 1649

... Be it ... enacted that whatsoever person or persons within
this province ... shall deny our Saviour, Jesus Christ, to be the son
of God, or shall deny the Holy Trinity (the Father, Son, and Holy
Ghost) ... shall be punished with death and confiscation or forfeiture
of all his or her lands. ...

... AND WHEREAS, The enforcing of the conscience ° in matters
of religion has frequently fallen out [turned out] to be of dangerous
consequence in those commonwealths where it has been practiced;
and for the more quiet and peaceable government of this province,

° **enforcing of the conscience:** recognition of the sense of one's obligation to
do right and be good.

and the better to preserve mutual love and amity amongst the inhabitants thereof. Be it therefore ... enacted ... that no person or persons whatsoever within this province ... professing to believe in Jesus Christ shall ... henceforth be any ways troubled, molested, or discountenanced [disapproved of] ... in respect of his or her religion nor in the free exercise thereof within this province ... nor any way compelled to the belief or exercise of any other religion against his or her consent, so as they be not unfaithful to the Lord Proprietary [proprietor], or molest or conspire against the civil government established or to be established in this province under him or his heirs. And that all and every person and persons that shall ... wrong, disturb, trouble, or molest any person whatsoever within this province professing to believe in Jesus Christ ... shall be compelled to pay treble damages to the party so wronged or molested, and for every such offense shall also forfeit twenty shillings sterling in money or the value thereof. ... Or if the parties so offending ... shall refuse or be unable to recompense the party so wronged or to satisfy such fine or forfeiture, then such offender shall be severely punished by public whipping and imprisonment during the pleasure of [as his will dictates] the Lord Proprietary, or his Lieutenant or chief governor of this province. ...

The Rhode Island Colonial Charter

"... no person ... shall be ... molested ...
for any differences in opinion in matters of
religion. ..."

In 1644, ten years after Roger Williams founded the colony of Rhode Island, the English Parliament granted a charter providing for a civil government by "voluntary consent" and elections "by the greatest part" of the people. Later, in 1663, Parliament replaced the original charter. The new charter, although not as democratic as the former one, gave more freedom to more people than existed in any of the other New

England colonies. The 1663 charter was, in fact, the only colonial charter providing for complete religious freedom. It marked a giant step forward in the history of human rights.

1663

... WHEREAS ... they [the colonists] have freely declared ... that a most flourishing civil state may stand and best be maintained ... with a full liberty in religious concernments [affairs] and that true piety rightly grounded upon gospel principles will give the best and greatest security to sovereignty and will lay in the hearts of men the strongest obligations to true loyalty:

Now know ye, that we, being willing to ... secure them in the free exercise and enjoyment of all their civil and religious rights ... and to preserve unto them that liberty, in the true Christian faith and worship of God, which they have sought ... to enjoy; ... do hereby publish, grant, ordain, and declare ... that no person within the said colony, at any time hereafter, shall be any wise molested, punished, disquieted, or called in question for any differences in opinion in matters of religion ... but that all and every person and persons may, from time to time, and at all times hereafter, freely and fully have and enjoy his and their own judgments and consciences in matters of religious concernments. ...

The Habeas Corpus Act
of the English Parliament

*"... if any person ... shall not be indicted ... he
shall be discharged from his imprisonment...."*

In 1679, with the passage of the Habeas Corpus Act, the English Parliament adopted one of the most far-reaching measures in the history of freedom. The law undertook to prevent arbitrary arrest and imprisonment by means of the writ of habeas corpus.°

The writ of habeas corpus is a legal document that compels a jailer to release a person from prison unless that person has been charged with, or convicted of, a crime. The importance of the writ becomes clear when you consider what could happen if this safeguard did not exist. A person could be arrested and held in jail indefinitely without any reason being given. A person could be imprisoned for years without a trial. A person could even be committed to a mental institution without being given an opportunity to prove his sanity.

The suspension of the writ in some of the colonies was one of the serious grievances that led the American colonies to revolt against Great Britain. It is not surprising that when the Constitution was adopted, this important human right was included among its provisions.

1679

... be it enacted ... that whenever any person ... shall bring any habeas corpus ... unto any sheriff ... jailer, minister, or other person ... the said officer ... shall within three days ... bring or cause to be brought the body of the party ... committed or restrained ... before the lord chancellor or lord keeper of the great seal of England ... or the judges or the barons ... or before such other person before whom the said writ is made returnable ° ... and shall ... then certify the true causes of his detainer [being kept in custody] or imprisonment ...

And if any person or persons committed as aforesaid ... shall not be indicted [charged with a crime] some time in the next term sessions ... the judges ... are hereby required upon motion [request for

° *habeas corpus:* a Latin expression meaning literally "you may have the body." Technically, it means that the "body" or person of the accused must be brought before a judge who determines whether or not the accused is being detained legally.

° *before whom ... returnable:* to whom a report concerning the action must be made.

a court ruling] in open court the last day of the term sessions ...
to set at liberty the prisoner upon bail ° ... And if any person or
persons committed as aforesaid ... shall not be indicted and tried
the second sessions ... after his commitment [arrest] ... he shall be
discharged from his imprisonment. ...

The English Bill of Rights

*"... suspending of laws ... without
consent of Parliament is illegal. ..."*

In 1688–89 the English people, weary of the arbitrary actions of their king, drove James II from the throne. The
"Glorious Revolution," as it has been called, brought an end
to the old theory of the divine right of kings and clearly established the principle of the supremacy of Parliament.

Parliament took steps to insure its victory by adopting the
English Bill of Rights. Later, American colonial legislatures
claimed the rights of Englishmen spelled out in this famous
document. And still later, a number of the historic liberties
included in the English Bill of Rights were incorporated in
the Constitution of the United States and in the American
Bill of Rights.

1689

... WHEREAS, The late King James II ... did endeavor to subvert [overthrow] and extirpate [wipe out] the Protestant religion and
the laws and liberties of this kingdom ... and *whereas* the said late
King James II having abdicated [given up] the government, and the
throne being vacant ...

° **bail:** security given to assure appearance of the released upon demand by the
court.

... the said lords ... being now assembled in a full and free representative of this nation, ... do in the first place ... declare:

1. *That* the pretended power of suspending of laws or the execution of laws by regal authority without consent of Parliament is illegal; ...

3. *That* the commission [authority] for erecting the late [recent] court of commissioners for ecclesiastical causes and all other commissions and courts of like nature are illegal and pernicious [corrupt]; ...

4. *That* levying money for or to the use of the crown by pretense of prerogative [right] without grant of Parliament ... is illegal;

5. *That* it is the right of the subjects to petition the king, and all commitments and prosecutions for such petitioning are illegal.

6. *That* ... raising or keeping a standing army within the kingdom in time of peace, unless it be with consent of Parliament, is against law. ...

8. *That* election of members of Parliament ought to be free;

9. *That* the freedom of speech and debates or proceedings in Parliament ought not to be impeached [challenged as to the validity thereof] or questioned in any court or place out of Parliament; °

10. *That* excessive bail ought not to be required, nor excessive fines imposed, nor cruel and unusual punishments inflicted.

11. *That* jurors ought to be duly impaneled and returned,° and jurors who pass upon men in trials for high treason ought to be freeholders [landholders];

12. *That* all grants and promises of fines and forfeitures of particular persons before conviction are illegal and void;

13. *And that,* for redress of all grievances and for the amending, strengthening, and preserving of the laws, Parliaments ought to be held frequently. ... Having, therefore, an entire confidence that his said Highness, the Prince of Orange, will perfect the deliverance so far advanced by him and will preserve them from the violation of their rights which they have here asserted and from all other attempts

---

° *out of Parliament:* This is now known as the principle of Congressional Immunity. See Article 1, Section 6, of the Constitution. Under this provision our Congressmen cannot be arrested or brought into court for what they say on the floor of Congress.

° *returned:* This means that proper attention should be paid to the selection of jurors and that said jurors should make "return" of their action upon a particular matter to the proper court authority.

upon their religion, rights, and liberties, the said lords ... and Com-
mons assembled at Westminster do resolve that William and Mary,
Prince and Princess of Orange, be and be declared King and Queen
of England, France, and Ireland, and the dominions thereunto belonging....

The Pennsylvania
Charter of Privileges

*"... no person ... who shall confess and acknowledge
One Almighty God ... shall be ... molested...."*

The Quakers, like the Catholics, had been persecuted in
Great Britain and in many of the colonies. Just as Lord Baltimore had been moved to found a haven for his co-religionists,
so William Penn established a refuge for his fellow Quakers.
In Penn's colony, however, religious toleration was extended
to all believers in God, to Christian and Jew alike.

The charter which incorporates this impressive advance in
human rights also proclaims a number of important political
principles, the most significant of which is government by
consent of the governed.

October 28, 1701

William Penn, Proprietary and Governor of the province of Penn-
sylvania and territories thereunto belonging:
To all to whom these presents shall come, send greeting....
Know ye, therefore, that for the further well-being and good gov-

ernment of the said province and territories . . . I, the said William Penn, do declare, grant, and confirm unto all the freemen, planters, and adventurers, and other inhabitants of this province and territories these following liberties, franchises [rights], and privileges . . . to be held, enjoyed, and kept . . . forever.

I. Because no people can be truly happy, though under the greatest enjoyment of civil liberties, if abridged [deprived] of the freedom of their consciences, as to their religious profession and worship: And Almighty God being the only Lord of conscience . . . I do hereby grant and declare that no person or persons inhabiting . . . this province or territories who shall confess and acknowledge *One* Almighty God, the Creator, Upholder, and Ruler of the world; and profess . . . themselves obliged to live quietly under the civil government shall be in any case molested or prejudiced [injured, or damaged, by judgment] in his or their person or estate because of his or their conscientious persuasion [belief] or practice, nor be compelled to frequent or maintain any religious worship, place, or ministry, contrary to his or their mind, or to do or suffer any other act or thing contrary to their religious persuasion.

And that all persons who also profess to believe in Jesus Christ, the Saviour of the World, shall be capable (notwithstanding their other persuasions and practices in point of conscience and religion) to serve this government in any capacity, both legislatively and executively. . . .

II. For the well governing of this province and territories, there shall be an assembly yearly chosen by the freemen thereof, to consist of four persons out of each county, of most note for virtue, wisdom, and ability. . . .

III. *That* the freemen in each respective county, at the time and place of meeting for electing their representatives to serve in assembly, may as often as there shall be occasion choose a double number of persons to present to the governor for sheriffs and coroners to serve for three years if . . . they behave themselves well; out of which respective elections and presentments, the governor shall nominate and commission one for each of the said offices. . . .

IV. *That* the laws of this government shall be in this style; viz. [namely], by the governor, with the consent and approbation of the freemen in general assembly met; and shall be, after confirmation by the governor, forthwith recorded in the Rolls Office [official list] and kept at Philadelphia, unless the governor and assembly shall agree to appoint another place.

V. *That* all criminals shall have the same privileges of witnesses and council as their prosecutors.

VI. *That* no person or persons shall or may, at any time hereafter, be obliged to answer any complaint, matter, or thing whatsoever relating to property before the governor and council, or in any other place, but in ordinary course of justice, unless appeals thereunto shall be hereafter by law appointed.° ...

And no act, law, or ordinance whatsoever shall at any time hereafter be made or done to alter, change, or diminish the form or effect of this charter, or of any part or clause therein, contrary to the true intent and meaning thereof without the consent of the governor ... and six ... of seven of the assembly met.

But because the happiness of mankind depends so much upon the enjoying of liberty of their consciences as aforesaid, I do hereby solemnly declare, promise, and grant, for me, my heirs and assigns ° that the first article of this charter relating to liberty of conscience, and every part and clause therein, according to the true intent and meaning thereof shall be kept and remain without any alteration inviolably forever.

And lastly, I, the said William Penn, Proprietary and Governor of the province of Pennsylvania and territories thereunto belonging, for myself, my heirs, and assigns, have solemnly declared, granted, and confirmed, and do hereby solemnly declare, grant, and confirm that neither I, my heirs, or assigns shall procure or do any thing or things whereby the liberties in this charter ... shall be infringed or broken. And if any thing shall be procured or done by any person or persons contrary to these presents, it shall be held of no force or effect.

IN WITNESS WHEREOF, I, the said William Penn, at Philadelphia in Pennsylvania, have unto this present charter of liberties set my hand and broad seal this twenty-eighth day of October, in the year of Our Lord one thousand seven hundred and one, being the thirteenth year of the reign of King William the Third, over England, Scotland, France and Ireland, etc., and the twenty-first year of my government. . . .

WILLIAM PENN

° *by law appointed:* unless appeal is made to another court.
° *heirs and assigns:* those to whom property may be transferred.

This Charter of Privileges being distinctly read in Assembly; and the whole and every part thereof being approved of and agreed to by us, we do thankfully receive the same from our Proprietary and Governor, at Philadelphia, this twenty-eighth day of October, one thousand seven hundred and one. Signed on behalf, and by order of the Assembly. . . .

[Signed by the Speaker of the Assembly and the Proprietary and Governor's Council.]

Andrew Hamilton's Defense of John Peter Zenger

"The loss of liberty to a generous mind is worse than death. . . ."

John Peter Zenger, printer of the New York Weekly Journal, was arrested and tried for libeling—holding up to public ridicule—Governor Cosby of New York and also for printing seditious articles—those which aroused opposition to the government. At that time, according to English law, a statement could be true and yet be libelous.

Defended by one of the greatest lawyers in colonial America, Zenger was acquitted by a jury which heard one of the most eloquent pleas in history for freedom to publish the truth. Described as the "morning star of that liberty which subsequently revolutionized America," this case has become the historic precedent for freedom of the press.

August 1735

May it please your honors ...

There is heresy in law as in religion, and both have changed very much; and we well know that it is not two centuries ago that a man would have been burned as a heretic for owning such opinions in matters of religion as are publicly written and printed at this day. They were fallible, it seems, and we take the liberty, not only to differ from them in religious opinion, but to condemn them and their opinions too; and I must presume that in taking these freedoms in thinking and speaking about matters of faith or religion, we are in the right; for, though it is said there are very great liberties of this kind taken in New York, yet I have heard of no information ° preferred by Mr. Attorney for any offense of this sort. From which I think it is pretty clear that in New York a man may make very free with his God, but he must take special care what he says of his Governor. It is agreed upon by all men that this is a reign of liberty, and while men keep within the bounds of truth, I hope they may with safety both speak and write their sentiments of the conduct of men of power; I mean of that part of their conduct only which affects the liberty or property of the people under their administration; were this to be denied, then the next step may make them slaves. For what notions can be entertained of slavery beyond that of suffering the greatest injuries and oppressions without the liberty of complaining; or if they do [complain], to be destroyed, body and estate, for so doing?

It is said, and insisted upon by Mr. Attorney, that government is a sacred thing; that it is to be supported and reverenced; it is government that protects our persons and estates; that prevents treasons, murders, robberies, riots, and all the train of evils that overturn kingdoms and states and ruin particular persons; and if those in the administration, especially the supreme magistrates, must have all their conduct censured by private men, government cannot subsist [continue to exist]. This is called a licentiousness [lawlessness] not to be tolerated. It is said that it brings the rulers of the people into con-

---

° *information:* an accusation against a person formally prepared by a government attorney.

tempt so that their authority is not regarded, and so that in the end the laws cannot be put in execution. These, I say, and such as these, are the general topics insisted upon by men in power and their advocates. But I wish it might be considered at the same time how often it has happened that the abuse of power has been the primary cause of these evils, and that it was the injustice and oppression of these great men which have commonly brought them into contempt with the people. The craft and art [cunning and skill] of these men are great, and who that is the least acquainted with history or with law can be ignorant of the specious pretenses [deceptive claims] which have often been made use of by men in power to introduce arbitrary rule and destroy the liberties of a free people. . . .

Gentlemen, the danger is great in proportion to the mischief that may happen through our too great credulity. A proper confidence in a court is commendable, but as the verdict (whatever it is) will be yours, you ought to refer no part of your duty to the discretion of other persons. If you should be of the opinion that there is no falsehood in Mr. Zenger's papers, you will, nay (pardon me for the expression), you ought to say so; because you do not know whether others (I mean the court) may be of that opinion. It is your right to do so, and there is much depending upon your resolution, as well as upon your integrity.

The loss of liberty to a generous mind is worse than death; and yet we know there have been those in all ages who, for the sake of preferment [promotion] or some imaginary honor, have freely lent a helping hand to oppress, nay, to destroy, their country. This brings to my mind that saying of the immortal Brutus, when he looked upon the creatures of Caesar, who were very great men, but by no means good men: "You Romans," said Brutus, "if yet I may call you so, consider what you are doing; remember that you are assisting Caesar to forge those very chains which one day he will make yourselves wear." This is what every man that values freedom ought to consider; he should act by judgment and not by affection or self-interest; for where those prevail, no ties of either country or kindred are regarded; as, upon the other hand, the man who loves his country prefers its liberty to all other considerations, well knowing that without liberty life is a misery. . . .

Power may justly be compared to a great river; while kept within its bounds, it is both beautiful and useful, but when it overflows its banks, it is then too impetuous to be stemmed; it bears down all before it and brings destruction and desolation wherever it comes. If, then, this be the nature of power, let us at least do our duty, and, like wise men who value freedom, use our utmost [greatest] care to support liberty, the only bulwark against lawless power, which, in all ages, has sacrificed to its wild lust and boundless ambition the blood of the best men that ever lived.

I hope to be pardoned, sir, for my zeal upon this occasion. It is an old and wise caution that when our neighbor's house is on fire, we ought to take care of our own. For though, blessed be God, I live in a government where liberty is well understood and freely enjoyed, yet experience has shown us all (I am sure it has to me) that a bad precedent in one government is soon set up for an authority in another; and therefore I cannot but think it mine and every honest man's duty that, while we pay all due obedience to men in authority, we ought, at the same time, to be upon our guard against power wherever we apprehend that it may affect ourselves or our fellow subjects.

I am truly very unequal to such an undertaking on many accounts. And you see I labor under the weight of many years and am borne down with great infirmities of body; yet old and weak as I am, I should think it my duty, if required, to go to the utmost [most distant] part of the land, where my service could be of any use in assisting to quench the flame of prosecutions . . . set on foot by the government to deprive a people of the right of remonstrating [objecting] and complaining . . . of the arbitrary attempts of men in power. Men who injure and oppress the people under their administration provoke them to cry out and complain, and then make that very complaint the foundation for new oppressions and prosecutions. I wish I could say there were no instances of this kind. But, to conclude, the question before the court, and you, gentlemen of the jury, is not of small nor private concern; it is not the cause of a poor printer, nor of New York alone, which you are now trying. No! It may in its consequence affect every free man that lives under a British government on the main continent of America. It is the best cause; it is the cause of liberty; and I make no doubt but your upright conduct, this day, will not only entitle you to the love and esteem of your fellow citizens, but every man who prefers freedom to a life of slavery will bless and honor you as men who have baffled the attempt of tyranny, and by an impartial and uncorrupt verdict have laid a noble foundation for securing to ourselves, our posterity, and our neighbors that to which nature and the laws of our country have given us a right—the liberty of both exposing and opposing arbitrary power (in these parts of the world at least) by speaking and writing truth.

The Albany Plan of Union

"... that ... one general government may be formed in America. ..."

In 1754, after the French and Indian War broke out, the Albany Congress was convened to unite the colonies against France and to enter into a treaty with the powerful Iroquois Confederation. At this meeting, Benjamin Franklin introduced his proposal for a self-governing federation within the British Empire. What Franklin sought to achieve was the creation of a central governing agency which would handle common problems, leaving to the local governments the power to handle their individual affairs. Rejected by both Britain and the colonies, this foresighted solution to the problems of colonial empire anticipated by many years the British Commonwealth of Nations. A reading of the document also discloses its influence on the thinking of those who drafted the Articles of Confederation and the Constitution of the United States.

July 10, 1754

It is proposed that humble application be made for an act of Parliament of Great Britain, by virtue of which one general government may be formed in America, including all the said colonies, within and under which government each colony may retain its present constitution, except in the particulars wherein a change may be directed by the said act, as hereafter follows.

1. That the said general government be administered by a Presi-dent-General, to be appointed and supported by the crown; and a Grand Council, to be chosen by the representatives of the people of the several colonies . . . in their respective assemblies.

2. That within—months after the passing [of] such act, the House of Representatives [in each of the colonies] that happen[s] to be sit-ting within that time, or that shall be especially for that purpose con-vened, may and shall choose members for the Grand Council, in the following proportion. . . .

Massachusetts Bay . . . 7	Pennsylvania 6
New Hampshire 2	Maryland 4
Connecticut 5	Virginia 7
Rhode Island 2	North Carolina 4
New York 4	South Carolina 4
New Jersey 3	Total members . . . 48

3. Who shall meet for the first time at the city of Philadelphia, be-ing called by the President-General as soon as conveniently may be after his appointment.

4. That there shall be a new election of the members of the Grand Council every three years; . . .

5. That after the first three years, when the proportion of money arising out of each colony to the general treasury can be known, the number of members to be chosen for each colony shall, from time to time, in all ensuing elections, be regulated by that proportion, yet . . . the number to be chosen by any one province [shall] be not more than seven, nor less than two.

6. That the Grand Council shall meet once in every year, and oftener if occasion require . . . or as they shall be called to meet . . . by the President-General on any emergency; he having first obtained in writing the consent of seven of the members to such call, and sent . . . timely notice to the whole.

7. That the Grand Council have power to choose their speaker; and shall neither be dissolved [declared out of existence], prorogued [closed for that session], nor continued . . . [in session] longer than six weeks at one time, without their own consent or the special com-mand of the crown. . . .

9. That the assent of the President-General be requisite to all acts of the Grand Council, and that it be his office and duty to cause them to be carried into execution.

10. That the President-General, with the advice of the Grand Council, hold or direct all Indian treaties, in which the general interest of the colonies may be concerned; and make peace or declare war with Indian nations.

11. That they make such laws as they judge necessary for regulating all Indian trade.

12. That they make all purchases from Indians, for the crown, of lands not now within the bounds of particular colonies. . . .

13. That they make new settlements on such purchases, by granting lands in the King's name, reserving a quitrent ° to the crown for the use of the general treasury.

14. That they make laws for regulating and governing such new settlements, till the crown shall think fit to form them into particular governments.

15. That they raise and pay soldiers and build forts for the defense of any of the colonies, and equip vessels of force to guard the coasts and protect the trade on the ocean, lakes, or great rivers; but they shall not impress [force into military service] men in any colony without the consent of the legislature.

16. That for these purposes they have power to make laws . . . and levy such general duties . . . or taxes, as to them shall appear most equal and just (considering the ability and other circumstances of the inhabitants in the several colonies), and such as may be collected with the least inconvenience to the people; rather discouraging luxury than loading industry with unnecessary burdens.

17. That they may appoint a General Treasurer and Particular Treasurer in each government when necessary; . . .

18. Yet no money . . . [shall be issued] but by joint orders of the President-General and Grand Council; except where sums have been appropriated to particular purposes, and the President-General . . . [has been] previously empowered by an act to draw such sums.

° quitrent: a fixed annual payment by the owners of land to the one who either gave them or sold them the land. The purpose of the quitrent was to show that complete ownership did not vest in the user of the land, but that there was a superior owner.

19. That the general accounts shall be yearly settled and reported to the several assemblies [of the colonies].

20. That a quorum [number needed to be present to transact business legally] of the Grand Council, empowered to act with the President-General . . . shall [consist] of twenty-five members; among whom there shall be one or more from a majority of the colonies.

21. That the laws made by them for the purposes aforesaid shall not be repugnant [in opposition to], but, as near as may be, agreeable to the laws of England, and shall be transmitted to the King in Council for approbation as soon as may be after their passing; and if not disapproved within three years after presentation . . . [shall] remain in force.

22. That, in case of the death of the President-General, the Speaker of the Grand Council for the time being shall succeed, and be vested [endowed] with the same powers and authorities, to continue till the King's pleasure be known.

23. That all military commission officers, whether for land or sea service, to act under this general constitution, shall be nominated by the President-General; but the approbation of the Grand Council is to be obtained before they receive their commissions. And all civil officers are to be nominated by the Grand Council and to receive the President-General's approbation before they officiate.

24. But, in case of vacancy by death or removal of any officer, civil or military, under this constitution, the Governor of the province in which such vacancy happens may appoint [a person to serve in that person's stead] till the pleasure of the President-General and Grand Council can be known.

25. That the particular military as well as civil establishments in each colony remain in their present state, the general constitution notwithstanding; and that on sudden emergencies any colony may defend itself and lay the accounts of expense . . . arising [from such defense] before the President-General and General Council, who may allow and order payment of the same, as far as they judge such accounts just and reasonable.

PART ONE

Creating
a New Nation

When Thomas Jefferson was born
in 1743 on the frontier of Virginia,
the thirteen American colonies were
part of the British Empire. From New
Hampshire south through Georgia,
there was a thin line of settlement
along the Atlantic coast. The people,
nine out of ten of whom were farmers, looked eastward to Great Britain
for political leadership.

During his lifetime, Jefferson took
a leading part in a far-reaching political revolution. When he died in 1826,
the United States was a proudly independent nation, a federal union of
24 states, and the advancing frontier
had crossed the Mississippi River.

James Otis' Speech Against the Writs of Assistance

"A man's house is his castle...."

During the French and Indian War, Great Britain, needing money to maintain her armed forces, decided to collect the customs duties which many colonists had been evading for years. In an effort to prevent smuggling, British officials resorted to the use of writs of assistance. These were general warrants to search any place at any time for smuggled goods.

When a British official in Boston applied for these writs, the colonial merchants hired two attorneys to argue against their issuance. One of these attorneys, the young and fiery James Otis, delivered on this occasion a memorable attack against this invasion of human rights. Although there was no official record of his address, John Adams, who happened to be present, took notes from which he later reconstructed the speech.

In his argument against the exercise of unlimited powers of Parliament over the colonies, Otis was appealing to a higher law—the law of nature, which Thomas Jefferson later appealed to in the Declaration of Independence. The Fourth Amendment to the Constitution of the United States stands as a tribute to Otis' warning against this type of oppressive governmental practice.

February 24, 1761

... In the first place, may it please your Honors, I will admit that writs of one kind may be legal; that is, special writs, directed to special officers and to search certain houses.... Your Honors will find in the old books [lawbooks] ... precedents of general warrants to

search suspected houses. But in more modern books you will find
only special warrants to search such and such houses specially named,
in which the complainant has before sworn that he suspects his goods
are concealed; and you will find it adjudged that special warrants only
are legal in the same manner I rely on it, that the writ prayed for in
this petition, being general, is illegal. It is a power that places the liberty of every man in the hands of every petty officer. I say I admit
that special writs of assistance, to search special places, may be
granted to certain persons on oath; but I deny that the writ now
prayed for can be granted, for I beg leave to make some observations
on the writ itself before I proceed to other acts of Parliament. In the
first place, the writ is universal, being directed "to all and singular
justices, sheriffs, constables, and all other officers and subjects"; so
that, in short, it is directed to every subject in the King's dominions.
Everyone with this writ may be a tyrant; if this commission be legal,
a tyrant in a legal manner also may control, imprison, or murder anyone within the realm. In the next place, it is perpetual; there is no return. A man is accountable to no person for his doings. Every man
may reign secure in his petty tyranny and spread terror and desolation around him. In the third place, a person with this writ, in the
daytime, may enter all houses, shops, etc., at will and command all to
assist him. Fourthly, by this writ not only deputies, etc., but even their
menial servants, are allowed to lord it over us. Now one of the most
essential branches of English liberty is the freedom of one's house. A
man's house is his castle; and while he is quiet, he is as well guarded
as a prince in his castle. This writ, if it should be declared legal,
would totally annihilate this privilege. Customhouse officers may enter our houses when they please; we are commanded to permit their
entry. Their menial servants may enter, may break locks, bars, and
everything in their way; and whether they break through malice or
revenge, no man, no court, can inquire. Bare suspicion without oath
is sufficient. This wanton [reckless] exercise of his power is not a
chimerical [fanciful] suggestion of a heated brain. I will mention
some facts. Mr. Pew had one of these writs, and when Mr. Ware succeeded him, he endorsed this writ over to Mr. Ware; so that these
writs are negotiable [transferable] from one officer to another; and
so your Honors have no opportunity of judging the persons to whom
this vast power is delegated. Another instance is this: Mr. Justice
Walley had called this same Mr. Ware before him, by a constable,

to answer for a breach of Sabbath-day acts, or that of profane swearing. As soon as he had finished, Mr. Ware asked him if he had done. He replied, "Yes." "Well then," said Mr. Ware, "I will show you a little of my power. I command you to permit me to search your house for uncustomed [smuggled] goods." And [Mr. Ware] went on to search his house from the garret to the cellar and then served the constable in the same manner. But to show another absurdity in this writ; if it should be established, I insist upon it, every person by the [statute] 14 Charles II has this power as well as customhouse officers. The words are, "It shall be lawful for any person or persons authorized," etc. What a scene does this open! Every man, prompted by revenge, ill humor, or wantonness to inspect the inside of his neighbor's house, may get a writ of assistance. Others will ask it from self-defense; one arbitrary exertion will provoke another, until society be involved in tumult and in blood.

Again, these writs are not returned. Writs in their nature are temporary things. When the purposes for which they are issued are answered, they exist no more; but these live forever; no one can be called to account. Thus reason and the constitution are both against this writ.... No acts of Parliament can establish such a writ.... But ... special writs may be granted *on oath and probable suspicion* ... an officer should show probable ground; should take his oath of it; should do this before a magistrate; and ... such magistrate, if he thinks proper, should issue a special warrant to a constable to search the places....

The Declaration and Resolves of the First Continental Congress

"... the foundation of ... all free government is a right in the people to participate in their legislative council. ..."

In 1773, events in the American colonies suddenly began to move with disconcerting speed. In angry reaction to the Tea Act of 1773, a number of Patriots in Boston staged the celebrated Tea Party. The British promptly met this challenge to their authority by adopting the Intolerable Acts which closed the Port of Boston, prohibited town meetings in Massachusetts, required the quartering of soldiers, and provided that colonial officials accused of crimes committed while enforcing British laws could be tried in England. Colonial leaders, equally quick to react, gathered in Philadelphia in September 1774. The First Continental Congress, as it was called, produced that series of declarations and resolutions which has been described with justification as the "Magna Carta of civil liberty in America."

October 14, 1774

... The good people of the several colonies of New Hampshire, Massachusetts Bay, Rhode Island, and Providence plantations, Connecticut, New York, New Jersey, Pennsylvania ... Delaware, Maryland, Virginia, North Carolina, and South Carolina, justly alarmed at these arbitrary proceedings of parliament ... have ... elected ... deputies to meet and sit in general Congress in the city of Philadelphia in order ... that their religion, laws, and liberties may not be subverted:

Whereupon the deputies so appointed being now assembled in a full and free representation of these colonies, taking into their most serious consideration the best means of attaining the ends aforesaid, do in the first place, as Englishmen their ancestors in like cases have usually done for asserting and vindicating [justifying] their rights and liberties, declare:

That the inhabitants of the English colonies in North America, by the immutable [unchangeable] laws of nature, the principles of the English constitution, and the several charters or compacts, have the following rights:

Resolved, N.C.D. [unanimously]

1. That they are entitled to life, liberty, and property, and they have never ceded [yielded] to any sovereign power whatever a right to dispose of either without their consent.

2. That our ancestors, who first settled these colonies, were at the time of their emigration from the mother country entitled to all the rights, liberties, and immunities [freedom from tax] of free and natural-born subjects within the realm of England.

3. That by such emigration they by no means forfeited, surrendered, or lost any of those rights, but that they were, and their descendants now are, entitled to the exercise and enjoyment of all such of them as their local and other circumstances enable them to exercise and enjoy.

4. That the foundation of English liberty and of all free government is a right in the people to participate in their legislative council: and as the English colonists are not represented and . . . [because of] their local and other circumstances cannot properly be represented in the British parliament, they are entitled to a free and exclusive power of legislation in their several provincial legislatures, where their right of representation can alone be preserved, in all cases of taxation and internal polity [government], subject only to the negative [veto] of their sovereign, in such manner as has been heretofore used and accustomed. But, from the necessity of the case and a regard to the mutual interest of both countries, we cheerfully consent to the operation of such acts of the British parliament as are bona fide restrained to the regulation of our external commerce for the purpose of securing the commercial advantages of the whole empire to the mother country, and the commercial benefits of its respective members, excluding every idea of taxation, internal or external, for raising a revenue on the subjects in America without their consent.

5. That the respective colonies are entitled to the common law of England and more especially to the great and inestimable privilege of

being tried by their peers of the vicinage [vicinity], according to the course of that law.

6. That they are entitled to the benefit of such of the English statutes as existed at the time of their colonization and which they have, by experience, respectively found to be applicable to their several local and other circumstances.

7. That these, his Majesty's colonies, are likewise entitled to all the immunities and privileges granted and confirmed to them by royal charters or secured by their several codes of provincial laws.

8. That they have a right peaceably to assemble, consider ... their grievances, and petition the king, and that all prosecutions, prohibitory proclamations, and commitments for the same are illegal.

9. That the keeping [of] a standing army in these colonies in times of peace [and] without the consent of the legislature of that colony in which such army is kept is against law.

10. It is ... necessary to good government and rendered essential by the English constitution that the ... branches of the legislature be independent of each other; that, therefore, the exercise of legislative power in several colonies by a council appointed during pleasure by the crown is unconstitutional, dangerous, and destructive to the freedom of American legislation.

All and each of which the aforesaid deputies, in behalf of themselves and their constituents, do claim, demand, and insist on, as their indubitable rights and liberties; which cannot be legally taken from them, altered, or abridged by any power whatever without their own consent [expressed] by their representatives in their several provincial legislatures.

In the course of our inquiry, we find many infringements and violations of the foregoing rights, which, from an ardent desire that harmony and mutual intercourse of affection and interest may be restored, we pass over for the present and proceed to state such acts and measures as have been adopted since the last war, which demonstrate a system formed to enslave America.

Resolved, That the following acts of parliament are infringements and violations of the rights of the colonists; and that the repeal of them is essentially necessary in order to restore harmony between Great Britain and the American colonies, ... viz.:

The several acts ... which impose duties for the purpose of raising a revenue in America. ...

Also the . . . acts passed in the last session of parliament for stopping the port and blocking up the harbor of Boston [and] for altering the charter and government of the Massachusetts Bay. . . .

Also the act passed the same session for establishing the Roman Catholic religion in the province of Quebec, abolishing the equitable system of English laws, and erecting a tyranny there to the great danger, from so great a dissimilarity of religion, law, and government, of the neighboring British colonies. . . .

Also the act passed the same session for the better providing [of] suitable quarters for officers and soldiers in his Majesty's service in North America.

Also, that the keeping [of] a standing army in several of these colonies in time of peace without the consent of the legislature of that colony in which the army is kept is against law.

To these grievous acts and measures Americans cannot submit, but in hopes that their fellow subjects in Great Britain will, on a revision of them, restore us to that state in which both countries found happiness and prosperity, we have for the present only resolved to pursue the following peaceable measures: (1) to enter into a nonimportation, nonconsumption, and nonexportation agreement or association; (2) to prepare an address to the people of Great Britain and a memorial [statement of facts] to the inhabitants of British America; (3) to prepare a loyal address to his Majesty agreeable to resolutions already entered into.

Patrick Henry's Speech Before the Virginia Convention

"I know not what course others may take; but as for me, give me liberty or give me death!"

Patrick Henry had attended the First Continental Congress as a delegate from Virginia. He returned to his native state convinced that war was inevitable. When conservative members of the Virginia Convention opposed the organization of the militia to act against British tyranny, charging that those who favored the action were guilty of treason, the fiery Virginian rose to deliver the most notable speech of his career. Although he had not written his speech, and although there was no secretary at the convention to make an exact copy, Patrick Henry spoke with such rousing eloquence that it was relatively easy for those who were moved by his words to reconstruct the speech from memory.

March 23, 1775

Mr. President: No man thinks more highly than I do of the patriotism, as well as abilities, of the very worthy gentlemen who have just addressed the House. But different men often see the same subjects in different lights; and, therefore, I hope that it will not be thought disrespectful to those gentlemen if, entertaining as I do, opinions of a character very opposite to theirs, I shall speak forth my sentiments freely and without reserve. This is no time for ceremony. The question before the House is one of awful moment [importance] to this country. For my own part I consider it as nothing less than a question of freedom or slavery; and in proportion to the magnitude of the subject ought to be the freedom of the debate. It is only in this way that we can hope to arrive at truth, and fulfill the great responsibility which we hold to God and our country. Should I keep back my opinions at such a time, through fear of giving offense, I should consider myself as guilty of treason toward my country, and of an act of disloyalty toward the majesty of heaven, which I revere above all earthly kings.

Mr. President, it is natural to man to indulge in the illusions of hope. We are apt to shut our eyes against a painful truth, and listen to the song of that siren till she transforms us into beasts. Is this the part of wise men, engaged in a great and arduous struggle for liberty? Are we disposed to be of the number of those who, having eyes, see not, and having ears, hear not the things which so nearly concern their temporal salvation? For my part, whatever anguish of spirit it may cost, I am willing to know the whole truth; to know the worst and to provide for it.

I have but one lamp by which my feet are guided, and that is the lamp of experience. I know of no way of judging of the future but by the past. And judging by the past, I wish to know what there has been in the conduct of the British ministry for the last ten years to justify those hopes with which gentlemen have been pleased to solace themselves and the House [convention]? Is it that insidious [treacherous] smile with which our petition has been lately received? Trust it not, sir; it will prove a snare to your feet. Suffer not yourselves to be betrayed with a kiss. Ask yourselves how this gracious reception of our petition comports [agrees] with those warlike preparations which cover our waters and darken our land. Are fleets and armies necessary to a work of love and reconciliation? Have we shown ourselves so unwilling to be reconciled that force must be called in to win back our love? Let us not deceive ourselves, sir. These are the implements of war and subjugation, the last arguments to which kings resort.

I ask, gentlemen, sir, what means this martial array if its purpose be not to force us to submission? . . . They are meant for us; they can be meant for no other. They are sent over to bind and rivet upon us those chains which the British ministry [has] been so long forging. And what have we to oppose to them? Shall we try argument? Sir, we have been trying that for the last ten years. Have we anything new to offer on the subject? Nothing . . . Sir, we have done everything that could be done to avert the storm which is now coming on. We have petitioned, we have remonstrated, we have supplicated, we have prostrated ourselves [thrown ourselves down] before the throne, and have implored its interposition [intervention] to arrest the tyrannical hands of the ministry and parliament. Our petitions have been slighted; our remonstrances have produced additional violence and insult; our supplications have been disregarded; and we have been spurned, with contempt, from the foot of the throne. In vain, after these things, may we indulge the fond hope of peace and reconciliation. There is no longer any room for hope. If we wish to be free, if we mean to preserve inviolate those inestimable privileges for which we have been so long contending, if we mean not basely to abandon the noble struggle in which we have been so long engaged and which we have pledged ourselves never to abandon until the glorious object of our contest shall be obtained, we must fight! I repeat it, sir—we must fight! . . .

They tell us, sir, that we are weak, unable to cope with so formidable an adversary. But when shall we be stronger? Will it be the next week or the next year? Will it be when we are totally disarmed and when a British guard shall be stationed in every house? Shall we gather strength by irresolution and inaction? Shall we acquire the means of effectual resistance by lying supinely [quietly] on our backs and hugging the delusive phantom of hope until our enemies shall have bound us hand and foot? Sir, we are not weak, if we make a proper use of those means which the God of nature hath placed in our power. Three millions of people armed in the holy cause of liberty and in such a country as that which we possess are invincible by any force which our enemy can send against us. Besides, sir, we shall not fight our battles alone. There is a just God who presides over the destinies of nations and who will raise friends to fight our battles for us. The battle, sir, is not to the strong alone. It is to the vigilant, the active, the brave. Besides, sir, we have no election [choice]. If we were base [mean] enough to desire it, it is now too late to retire from the contest. There is no retreat but in submission and slavery! Our chains are forged. Their clanking may be heard on the plains of Boston! The war is inevitable—and let it come! I repeat it, sir—let it come!

It is in vain, sir, to extenuate [prolong] the matter. Gentlemen may cry peace, peace. But there is no peace. The war is actually begun! The next gale that sweeps from the north will bring to our ears the clash of resounding arms! Our brethren are already in the field! Why stand we here idle? What is it that gentlemen wish? What would they have? Is life so dear, or peace so sweet, as to be purchased at the price of chains and slavery? Forbid it, Almighty God! I know not what course others may take; but as for me, give me liberty or give me death!

Thomas Paine's "Common Sense"

"O ye that love mankind! Ye that
dare oppose not only the tyranny
but the tyrant, stand forth!"

There were no television sets or radios in 1776 to broadcast the events that were plunging the American colonies and their mother country into the maelstrom of war. But there were newspapers to tell the story and pamphlets to explore the arguments. The most famous of the pamphleteers was Thomas Paine, whose ringing words and phrases encouraged the Americans to declare their independence and to fight for ultimate victory.

Common Sense has been described as a spark dropped in a keg of powder. It played upon the emotions of Americans for whom the blood shed at Lexington, Concord, and Bunker Hill was still a fresh and painful memory. Paine argued that there were immediate advantages to be gained by separating from Great Britain. Then, placing the struggle on a nobler level, he exclaimed, "The cause of America is in a great measure the cause of mankind." Those who read Common Sense (and eventually 150,000 copies were sold) realized that they were standing at a crossroads in history. Paine's ideas inspired them to take the road which led to the Declaration of Independence.

January 1776

... In the following pages I offer nothing more than simple facts, plain arguments, and common sense: ...

Volumes have been written on the subject of the struggle between England and America. Men of all ranks have embarked in the controversy, from different motives, and with various designs; but all have been ineffectual, and the period of debate is closed. Arms as the last resource decide the contest; the appeal was the choice of the King, and the continent has accepted the challenge....

The sun never shone on a cause of greater worth. 'Tis not the affair of a city, a county, a province, or a kingdom; but of a continent—of at least one eighth part of the habitable globe. 'Tis not the concern of a day, a year, or an age; posterity are virtually [in effect] involved in the contest and will be more or less affected even to the end of time by the proceedings now. Now is the seedtime of continental union, faith, and honor. The least fracture now will be like a name engraved with the point of a pin on the tender rind [bark] of a young oak; the wound will enlarge with the tree, and posterity [will] read it in full-grown characters.

By referring the matter from argument to arms, a new era for politics is struck [begun]—a new method of thinking has arisen....

As much has been said of the advantages of reconciliation, which, like an agreeable dream, has passed away and left us as we were; it is but right that we should examine the contrary side of the argument and inquire into some of the many material injuries which these colonies sustain, and always will sustain, by being connected with and dependent on Great Britain. [It is right to] examine that connection and dependence on the principles of nature and common sense; to see what we have to trust to if separated and what we are to expect if dependent.

I have heard it asserted by some that as America has flourished under her former connection with Great Britain, the same connection is necessary toward [to] her future happiness, and will always have the same effect. Nothing can be more fallacious than this kind of argument. We may as well assert that because a child has thrived upon milk, it is never to have meat, or that the first twenty years of our lives [are] to become a precedent for the next twenty. But even this is admitting more than is true, for I answer roundly [plainly] that America would have flourished as much, and probably much more, had no European power taken any notice of her. The commerce by which she has enriched herself are the necessaries of life and will always have a market while eating is the custom in Europe. . . .

Alas! We have been long led away by ancient prejudices and [have] made large sacrifices to superstition. We have boasted the protection of Great Britain, without considering that her motive was *interest* not *attachment* and that she did not protect us from *our enemies* on *our account*, but from *her enemies* on *her own account*. . . .
. . . France and Spain never were, nor perhaps ever will be, our enemies as *Americans*, but as . . . *subjects of Great Britain*.

But Britain is the parent country say some. Then the more shame upon her conduct. Even brutes do not devour their young, nor savages make war upon their families; wherefore, the assertion, if true, turns to her reproach; but it happens not to be true, or only partly so, . . . Europe and not England is the parent country of America. This New World has been the asylum [a place of security] for the persecuted lovers of civil and religious liberty from *every part* of Europe. Hither have they fled, not from the tender embraces of the mother, but from the cruelty of the monster; and it is so far true of England that the same tyranny which drove the first emigrants from home pursues their descendants still.

In this extensive quarter of the globe, we forget the narrow limits of three hundred and sixty miles (the extent of England) and carry our friendship on a larger scale; we claim brotherhood with every European Christian and triumph in the generosity of the sentiment. . . .

'Tis repugnant to reason, to the universal order of things, to all examples from former ages, to suppose that this continent can long remain subject to any external power. The most sanguine [hopeful] in Britain do not think so. The utmost stretch of human wisdom cannot at this time compass [make up] a plan, short of separation, which can promise the continent even a year's security. . . .

A government of our own is our natural right; and when a man seriously reflects on the precariousness [uncertainty] of human affairs, he will become convinced that it is infinitely wiser and safer to form ı constitution of our own, in a cool, deliberate manner, while we have it in our power, than to trust such an interesting event to time and chance. . . .

O ye that love mankind! Ye that dare oppose not only the tyranny but the tyrant, stand forth! Every spot of the old world is overrun with oppression. Freedom has been hunted round the globe. Asia and Africa have long expelled her. Europe regards her like a stranger, and England has given her warning to depart. O! Receive the fugitive, and prepare in time an asylum for mankind. . . .

On these grounds I rest the matter. And as no offer has yet been made to refute the doctrine contained in the former editions of this pamphlet, it is a negative proof that either the doctrine cannot be refuted, or that the party in favor of it are too numerous to be opposed. *Wherefore,* instead of gazing at each other with suspicious or doubtful curiosity, let each of us hold out to his neighbor the hearty hand of friendship, and unite in drawing a line, which, like an act of oblivion [pardon], shall bury in forgetfulness every former dissension. Let the names of Whig and Tory be extinct; and let none other be heard among us, than those of *a good citizen, an open and resolute friend,* and *a virtuous supporter of the* RIGHTS OF MANKIND, and of the FREE AND INDEPENDENT STATES OF AMERICA.

The Declaration of Independence

". . . all men are created equal . . . [and] are endowed by their Creator with certain unalienable rights . . . life, liberty, and the pursuit of happiness. . . ."

One of the noblest documents in the history of mankind, the Declaration of Independence, proclaims in memorable language man's aspiration for freedom. Jefferson said that he had intended it "to be an expression of the American mind," but it has turned out to be an expression of the ideals of all who seek those fundamental human rights which go with human dignity. It is probably the best summary of the watchwords of democracy in political literature.

Adopted by the Continental Congress fifteen months after the battles of Lexington and Concord, the Declaration marked a complete break between the colonies and the mother country. It represented a formal declaration of war and a new conception of government.

July 4, 1776

When, in the course of human events, it becomes necessary for one people to dissolve the political bands which have connected them with another, and to assume, among the powers of the earth, the separate and equal station to which the laws of nature and of nature's God entitle them, a decent respect to the opinions of mankind requires that they should declare the causes which impel them to the separation.

We hold these truths to be self-evident: that all men are created equal, that they are endowed by their Creator with certain unalienable rights, that among these are life, liberty, and the pursuit of happiness.

That, to secure these rights, governments are instituted among men, deriving their just powers from the consent of the governed; that whenever any form of government becomes destructive of these ends, it is the right of the people to alter or to abolish it, and to institute new government, laying its foundation on such principles, and organizing its powers in such form, as to them shall seem most likely to effect their safety and happiness. Prudence, indeed, will dictate that governments long established should not be changed for light and transient causes; and accordingly all experience hath shown that mankind are more disposed to suffer while evils are sufferable, than to right themselves by abolishing the forms to which they are accustomed. But when a long train of abuses and usurpations, pursuing invariably the same object, evinces a design to reduce them under absolute despotism, it is their right, it is their duty, to throw off such government, and to provide new guards for their future security.

Such has been the patient sufferance of these colonies; and such is now the necessity which constrains them to alter their former systems of government. The history of the present king of Great Britain is a history of repeated injuries and usurpations, all having in direct object the establishment of an absolute tyranny over these states. To prove this, let facts be submitted to a candid world.

He has refused his assent to laws the most wholesome and necessary for the public good.

He has forbidden his governors to pass laws of immediate and pressing importance, unless suspended in their operation till his assent should be obtained; and when so suspended, he has utterly neglected to attend to them.

He has refused to pass other laws for the accommodation of large districts of people, unless those people would relinquish the right of representation in the legislature, a right inestimable to them, and formidable to tyrants only.

He has called together legislative bodies at places unusual, uncomfortable, and distant from the depository of their public records, for the sole purpose of fatiguing them into compliance with his measures.

He has dissolved representative houses repeatedly, for opposing, with manly firmness, his invasions on the rights of the people.

He has refused, for a long time after such dissolutions, to cause others to be elected; whereby the legislative powers, incapable of annihilation, have returned to the people at large for their exercise; the state remaining, in the meantime, exposed to all the dangers of invasion from without and convulsions within.

He has endeavored to prevent the population of these states; for that purpose obstructing the laws of naturalization of foreigners, refusing to pass others to encourage their migration hither, and raising the conditions of new appropriations of lands.

He has obstructed the administration of justice, by refusing his assent to laws for establishing judiciary powers.

He has made judges dependent on his will alone for the tenure of their offices, and the amount and payment of their salaries.

He has erected a multitude of new offices, and sent hither swarms of officers to harass our people and eat out their substance.

He has kept among us, in times of peace, standing armies, without the consent of our legislature.

He has affected to render the military independent of, and superior to, the civil power.

He has combined with others to subject us to a jurisdiction foreign to our constitution and unacknowledged by our laws, giving his assent to their acts of pretended legislation:

For quartering large bodies of armed troops among us;

For protecting them, by a mock trial, from punishment for any murders which they should commit on the inhabitants of these states;

For cutting off our trade with all parts of the world;

For imposing taxes on us without our consent;

For depriving us, in many cases, of the benefits of trial by jury;

For transporting us beyond seas, to be tried for pretended offenses;

For abolishing the free system of English laws in a neighboring province, establishing therein an arbitrary government, and enlarging its boundaries, so as to render it at once an example and fit instrument for introducing the same absolute rule into these colonies;

For taking away our charters, abolishing our most valuable laws, and altering, fundamentally, the forms of our governments;

For suspending our own legislature, and declaring themselves invested with power to legislate for us in all cases whatsoever.

He has abdicated government here, by declaring us out of his protection and waging war against us.

He has plundered our seas, ravaged our coasts, burned our towns, and destroyed the lives of our people.

He is at this time transporting large armies of foreign mercenaries to complete the works of death, desolation, and tyranny already begun with circumstances of cruelty and perfidy scarcely paralleled in the most barbarous ages, and totally unworthy the head of a civilized nation.

He has constrained our fellow-citizens, taken captive on the high seas, to bear arms against their country, to become the executioners of their friends and brethren, or to fall themselves by their hands.

He has excited domestic insurrections among us, and has endeavored to bring on the inhabitants of our frontiers the merciless Indian savages, whose known rule of warfare is an undistinguished destruction of all ages, sexes, and conditions.

In every stage of these oppressions we have petitioned for redress in the most humble terms; our repeated petitions have been answered only by repeated injury. A prince whose character is thus marked by every act which may define a tyrant is unfit to be the ruler of a free people.

Nor have we been wanting in attention to our British brethren. We have warned them, from time to time, of attempts by their legislature to extend an unwarrantable jurisdiction over us. We have reminded them of the circumstances of our emigration and settlement here. We have appealed to their native justice and magnanimity; and we have conjured them, by the ties of our common kindred, to disavow these usurpations, which would inevitably interrupt our connections and correspondence. They, too, have been deaf to the voice of justice and of consanguinity. We must, therefore, acquiesce in the necessity which denounces our separation, and hold them, as we hold the rest of mankind, enemies in war, in peace, friends.

We, therefore, the representatives of the United States of America, in General Congress assembled, appealing to the Supreme Judge of the world for the rectitude of our intentions, do, in the name and by authority of the good people of these colonies, solemnly publish and declare, that these united colonies are, and of right ought to be, free and independent states; that they are absolved from all allegiance to the British crown, and that all political connection between them and the state of Great Britain is, and ought to be, totally dissolved; and that, as free and independent states, they have full power to levy war, conclude peace, contract alliances, establish commerce, and to do all other acts and things which independent states may of right do. And, for the support of this declaration, with a firm reliance on the protection of Divine Providence, we mutually pledge to each other our lives, our fortunes, and our sacred honor.

John Hancock (MASSACHUSETTS)

[Signed by representatives of the thirteen colonies.]

Thomas Paine's "The Crisis"

"These are the times that try men's souls."

Only a few months had passed since the Continental Congress had adopted the Declaration of Independence and Patriots throughout the colonies had celebrated their newly proclaimed liberty with the ringing of bells and wild celebrations around blazing bonfires. Now, with winter approaching, jubilation had given way to despair. The colonial cause seemed doomed to defeat. Washington's army, reduced to a ragged band of hardly more than five thousand men, was encamped in hastily constructed shelters on the west bank of the Delaware River.

Such was the desperate situation that prompted Thomas Paine to write The Crisis. When read to the cold and hungry troops, Paine's stirring words helped to revive their flagging spirits. The colonial victories at Trenton in the dawn of a bleak Christmas morning and at Princeton a few days later marked a turning point in the war.

December 1776

These are the times that try men's souls. The summer soldier and the sunshine patriot will, in this crisis, shrink from the service of their country; but he that stands it now deserves the love and thanks of man and woman. Tyranny, like hell, is not easily conquered; yet we have this consolation with us, that the harder the conflict, the more glorious the triumph. What we obtain too cheap, we esteem too lightly; it is dearness [costliness] only that gives everything its value. Heaven knows how to put a proper price upon its goods; and it would be strange indeed if so celestial [divine] an article as FREEDOM should not be highly rated. Britain, with an army to enforce her tyranny, has declared that she has a right (not only to TAX) but "to BIND us in

ALL CASES WHATSOEVER," and if being bound in that manner is not slavery, then is there not such a thing as slavery upon earth. Even the expression is impious [lacking in respect]; for so unlimited a power can belong only to God.

Whether the independence of the continent was declared too soon or delayed too long, I will not now enter into as an argument; my own simple opinion is that had it been eight months earlier, it would have been much better. . . .

I have as little superstition in me as any man living, but my secret opinion has ever been, and still is, that God Almighty will not give up a people to military destruction or leave them unsupportedly to perish, who have so earnestly and so repeatedly sought to avoid the calamities of war, by every decent method which wisdom could invent. Neither have I so much of the infidel [non-Christian] in me as to suppose that He has relinquished the government of the world and given us up to the care of devils; and as I do not, I cannot see on what grounds the king of Britain can look up to heaven for help against us; a common murderer, a highwayman, or a housebreaker has as good a pretense as he.

'Tis surprising to see how rapidly a panic will sometimes run through a country. All nations and ages have been subject to them. Britain has trembled like an ague at the report of a French fleet of flat-bottomed boats; and in the fourteenth [fifteenth] century ° the whole English army, after ravaging the kingdom of France, was driven back like men petrified with fear; and this brave exploit was performed by a few broken forces collected and headed by a woman, Joan of Arc. Would that heaven might inspire some Jersey maid to spirit up [arouse] her countrymen and save her fair fellow sufferers from ravage and ravishment! Yet panics, in some cases, have their uses; they produce as much good as hurt. Their duration is always short; the mind soon grows through them and acquires a firmer habit than before. But their peculiar advantage is that they are the touchstones [tests] of sincerity and hypocrisy and bring things and men to light which might otherwise have lain forever undiscovered. In fact, they have the same effect on secret traitors which an imaginary apparition would have upon a private murderer. They sift out the hidden thoughts of man and hold them up in public to the world.

° Paine was thinking of the 1400's, but mistakenly called them the fourteenth century.

Many a disguised Tory has lately shown his head, that shall peni-
tentially solemnize [regretfully remember] with curses the day on
which Howe [General Howe of the British Army] arrived upon the
Delaware. . . .

I shall conclude this paper with some miscellaneous remarks on the
state of our affairs and shall begin with asking the following question: Why is it that the enemy have left the New England provinces
and made these middle ones the seat of the war? The answer is easy:
New England is not infested with Tories, and we are. . . . And what
is a Tory? Good God! What is he? I should not be afraid to go with
a hundred Whigs against a thousand Tories, were they to attempt to
get into arms. Every Tory is a coward; for servile [submissive], slavish,
self-interested fear is the foundation of Toryism; and a man under
such influence, though he may be cruel, never can be brave. . . .

I once felt all that kind of anger which a man ought to feel against
the mean principles that are held by the Tories; a noted one, who
kept a tavern at Amboy, was standing at his door, with as pretty a
child in his hand, about eight or nine years old, as I ever saw, and
after speaking his mind freely as he thought was prudent, finished
with this unfatherly expression, "Well! Give me peace in my day."
Not a man lives on the continent but fully believes that a separation
must sometime or other finally take place, and a generous parent
should have said, "If there must be trouble, let it be in my day that
my child may have peace," and this single reflection, well applied, is
sufficient to awaken every man to duty. Not a place upon earth might
be so happy as America. Her situation is remote from all the wran-
gling world, and she has nothing to do but to trade with them. A man
can distinguish himself between temper and principle, and I am as
confident, as I am that God governs the world, that America will
never be happy till she gets clear of foreign dominion. Wars, without
ceasing, will break out till that period arrives, and the continent must
in the end be conqueror; for though the flame of liberty may sometimes cease to shine, the coal can never expire. . . .

I turn with the warm ardor of a friend to those who have nobly
stood, and are yet determined to stand the matter out; I call not
upon a few but upon all; not on this state or that state, but on every
state: Up and help us; lay your shoulders to the wheel; better have
too much force than too little when so great an object is at stake.
Let it be told to the future world that in the depth of winter, when

nothing but hope and virtue could survive, the city and the country, alarmed at one common danger, came forth to meet and to repulse it. Say not that thousands are gone, [but] turn out your tens of thousands; throw not the burden of the day upon Providence, but *"show your faith by your works,"* that God may bless you. It matters not where you live or what rank of life you hold; the evil or the blessing will reach you all. The far and the near, the home counties and the back, the rich and the poor, will suffer or rejoice alike. The heart that feels not now is dead; the blood of his children will curse his cowardice who shrinks back at a time when a little might have saved the whole and made them happy. I love the man that can smile in trouble, that can gather strength from distress and grow brave by reflection. 'Tis the business of little minds to shrink; but he whose heart is firm and whose conscience approves his conduct will pursue his principles unto death. My own line of reasoning is to myself as straight and clear as a ray of light. Not all the treasures of the world, so far as I believe, could have induced me to support an offensive war, for I think it murder; but if a thief breaks into my house, burns and destroys my property, and kills or threatens to kill me or those that are in it and to *"bind me in all cases whatsoever"* to his absolute will, am I to suffer it? What signifies . . . to me whether he who does it is a king or a common man; my countryman or not my countryman; whether it be done by an individual villain or an army of them? If we reason to the root of things, we shall find no difference; neither can any just cause be assigned [determined] why we should punish in the one case and pardon in the other. Let them call me rebel and welcome. I feel no concern from it; . . .

There are cases which cannot be overdone by language, and this is one. There are persons, too, who see not the full extent of the evil which threatens them; they solace themselves with hopes that the enemy, if he succeed, will be merciful. It is the madness of folly to expect mercy from those who have refused to do justice; and even mercy, where conquest is the object, is only a trick of war; the cunning of the fox is as murderous as the violence of the wolf, and we ought to guard equally against both. . . .

I thank God that I fear not. I see no real cause for fear. I know our situation well and can see the way out of it. While our army was collected, Howe dared not risk a battle; and it is no credit to him that he decamped from the White Plains and waited a mean opportunity to ravage the defenseless Jerseys; but it is great credit to us that, with a handful of men, we sustained an orderly retreat for near an hundred miles, brought off our ammunition, all our field pieces, the greatest part of our stores, and had four rivers to pass. None can say that our retreat was precipitate [abrupt], for we were near three weeks in performing it, [in order] that the country might have time to come in. Twice we marched back to meet the enemy and remained out till dark. The sign of fear was not seen in our camp, and had not some cowardly and disaffected [discontented] inhabitants spread false alarms through the country, the Jerseys had never been ravaged. Once more we are again collected and collecting; our new army at both ends of the continent is recruiting fast, and we shall be able to open the next campaign with sixty thousand men, well armed and clothed. This is our situation, and who will may know it. By perseverance and fortitude we have the prospect of a glorious issue; by cowardice and submission, a sad choice of a variety of evils. . . . And if there yet remains one thoughtless wretch who believes it not, let him suffer it unlamented.

The Articles of Confederation

"Each state retains its sovereignty, freedom, and independence. . . ."

With the Declaration of Independence, the colonies cut the ties binding them to Great Britain. Now, with this decisive step behind them, the thirteen independent states faced the formidable problem of organizing a central government under which they could carry on the war effort and, with victory achieved, move into the future as a united people. In response to a resolution presented by Richard Henry Lee, who had also taken the initiative in moving for a declaration of independence, the Second Continental Congress undertook to solve the problem by appointing a committee to draft a constitution.

The constitution, known as the Articles of Confederation, was adopted on November 15, 1777, but, as a result of a controversy over the claims to western lands, was not ratified by the thirteen states until 1781. This constitution was a remarkable achievement in that it did create a union; it did provide a central government under which the colonies fought the war and won the victory; and it did enact the Land Ordinance of 1785 and the Northwest Ordinance. As the years passed, however, the weaknesses of a loose confederation became increasingly apparent, and more and more of America's leaders began to consider the advantages of a stronger central government, or a federal union.

March 1, 1781

...We, the undersigned delegates of the states...agree to certain Articles of Confederation and perpetual Union between the States....

Article 1. The style [title] of this confederacy shall be "The United States of America."

Article 2. Each state retains its sovereignty, freedom, and independence, and every power, jurisdiction [authority to act], and right which is not by this confederation expressly delegated to the United States in Congress assembled.

Article 3. The said states hereby severally enter into a firm league of friendship with each other for their common defense, the security of their liberties, and their mutual and general welfare, binding themselves to assist each other against all force offered to [them] or attacks made upon them or [upon] any of them on account of religion, sovereignty, trade, or any other pretense whatever.

Article 4. The better to secure and perpetuate [cause to endure] mutual friendship and intercourse [business connections] among the people of the different states in this union, the free inhabitants of each of these states ... shall be entitled to all privileges and immunities of free citizens in the several states; ...

If any person guilty of, or charged with, treason, felony [crime], or other high misdemeanor in any state shall flee from justice, he shall, upon demand of the governor or executive power of the state from which he fled, be delivered up and removed to the state having jurisdiction of his offense.

Full faith and credit shall be given in each of these states to the records, acts, and judicial proceedings of the courts and magistrates of every other state.

Article 5. ... Delegates shall be annually appointed in such manner as the legislature of each state shall direct to meet in Congress on the first Monday in November in every year....

No state shall be represented in Congress by less than two [members], nor by more than seven members; and no person shall be capable of being a delegate for more than three years in any term of six years; nor shall any person, being a delegate, be capable of holding any office under the United States, for which he, or another for his benefit, receives any salary, fees, or emolument [payment] of any kind....

In determining questions in the United States, in Congress assembled, each state shall have one vote.

Freedom of speech and debate in Congress shall not be impeached or questioned in any court or place out of Congress, and the members of Congress shall be protected in their persons from arrests and imprisonments during the time of their going to and from and attendance on Congress, except for treason, felony, or breach of the peace.

Article 6. No state without the consent of the United States in Congress assembled shall send any embassy [ambassador] to, or receive any embassy from, or enter into any conference, agreement, or alliance or treaty with any king, prince, or state; nor shall any person holding any office of profit or trust under the United States, or any of ... [the states], accept ... any present, emolument, office, or title of any kind whatever from any king, prince, or foreign state; nor shall the United States in Congress assembled, or any of ... [the states], grant any title of nobility.

No two or more states shall enter into any treaty, confederation, or alliance whatever between them without the consent of the United States in Congress assembled....

No state shall lay any imposts [taxes on trade] or duties which may interfere with any stipulations [conditions] in treaties entered into by the United States in Congress assembled....

No vessels of war shall be kept up in time of peace by any state except such number only as shall be deemed necessary by the United

States in Congress assembled for the defense of such state or its trade; nor shall any body of forces be kept up by any state in time of peace except such number only as in the judgment of the United States in Congress assembled shall be deemed requisite to garrison [furnish with soldiers] the forts necessary for the defense of such state; but every state shall always keep up a well-regulated and disciplined militia, . . . a due number of field pieces and tents, and a proper quantity of arms, ammunition, and camp equipage [equipment].

No state shall engage in any war without the consent of the United States in Congress assembled, unless such state be actually invaded by enemies, or shall have received certain advice of a resolution being formed by some nation of Indians to invade such state, and the danger is so imminent as not to admit of a delay till the United States in Congress assembled can be consulted. . . .

Article 7. When land forces are raised by any state for the common defense, all officers of or under the rank of colonel shall be appointed by the legislature of each state respectively by whom such forces shall be raised or in such manner as such state shall direct. . . .

Article 8. All charges of war, and all other expenses that shall be incurred for the common defense or general welfare and allowed by the United States in Congress assembled shall be defrayed out of a common treasury, which shall be supplied by the several states, in proportion to the value of all land within each state, granted to or surveyed for any person, as such land and the buildings and improvements thereon shall be estimated according to such mode as the United States in Congress assembled shall from time to time direct and appoint. The taxes for paying that proportion shall be laid and levied by the authority and direction of the legislatures of the several states within the time agreed upon by the United States in Congress assembled.

Article 9. The United States in Congress assembled shall have the sole and exclusive right and power of determining on peace and war, except in the cases mentioned in the sixth article; of sending and receiving ambassadors; [of] entering into treaties and alliances . . . ; of granting letters of marque and reprisal ° in times of peace; [of]

° *letters of marque and reprisal:* licenses issued by the government to privateers —armed ships privately owned—allowing them to attack enemy ships during wartime.

appointing courts for the trial of piracies and felonies committed on the high seas. . . .

The United States in Congress assembled shall also be the last resort on appeal in all disputes and differences now subsisting or that hereafter may arise between two or more states concerning boundary, jurisdiction, or any other cause whatever. . . .

The United States in Congress assembled shall also have the sole and exclusive right and power of regulating the alloy [comparative purity] and value of coin struck by their own authority or by that of the respective states; fixing the standard of weights and measures throughout the United States; regulating the trade and managing all affairs with the Indians, [who are] not members of any of the states, provided that the legislative right of any state within its own limits be not infringed or violated; establishing and regulating post offices from one state to another, throughout all the United States, and exacting such postage on the papers passing through the same as may be requisite to defray the expenses of the said office; appointing all officers of the land forces in the service of the United States, except regimental officers; appointing all the officers of the naval forces and commissioning all officers whatever in the Service of the United States; making rules for the government and regulation of the said land and naval forces and directing their operations.

The United States in Congress assembled shall have authority to appoint a committee to sit in the recess [intermission] of Congress, to be denominated [named] "A Committee of the States," and to consist of one delegate from each state; and to appoint such other committees and civil officers as may be necessary for managing the general affairs of the United States under their direction; to appoint one of their number to preside, provided that no person be allowed to serve in the office of President more than one year in any term of three years; to ascertain the necessary sums of money to be raised for the service of the United States, and to appropriate and apply the same for defraying the public expenses; to borrow money or emit [print and circulate] bills on the credit of the United States, transmitting every half year to the respective states an account of the sums of money so borrowed or emitted; to build and equip a navy; to agree upon the number of land forces and to make requisitions from each state for its quota, in proportion to the number of white inhabitants in such state; which requisition shall be binding, and thereupon the legislature of each state shall appoint the regimental officers, raise the men and clothe, arm, and equip them in a soldier-like manner, at the expense of the United States and the officers and men so clothed, armed, and equipped shall march to the place appointed, and within the time agreed on by the United States in Congress assembled....

The United States in Congress assembled shall never engage in a war, nor grant letters of marque and reprisal in time of peace, nor enter into any treaties or alliances, nor coin money, nor regulate the value thereof, nor ascertain the sums and expenses necessary for the defense and welfare of the United States, or [of] any of them, nor emit bills, nor borrow money on the credit of the United States, nor appropriate money, nor agree upon the number of vessels of war to be built or purchased, or the number of land or sea forces to be raised, nor appoint a commander in chief of the army or navy unless nine states assent to the same; nor shall a question on any other point, except for adjourning from day to day, be determined unless by the votes of a majority of the United States in Congress assembled.

The Congress of the United States shall have power to adjourn to any time within the year and to any place within the United States so that no period of adjournment be for a longer duration than the space of six months, and shall publish the journal of their proceedings monthly, except such parts thereof relating to treaties, alliances, or military operations as in their judgment require secrecy; and the yeas and nays of the delegates of each state on any question shall be entered on the journal when it is desired by any delegate; and the delegates of a state, or any of them, at his or their request shall be furnished with a transcript [copy] of the said journal, except such parts as are above excepted, to lay before the legislatures of the several states.

Article 10. The Committee of the States, or any nine of them, shall be authorized to execute in the recess of Congress such of the powers of Congress as the United States in Congress assembled, by the consent of nine states, shall from time to time think expedient [necessary] to vest [furnish] them with; provided that no power be delegated to the said Committee for the exercise of which, by the Articles of Confederation, the voice of nine states in the Congress of the United States assembled is requisite.

Article 11. Canada acceding [agreeing] to this Confederation, and joining in the measures of the United States, shall be admitted into, and entitled to all the advantages of, this union: but no other colony shall be admitted into the same, unless such admission be agreed to by nine states.

Article 12. All bills of credit emitted, monies borrowed, and debts contracted by, or under, the authority of Congress, before the assembling of the United States, in pursuance [carrying out] of the present Confederation, shall be deemed and considered as a charge against the United States, for payment and satisfaction whereof the said United States and the public faith are hereby solemnly pledged.

Article 13. Every state shall abide by the determinations [decisions] of the United States in Congress assembled on all questions which by this Confederation are submitted to them. And the Articles of this Confederation shall be inviolably observed by every state, and the union shall be perpetual; nor shall any alteration at any time hereafter be made in any of them; unless such alteration be agreed to in a Congress of the United States and be afterward confirmed by the legislatures of every state.

. . . KNOW YE that we the undersigned delegates, by virtue of the power and authority to us given for that purpose, do by these presents, in the name and in behalf of our respective constituents [residents in the districts represented], fully and entirely ratify and confirm each and every of the said Articles of Confederation and Perpetual Union, and all and singular the matters and things therein contained: And we do further solemnly plight [pledge] and engage the faith of our respective constituents that they shall abide by the determinations of the United States in Congress assembled on all questions which by the said Confederation are submitted to them. And that the Articles thereof shall be inviolably observed by the states we respectively represent, and that the union shall be perpetual. In witness whereof we have hereunto set our hands in Congress. Done at Philadelphia in the state of Pennsylvania the ninth day of July in the Year of Our Lord one thousand seven hundred and seventy-eight, and in the third year of the independence of America.

[Signed by representatives of the thirteen states.]

The Land Ordinance

*"There shall be reserved the lot No. 16 of every
township for the maintenance of public schools...."*

The Ordinance of 1785 provided for a regular, systematic
development of the western lands. Its rectangular surveys and
six-mile-square townships gave a checkerboard pattern to
many of the new states.

The law served several useful purposes. It brought money
into the treasury from the sale of public lands; it eliminated
many boundary disputes; and it provided for orderly and
compact settlement of the wilderness. Until the Homestead
Act of 1862, this legislation set the pattern for our public
land system.

May 20, 1785

Be it ordained [established by law] by the United States in Congress assembled that the territory ceded by individual states to the
United States, which has been purchased from the Indian inhabitants, shall be disposed of in the following manner:

A surveyor from each state shall be appointed by Congress or a
Committee of the States....

The surveyors, as they are respectively qualified, shall proceed to
divide the said territory into townships of six miles square by lines
running due north and south and [by] others crossing these at right
angles, as near as may be....

The first line, runing due north and south as aforesaid, shall begin
on the River Ohio at a point that shall be found to be due north from
the western termination of a line which has been run as the southern
boundary of the state of Pennsylvania; and the first line, running
east and west, shall begin at the same point and shall extend through-

out the whole territory.... The geographer shall designate the townships or fractional parts of townships by numbers progressively from south to north; always beginning each range with No. 1; and the ranges shall be distinguished by their progressive numbers to the westward. The first range, extending from the Ohio to the Lake Erie, being marked No. 1....

The plats [maps] of the townships, respectively, shall be marked by subdivisions into lots of one mile square, or 640 acres ... and numbered from 1 to 36....

...the Secretary of War shall take by lot a number of townships ... for the use of the late Continental army....

...none of the lands within the said territory [shall] be sold under the price of one dollar the acre, to be paid in specie [coin], or loan-office certificates reduced to specie value by the scale of depreciation, or certificates of liquidated debts of the United States, including interest....

There shall be reserved for the United States out of every township ... four lots .... There shall be reserved the lot No. 16 of every township for the maintenance of public schools within the said township ....

AND WHEREAS, Congress ... stipulated grants of land to certain officers and soldiers of the late Continental army ... for complying with such engagements; be it ordained that the Secretary of War ... determine who are the objects of the above resolutions and engagements ... and cause the townships, hereinbefore reserved for the use of the late Continental army, to be drawn for in such manner as he shall deem expedient....

The Virginia Statute for Religious Freedom

". . . truth is great and will prevail if left to herself . . ."

Jefferson hated every kind of tyranny over the minds of men. His crusade brought him into conflict with the Anglican Church, the established church in Virginia. He wanted, in his own words, "freedom for the Jew and the Gentile, the Christian and the Mohammedan, the Hindu and infidel of every denomination."

After long and often bitter debate, the Virginia legislature finally adopted the law Jefferson had drafted. Five years later, when the First Amendment to the Constitution became part of "the supreme law of the land," the principle of the separation of church and state was established as a basic rule of our national government.

January 16, 1786

I. Well aware that Almighty God has created the mind free; *that* all attempts to influence it by temporal [civil] punishments or burdens or by civil incapacitations [lack of fitness for office], tend only to . . . [produce] habits of hypocrisy and meanness and are a departure from the plan of the Holy Author of our religion, who, being Lord both of body and mind, yet chose not to propagate [spread abroad] it by coercions [force] on either, as was in his Almighty power to do; *that* the impious presumption of legislators and rulers, civil as well as ecclesiastical, who, being themselves but fallible and uninspired men, have assumed dominion [rule] over the faith of others, setting up their own opinions and modes of thinking as the only true and infallible [ones], and, as such, endeavoring to impose them on others, have established and maintained false religions over the greatest part of the world and through all time; *that* to compel a man to furnish contributions of money for the propagation of opinions which he disbelieves is sinful and tyrannical; *that* even ... forcing him to support this or that teacher of his own religious persuasion is depriving him of the comfortable liberty of giving his contributions to the particular pastor whose morals he would make his pattern and whose powers he feels most persuasive to righteousness ... ; *that* our civil rights have no dependence on our religious opinions any more than [on] our opinions in physics or geometry; *that* therefore the proscribing [of] any citizen as unworthy [of] the public confidence by laying upon him an incapacity of being called to offices of trust and emolument unless he profess or renounce this or that religious opinion is depriving him injuriously of those privileges and advantages to which in common with his fellow citizens he has a natural right; ... *that* to suffer the civil magistrate to intrude his powers into the field of opinion and to restrain the profession or propagation of principles on supposition of their ill tendency is a dangerous fallacy which at once destroys all religious liberty, because he [the magistrate], being, of course, judge of that tendency, will make his opinions the rule of judgment and approve or condemn the sentiments of others only as they shall square with, or differ from, his own; *that* it is time enough for the rightful purposes of civil government for its officers to interfere when principles break out into overt [open, or public] acts against peace and good order; and, finally, *that* truth is great and will prevail if left to herself, that she is the proper and sufficient antagonist to error and has nothing to fear from the conflict, unless by human interposition disarmed of her natural weapons, free argument and debate, [for] errors [cease] to be dangerous when it is permitted freely to contradict them.

II. *Be it enacted by the General Assembly* that no man shall be compelled to frequent or support any religious worship, place, or ministry whatsoever, nor shall be enforced, restrained, molested, or burdened in his body or goods, nor shall otherwise suffer on account of his religious opinions or belief; but that all men shall be free to profess, and by argument to maintain, their opinion in matters of religion, and that the same shall in no wise diminish, enlarge, or affect their civil capacities.

III. And though we well know that this assembly, elected by the people for the ordinary purposes of legislation only, [has] no power to restrain the acts of succeeding assemblies, constituted with powers equal to her own, and that therefore to declare this act to be irrevocable would be of no effect in law; yet, as we are free to declare, and do declare, that the rights hereby asserted are of the natural rights of mankind, and that if any act shall hereafter be passed to repeal the present or to narrow its operation, such act will be an infringement [violation] of natural rights.

The Northwest Ordinance

"...such state shall be admitted...on an equal footing with the original states..."

When the original thirteen states formed their first union under the Articles of Confederation, they found themselves in possession of a vast tract of land between the Appalachian Mountains and the Mississippi River. What should be done with it? Should the territory be treated as an American colony and its settlers regarded as second-class citizens? Or, should the land be carved into new states? America's leaders answered these questions when they adopted the Northwest Ordinance, or, as it is sometimes called, the Ordinance of 1787. With this great law, Americans took a significant step forward in the democratic tradition. New states were to be carved out of the old Northwest Territory and they were to be admitted into the union on the same basis as the original thirteen states. In addition, the newly created states were to adopt bills of rights, abolish slavery, treat the Indians fairly, and encourage education.

Is it any wonder that Daniel Webster doubted whether "any single law of any lawgiver, ancient or modern, has produced effects of more distinct, marked, and lasting character than the Ordinance of 1787"?

July 13, 1787

Be it ordained by the United States in Congress assembled ...
there shall be appointed from time to time by Congress a governor,
whose commission shall continue in force for the term of three years,
unless sooner revoked by Congress; ...

There shall be appointed from time to time by Congress a secretary, whose commission shall continue in force for four years unless
sooner revoked; ... There shall also be appointed a court to consist
of three judges, any two of whom to form a court,° who shall have
a common-law jurisdiction [control over ordinary affairs] and reside
in the district, ... and their commissions shall continue in force during good behavior.

The governor and judges, or a majority of them, shall adopt and
publish in the district such laws of the original states, criminal and
civil, as may be necessary and best suited to the circumstances of the
district and report them to Congress from time to time: which laws
shall be in force in the district until the organization of the General
Assembly therein, unless disapproved of by Congress; ...

The governor, for the time being, shall be commander in chief
of the militia [and shall] appoint and commission all officers in the
same below the rank of general officers [officers above the rank of
colonel]; all general officers shall be appointed and commissioned by
Congress.

So soon as there shall be five thousand free male inhabitants of
full age in the district, upon giving proof thereof to the governor, they
shall receive authority, with time and place, to elect representatives
from their counties or townships to represent them in the General
Assembly, provided that for every five hundred free male inhabitants,
there shall be one representative, and so on, ... until the number of
representatives shall amount to twenty-five; ... provided, also, that a
freehold in fifty acres of land in the district, having been a citizen
of one of the states and being resident in the district, or the like
freehold and two years residence in the district, shall be necessary to
qualify a man as an elector of a representative.

° *any two of whom to form a court:* may hold court without the third judge.

The representatives thus elected shall serve for the term of two years; and in case of the death of a representative, or removal from office, the governor shall issue a writ to the county or township for which he was a member, to elect another in his stead to serve for the residue [remainder] of the term.

The General Assembly, or legislature, shall consist of the governor, legislative council,° and a house of representatives. The legislative council shall consist of five members, to continue in office five years ... the governor, legislative council, and house of representatives shall have authority to make laws in all cases for the government of the district, not repugnant to the principles and articles in this ordinance....

And for extending the fundamental principles of civil and religious liberty, which form the basis whereon these republics, their laws and constitutions are erected; to fix and establish those principles as the basis of all laws, constitutions, and governments, which forever hereafter shall be formed in the said territory; to provide also for the establishment of states, and permanent government therein, and for their admission to a share in the federal councils on an equal footing with the original states, at as early periods as may be consistent with the general interest:

It is hereby ordained and declared by the authority aforesaid that the following articles shall be considered as articles of compact between the original states and the people and states in the said territory, and forever remain unalterable, unless by common consent, to wit:

Article 1. No person, demeaning [behaving] himself in a peaceable and orderly manner, shall ever be molested on account of his mode of worship or religious sentiments in the said territory.

Article 2. The inhabitants of the said territory shall always be entitled to the benefits of the writ of habeas corpus ° and of the trial by jury; of a proportionate representation of the people in the legislature; and of judicial proceedings according to the course of the common law. All persons shall be bailable,° unless for capital offenses [those punishable by death], where the proof shall be evident, or the

° *legislative council:* was nominated by the house of representatives and appointed by the Congress.
° See the English Habeas Corpus Act of 1679, page 19.
° *bailable:* entitled to seek release on bail.

presumption [probability] great. All fines shall be moderate; and no cruel or unusual punishments shall be inflicted. No man shall be deprived of his liberty or property, but by the judgment of his peers or the law of the land; and should the public exigencies [instantly important] make it necessary, for the common preservation, to take any person's property, or to demand his particular services, full compensation shall be made for the same. And, in the just preservation of rights and property, it is understood and declared that no law ought ever to be made or have force in the said territory, that shall, in any manner whatever, interfere with or affect private contracts or engagements, bona fide, and without fraud previously formed.

Article 3. Religion, morality, and knowledge being necessary to good government and the happiness of mankind, schools and the means of education shall forever be encouraged. The utmost good faith shall always be observed toward the Indians; their lands and property shall never be taken from them without their consent; and in their property, rights, and liberty they shall never be invaded or disturbed unless in just and lawful wars authorized by Congress; but laws founded in justice and humanity shall from time to time be made for preventing wrongs being done to them, and for preserving peace and friendship with them.

Article 4. The said territory and the states which may be formed therein, shall forever remain a part of this Confederacy of the United States of America, subject to the Articles of Confederation, and to such alterations therein as shall be constitutionally made; and to all the acts and ordinances of the United States in Congress assembled, conformable [agreeable] thereto. . . .

No tax shall be imposed on lands the property of the United States; and, in no case, shall nonresident proprietors be taxed higher than residents. The navigable waters leading into the Mississippi and St. Lawrence, and the carrying places between the same, shall be common highways and forever free, as well to the inhabitants of the said territory as to the citizens of the United States, and those of any other states that may be admitted into the Confederacy, without any tax, impost, or duty therefor.

Article 5. There shall be formed in the said territory, not less than three nor more than five states; . . . And, whenever any of the said states shall have sixty thousand free inhabitants therein, such state shall be admitted by its delegates into the Congress of the United

States on an equal footing with the original states in all respects whatever, and shall be at liberty to form a permanent constitution and state government: *Provided* the constitution and government so to be formed shall be republican ° and in conformity to the principles contained in these articles; and, so far as it can be consistent with the general interest of the Confederacy, such admission shall be allowed at an earlier period, and when there may be a smaller number of free inhabitants in the state than sixty thousand.

Article 6. There shall be neither slavery nor involuntary servitude in the said territory, otherwise than in punishment of crimes whereof the party shall have been duly convicted: *Provided*, always, that any person escaping into the same, from whom labor or service is lawfully claimed in any one of the original states, such fugitive may be lawfully reclaimed and conveyed to the person claiming his or her labor or services as aforesaid. . . .

The Constitution of the United States and the Amendments

"This Constitution . . . shall be the supreme law of the land . . ."

The Constitution of the United States represents the classic solution to one of mankind's greatest political problems: How can a group of small states combine into a strong union without losing their individuality and surrendering their control over local affairs? The Fathers of the Constitution—the fifty-five delegates who met at Philadelphia during the hot summer days of 1787—answered this question with a document which called for a federal plan of government, a system

° **government . . . shall be republican:** form of government in which the sovereign people elect representatives responsible to the people.

of separation of powers with checks and balances, and a procedure for orderly change to meet the exigencies of the future. Adopted on September 17, 1787, it was ratified in June 1788. Since that time the Constitution has served as a model for many new-born nations.

A serious objection to the new Constitution, however, was its lack of a "bill of rights." Determined to safeguard their hard-won rights, many Americans accepted the new government on the condition that provision be made for the protection of their fundamental liberties against usurpation by the newly created central government. On December 15, 1791, the first ten amendments to the Constitution were ratified. Gradually, over the years, more amendments were added as political, economic, and social problems called for solution.

September 17, 1787

PREAMBLE

We, the people of the United States, in order to form a more perfect Union, establish justice, insure domestic tranquillity, provide for the common defense, promote the general welfare, and secure the blessings of liberty to ourselves and our posterity, do ordain and establish this CONSTITUTION for the United States of America.

Article 1

Section 1. All legislative powers herein granted shall be vested in a Congress of the United States, which shall consist of a Senate and House of Representatives.

Section 2. 1. The House of Representatives shall be composed of members chosen every second year by the people of the several states, and the electors in each state shall have the qualifications requisite for electors of the most numerous branch of the state legislature.

2. No person shall be a Representative who shall not have attained to the age of twenty-five years, and been seven years a citizen of the United States, and who shall not, when elected, be an inhabitant of that state in which he shall be chosen.

3. Representatives [and direct taxes] ° shall be apportioned among the several states which may be included within this Union, according to their respective numbers, [which shall be determined by adding to the whole number of free persons, including those bound to service for a term of years, and excluding Indians not taxed, three-fifths of all other persons]. The actual enumeration shall be made within three years after the first meeting of the Congress of the United States, and within every subsequent term of ten years, in such manner as they shall by law direct. The number of Representatives shall not exceed 1 for every 30,000, but each state shall have at least 1 Representative; [and until such enumeration shall be made, the state of New Hampshire shall be entitled to choose 3; Massachusetts, 8; Rhode Island and Providence Plantations, 1; Connecticut, 5; New York, 6; New Jersey, 4; Pennsylvania, 8; Delaware, 1; Maryland, 6; Virginia, 10; North Carolina, 5; South Carolina, 5; and Georgia, 3].

4. When vacancies happen in the representation from any state, the executive authority thereof shall issue writs of election to fill such vacancies.

5. The House of Representatives shall choose their Speaker and other officers; and shall have the sole power of impeachment.

Section 3. 1. The Senate of the United States shall be composed of two Senators from each state, [chosen by the legislature thereof,] for six years, and each Senator shall have one vote.

2. [Immediately after they shall be assembled in consequence of the first election, they shall be divided as equally as may be into three classes. The seats of the Senators of the first class shall be vacated at the expiration of the second year, of the second class at the expiration of the fourth year, and of the third class at the expiration of the sixth year, so that one-third may be chosen every second year; and if vacancies happen by resignation, or otherwise, during the recess of the legislature of any state, the executive thereof may make temporary appointments until the next meeting of the legislature, which shall then fill such vacancies.]

3. No person shall be a Senator who shall not have attained to the age of thirty years, and been nine years a citizen of the United States, and who shall not, when elected, be an inhabitant of that state for which he shall be chosen.

° Portions of the text printed in brackets have gone out of date or have been changed by amendment.

4. The Vice-President of the United States shall be president of the Senate, but shall have no vote, unless they be equally divided.

5. The Senate shall choose their other officers, and also a president *pro tempore*, in the absence of the Vice-President, or when he shall exercise the office of President of the United States.

6. The Senate shall have the sole power to try all impeachments. When sitting for that purpose, they shall be on oath or affirmation. When the President of the United States is tried, the Chief Justice shall preside; and no person shall be convicted without the concurrence of two-thirds of the members present.

7. Judgment in cases of impeachment shall not extend further than to removal from office, and disqualification to hold and enjoy any office of honor, trust, or profit under the United States; but the party convicted shall nevertheless be liable and subject to indictment, trial, judgment, and punishment, according to law.

Section 4. 1. The times, places, and manner of holding elections for Senators and Representatives shall be prescribed in each state by the legislature thereof; but the Congress may at any time by law make or alter such regulations, except as to the places of choosing Senators.

2. The Congress shall assemble at least once in every year, [and such meeting shall be on the first Monday in December,] unless they shall by law appoint a different day.

Section 5. 1. Each house shall be the judge of the elections, returns, and qualifications of its own members, and a majority of each shall constitute a quorum to do business; but a smaller number may adjourn from day to day, and may be authorized to compel the attendance of absent members, in such manner, and under such penalties, as each house may provide.

2. Each house may determine the rules of its proceedings, punish its members for disorderly behavior, and with the concurrence of two-thirds, expel a member.

3. Each house shall keep a journal of its proceedings, and from time to time publish the same, excepting such parts as may in their judgment require secrecy; and the yeas and nays of the members of either house on any question shall, at the desire of one-fifth of those present, be entered on the journal.

4. Neither house, during the session of Congress, shall, without the consent of the other, adjourn for more than three days, nor to any other place than that in which the two houses shall be sitting.

Section 6. 1. The Senators and Representatives shall receive a compensation for their services, to be ascertained by law and paid out of the Treasury of the United States. They shall in all cases except treason, felony, and breach of the peace, be privileged from arrest during their attendance at the session of their respective houses, and in going to and returning from the same; and for any speech or debate in either house, they shall not be questioned in any other place.

2. No Senator or Representative shall, during the time for which he was elected, be appointed to any civil office under the authority of the United States, which shall have been created, or the emoluments whereof shall have been increased, during such time; and no person holding any office under the United States shall be a member of either house during his continuance in office.

Section 7. 1. All bills for raising revenue shall originate in the House of Representatives; but the Senate may propose or concur with amendments as on other bills.

2. Every bill which shall have passed the House of Representatives and the Senate, shall, before it become a law, be presented to the President of the United States; if he approve, he shall sign it, but if not, he shall return it, with his objections, to that house in which it shall have originated, who shall enter the objections at large on their journal, and proceed to reconsider it. If after such reconsideration two-thirds of that house shall agree to pass the bill, it shall be sent, together with the objections, to the other house, by which it shall likewise be reconsidered, and, if approved by two-thirds of that house, it shall become a law. But in all such cases the votes of both houses shall be determined by yeas and nays, and the names of the persons voting for and against the bill shall be entered on the journal of each house respectively. If any bill shall not be returned by the President within ten days (Sundays excepted) after it shall have been presented to him, the same shall be a law, in like manner as if he had signed it, unless the Congress by their adjournment prevent its return, in which case it shall not be a law.

3. Every order, resolution, or vote to which the concurrence of the Senate and House of Representatives may be necessary (except on a question of adjournment) shall be presented to the President of the United States; and before the same shall take effect, shall be approved by him, or being disapproved by him, shall be repassed by two-thirds

of the Senate and House of Representatives, according to the rules and limitations prescribed in the case of a bill.

Section 8. The Congress shall have power

1. To lay and collect taxes, duties, imposts, and excises, to pay the debts and provide for the common defense and general welfare of the United States; but all duties, imposts, and excises shall be uniform throughout the United States;

2. To borrow money on the credit of the United States;

3. To regulate commerce with foreign nations, and among the several states, and with the Indian tribes;

4. To establish a uniform rule of naturalization, and uniform laws on the subject of bankruptcies throughout the United States;

5. To coin money, regulate the value thereof, and of foreign coin, and fix the standard of weights and measures;

6. To provide for the punishment of counterfeiting the securities and current coin of the United States;

7. To establish post offices and post roads;

8. To promote the progress of science and useful arts by securing for limited times to authors and inventors the exclusive right to their respective writings and discoveries;

9. To constitute tribunals inferior to the Supreme Court;

10. To define and punish piracies and felonies committed on the high seas and offenses against the law of nations;

11. To declare war, [grant letters of marque and reprisal,] and make rules concerning captures on land and water;

12. To raise and support armies, but no appropriation of money to that use shall be for a longer term than two years;

13. To provide and maintain a navy;

14. To make rules for the government and regulation of the land and naval forces;

15. To provide for calling forth the militia to execute the laws of the Union, suppress insurrections, and repel invasions;

16. To provide for organizing, arming, and disciplining the militia, and for governing such part of them as may be employed in the service of the United States, reserving to the states, respectively, the appointment of the officers, and the authority of training the militia according to the discipline prescribed by Congress;

17. To exercise exclusive legislation in all cases whatsoever, over such district (not exceeding ten miles square) as may, by cession of

particular states, and the acceptance of Congress, become the seat of government of the United States, and to exercise like authority over all places purchased by the consent of the legislature of the state in which the same shall be, for the erection of forts, magazines, arsenals, dock-yards, and other needful buildings;—and

18. To make all laws which shall be necessary and proper for carrying into execution the foregoing powers, and all other powers vested by this Constitution in the government of the United States, or in any department or officer thereof.

Section 9. 1. [The migration or importation of such persons as any of the states now existing shall think proper to admit shall not be prohibited by the Congress prior to the year 1808; but a tax or duty may be imposed on such importation, not exceeding $10 for each person.]

2. The privilege of the writ of *habeas corpus* shall not be suspended, unless when in cases of rebellion or invasion the public safety may require it.

3. No bill of attainder or *ex post facto* law shall be passed.

4. No capitation or other direct tax shall be laid, unless in proportion to the census or enumeration hereinbefore directed to be taken.

5. No tax or duty shall be laid on articles exported from any state.

6. No preference shall be given by any regulation of commerce or revenue to the ports of one state over those of another; nor shall vessels bound to, or from, one state, be obliged to enter, clear, or pay duties in another.

7. No money shall be drawn from the Treasury, but in consequence of appropriations made by law; and a regular statement and account of the receipts and expenditures of all public money shall be published from time to time.

8. No title of nobility shall be granted by the United States; and no person holding any office of profit or trust under them, shall, without the consent of the Congress, accept of any present, emolument, office, or title, of any kind whatever, from any king, prince, or foreign state.

Section 10. 1. No state shall enter into any treaty, alliance, or confederation; grant letters of marque and reprisal; coin money; emit bills of credit; make anything but gold and silver coin a tender in payment of debts; pass any bill of attainder, *ex post facto* law, or law impairing the obligation of contracts, or grant any title of nobility.

2. No state shall, without the consent of the Congress, lay any

imposts or duties on imports or exports, except what may be absolutely necessary for executing its inspection laws; and the net produce of all duties and imposts, laid by any state on imports or exports, shall be for the use of the Treasury of the United States; and all such laws shall be subject to the revision and control of the Congress.

3. No state shall, without the consent of Congress, lay any duty of tonnage, keep troops, or ships of war in time of peace, enter into any agreement or compact with another state, or with a foreign power, or engage in war, unless actually invaded, or in such imminent danger as will not admit of delay.

Article 2

Section 1. 1. The executive power shall be vested in a President of the United States of America. He shall hold his office during the term of four years, and together with the Vice-President, chosen for the same term, be elected as follows:

2. Each state shall appoint, in such manner as the legislature thereof may direct, a number of electors, equal to the whole number of Senators and Representatives to which the state may be entitled in the Congress; but no Senator or Representative, or person holding an office of trust or profit under the United States, shall be appointed an elector.

3. [The electors shall meet in their respective states, and vote by ballot for two persons, of whom one at least shall not be an inhabitant of the same state with themselves. And they shall make a list of all the persons voted for, and of the number of votes for each; which list they shall sign and certify, and transmit sealed to the seat of the government of the United States, directed to the president of the Senate. The president of the Senate shall, in the presence of the Senate and House of Representatives, open all the certificates, and the votes shall then be counted. The persons having the greatest number of votes shall be the President, if such number be a majority of the whole number of electors appointed; and if there be more than one who have such majority, and have an equal number of votes, then the House of Representatives shall immediately choose by ballot one of them for President; and if no person have a majority, then from the five highest on the list the said House shall in like manner choose the President. But in choosing the President the votes shall be taken by states, the representation from each state having one vote. A quorum

for this purpose shall consist of a member or members from two-thirds of the states, and a majority of all the states shall be necessary to a choice. In every case, after the choice of the President, the person having the greatest number of votes of the electors shall be the Vice President. But if there should remain two or more who have equal votes, the Senate shall choose from them by ballot the Vice-President.]

4. The Congress may determine the time of choosing the electors and the day on which they shall give their votes; which day shall be the same throughout the United States.

5. No person except a natural-born citizen [or a citizen of the United States, at the time of the adoption of this Constitution,] shall be eligible to the office of President; neither shall any person be eligible to that office who shall not have attained to the age of thirty-five years, and been fourteen years a resident within the United States.

6. In case of the removal of the President from office, or of his death, resignation, or inability to discharge the powers and duties of the said office, the same shall devolve on the Vice-President, and the Congress may by law provide for the case of removal, death, resignation, or inability, both of the President and Vice-President, declaring what officer shall then act as President, and such officer shall act accordingly, until the disability be removed, or a President shall be elected.

7. The President shall, at stated times, receive for his services, a compensation, which shall neither be increased nor diminished during the period for which he shall have been elected, and he shall not receive within that period any other emolument from the United States, or any of them.

8. Before he enter on the execution of his office, he shall take the following oath or affirmation:—"I do solemnly swear (or affirm) that I will faithfully execute the office of President of the United States, and will to the best of my ability, preserve, protect, and defend the Constitution of the United States."

Section 2. 1. The President shall be Commander in Chief of the Army and Navy of the United States, and of the militia of the several states, when called into the actual service of the United States; he may require the opinion, in writing, of the principal officer in each of the executive departments, upon any subject relating to the duties of their respective offices, and he shall have power to grant reprieves and pardons for offenses against the United States, except in cases of impeachment.

2. He shall have power, by and with the advice and consent of the Senate, to make treaties, provided two-thirds of the Senators present concur; and he shall nominate, and by and with the advice and consent of the Senate, shall appoint ambassadors, other public ministers and consuls, judges of the Supreme Court, and all other officers of the United States, whose appointments are not herein otherwise provided for, and which shall be established by law; but the Congress may by law vest the appointment of such inferior officers, as they think proper, in the President alone, in the courts of law, or in the heads of departments.

3. The President shall have power to fill up all vacancies that may happen during the recess of the Senate, by granting commissions which shall expire at the end of their next session.

Section 3. He shall from time to time give to the Congress information of the state of the Union, and recommend to their consideration such measures as he shall judge necessary and expedient; he may, on extraordinary occasions, convene both houses, or either of them, and in case of disagreement between them, with respect to the time of adjournment, he may adjourn them to such time as he shall think proper; he shall receive ambassadors and other public ministers; he shall take care that the laws be faithfully executed, and shall commission all the officers of the United States.

Section 4. The President, Vice-President, and all civil officers of the United States, shall be removed from office on impeachment for, and conviction of, treason, bribery, or other high crimes and misdemeanors.

Article 3

Section 1. The judicial power of the United States shall be vested in one Supreme Court and in such inferior courts as the Congress may from time to time ordain and establish. The judges, both of the Supreme and inferior courts, shall hold their offices during good behavior, and shall, at stated times, receive for their services a compensation, which shall not be diminished during their continuance in office.

Section 2. 1. The judicial power shall extend to all cases, in law and equity, arising under this Constitution, the laws of the United States, and treaties made or which shall be made, under their authority; to all cases affecting ambassadors, other public ministers and consuls; to all cases of admiralty and maritime jurisdiction; to controversies to which the United States shall be a party; to controversies between two or more states; [between a state and citizens of another state;] between citizens of different states; between citizens of the same state claiming lands under grants of different states, and between a state, or the citizens thereof, and foreign states, citizens, or subjects.

2. In all cases affecting ambassadors, other public ministers and consuls, and those in which a state shall be a party, the Supreme Court shall have original jurisdiction. In all the other cases before mentioned, the Supreme Court shall have appellate jurisdiction, both as to law and fact, with such exceptions, and under such regulations as the Congress shall make.

3. The trial of all crimes, except in cases of impeachment, shall be by jury; and such trial shall be held in the state where the said crimes shall have been committed; but when not committed within any state, the trial shall be at such place or places as the Congress may by law have directed.

Section 3. 1. Treason against the United States shall consist only in levying war against them, or in adhering to their enemies, giving them aid and comfort. No person shall be convicted of treason unless on the testimony of two witnesses to the same overt act, or on confession in open court.

2. The Congress shall have power to declare the punishment of treason, but no attainder of treason shall work corruption of blood or forfeiture except during the life of the person attainted.

Article 4

Section 1. Full faith and credit shall be given in each state to the public acts, records, and judicial proceedings of every other state. And the Congress may by general laws prescribe the manner in which such acts, records, and proceedings shall be proved, and the effect thereof.

Section 2. 1. The citizens of each state shall be entitled to all privileges and immunities of citizens in the several states.

2. A person charged in any state with treason, felony, or other crime, who shall flee from justice, and be found in another state, shall

on demand of the executive authority of the state from which he fled, be delivered up, to be removed to the state having jurisdiction of the crime.

3. [No person held in service or labor in one state, under the laws thereof, escaping into another, shall in consequence of any law or regulation therein, be discharged from such service or labor, but shall be delivered up on claim of the party to whom such service or labor may be due.]

Section 3. 1. New states may be admitted by the Congress into this Union; but no new state shall be formed or erected within the jurisdiction of any other state; nor any state be formed by the junction of two or more states, or parts of states, without the consent of the legislatures of the states concerned as well as of the Congress.

2. The Congress shall have power to dispose of and make all needful rules and regulations respecting the territory or other property belonging to the United States; and nothing in this Constitution shall be so construed as to prejudice any claims of the United States, or of any particular state.

Section 4. The United States shall guarantee to every state in this Union a republican form of government, and shall protect each of them against invasion; and on application of the legislature, or of the executive (when the legislature cannot be convened) against domestic violence.

Article 5

The Congress, whenever two-thirds of both houses shall deem it necessary, shall propose amendments to this Constitution, or, on the application of the legislatures of two-thirds of the several states, shall call a convention for proposing amendments, which in either case shall be valid to all intents and purposes, as part of this Constitution, when ratified by the legislatures of three-fourths of the several states, or by conventions in three-fourths thereof, as the one or the other mode of ratification may be proposed by the Congress; provided that [no amendments which may be made prior to the year 1808 shall in any manner affect the first and fourth clauses in the Ninth Section of the First Article; and that] no state, without its consent, shall be deprived of its equal suffrage in the Senate.

Article 6

1. All debts contracted and engagements entered into, before the adoption of this Constitution, shall be as valid against the United States under this Constitution as under the Confederation.

2. This Constitution, and the laws of the United States which shall be made in pursuance thereof, and all treaties made, or which shall be made, under the authority of the United States, shall be the supreme law of the land; and the judges in every state shall be bound thereby, anything in the constitution or laws of any state to the contrary notwithstanding.

3. The Senators and Representatives before mentioned, and the members of the several state legislatures, and all executive and judicial officers, both of the United States and of the several states, shall be bound by oath or affirmation, to support this Constitution; but no religious test shall ever be required as a qualification to any office or public trust under the United States.

Article 7

The ratification of the convention of nine states shall be sufficient for the establishment of this Constitution between the states so ratifying the same.

DONE in Convention by the unanimous consent of the States present the seventeenth day of September in the year of our Lord one thousand seven hundred and eighty-seven and of the independence of the United States of America the twelfth. In witness whereof we have hereunto subscribed our names,

GEORGE WASHINGTON
President and deputy from Virginia

[Signed by representatives of the thirteen states.]

AMENDMENTS

(The first ten Amendments were adopted December 15, 1791, and form what is known as the "Bill of Rights.")

Amendment 1

Congress shall make no law respecting an establishment of religion, or prohibiting the free exercise thereof; or abridging the freedom of speech, or of the press; or the right of the people peaceably to assemble, and to petition the government for a redress of grievances.

Amendment 2

A well-regulated militia, being necessary to the security of a free state, the right of the people to keep and bear arms shall not be infringed.

Amendment 3

No soldier shall, in time of peace, be quartered in any house, without the consent of the owner; nor in time of war, but in a manner to be prescribed by law.

Amendment 4

The right of the people to be secure in their persons, houses, papers, and effects, against unreasonable searches and seizures, shall not be violated; and no warrants shall issue but upon probable cause, supported by oath or affirmation, and particularly describing the place to be searched and the persons or things to be seized.

Amendment 5

No person shall be held to answer for a capital, or otherwise infamous, crime, unless on a presentment or indictment of a grand jury, except in cases arising in the land or naval forces, or in the militia, when in actual service in time of war or public danger; nor shall any person be subject for the same offense to be twice put in jeopardy of life or limb; nor shall be compelled, in any criminal case, to be a witness against himself; nor be deprived of life, liberty, or property, without due process of law; nor shall private property be taken for public use without just compensation.

Amendment 6

In all criminal prosecutions, the accused shall enjoy the right to a speedy and public trial, by an impartial jury of the state and district wherein the crime shall have been committed, which district shall have been previously ascertained by law, and to be informed of the nature and cause of the accusation; to be confronted with the witnesses against him; to have compulsory process for obtaining witnesses in his favor; and to have the assistance of counsel for his defense.

Amendment 7

In suits at common law, where the value in controversy shall exceed twenty dollars, the right of trial by jury shall be preserved, and no fact tried by a jury shall be otherwise re-examined in any court of the United States than according to the rules of the common law.

Amendment 8

Excessive bail shall not be required, nor excessive fines imposed, nor cruel and unusual punishments inflicted.

Amendment 9

The enumeration in the Constitution of certain rights shall not be construed to deny or disparage others retained by the people.

Amendment 10

The powers not delegated to the United States by the Constitution, nor prohibited by it to the states, are reserved to the states respectively, or to the people.

Amendment 11 (1798)

The judicial power of the United States shall not be construed to extend to any suit in law or equity, commenced or prosecuted against one of the United States, by citizens of another state, or by citizens or subjects of any foreign state.

Amendment 12 (1804)

The electors shall meet in their respective states, and vote by ballot for President and Vice-President, one of whom, at least, shall not be an inhabitant of the same state with themselves; they shall name in their ballots the person voted for as President, and in distinct ballots the person voted for as Vice-President, and they shall make distinct lists of all persons voted for as President, and of all persons voted for as Vice-President, and of the number of votes for each, which lists they shall sign and certify, and transmit, sealed, to the seat of government of the United States, directed to the president of the Senate; the president of the Senate shall, in the presence of the Senate and House of Representatives, open all the certificates and the votes shall then be counted; the person having the greatest number of votes for President shall be the President, if such number be a majority of the whole number of electors appointed; and if no person have such majority, then from the persons having the highest numbers not exceeding three on the list of those voted for as President, the House of Representatives shall choose immediately, by ballot, the President. But in choosing the President, the votes shall be taken by states, the representation from each state having one vote; a quorum for this purpose shall consist of a member or members from two-thirds of the states, and a majority of all the states shall be necessary to a choice. [And if the House of Representatives shall not choose a President whenever the right of choice shall devolve upon them, before the fourth day of March next following, then the Vice-President shall act as President, as in the case of the death or other constitutional disability of the President.] The person having the greatest number of votes as Vice-President shall be the Vice-President, if such number be a majority of the whole number of electors appointed, and if no person have a majority, then, from the two highest numbers on the list, the Senate shall choose the Vice-President; a quorum for the purpose shall consist of two-thirds of the whole number of Senators, and a majority of the whole number shall be necessary to a choice. But no person constitutionally ineligible to the office of President shall be eligible to that of Vice-President of the United States.

Amendment 13 (1865)

Section 1. Neither slavery nor involuntary servitude, except as a punishment for crime whereof the party shall have been duly convicted, shall exist within the United States, or any place subject to their jurisdiction.

Section 2. Congress shall have power to enforce this article by appropriate legislation.

Amendment 14 (1868)

Section 1. All persons born or naturalized in the United States and subject to the jurisdiction thereof are citizens of the United States and of the state wherein they reside. No state shall make or enforce any law which shall abridge the privileges or immunities of citizens of the United States; nor shall any state deprive any person of life, liberty, or property, without due process of law; nor deny to any person within its jurisdiction the equal protection of the laws.

Section 2. Representatives shall be apportioned among the several states according to their respective numbers, counting the whole number of persons in each state, excluding Indians not taxed. But when the right to vote at any election for the choice of electors for President and Vice-President of the United States, Representatives in Congress, the executive and judicial officers of a state, or the members of the legislature thereof, is denied to any of the male inhabitants of such state, being twenty-one years of age and citizens of the United States, or in any way abridged, except for participation in rebellion, or other crime, the basis of representation therein shall be reduced in the proportion which the number of such male citizens shall bear to the whole number of male citizens twenty-one years of age in such state.

Section 3. No person shall be a Senator or Representative in Congress, or elector of President and Vice-President, or hold any office, civil or military, under the United States, or under any state, who, having previously taken an oath, as a member of Congress, or as an officer of the United States, or as a member of any state legislature, or as an executive or judicial officer of any state, to support the Constitution of the United States, shall have engaged in insurrection or rebellion against the same, or given aid or comfort to the enemies thereof. But Congress may, by vote of two-thirds of each house, remove such disability.

Section 4. The validity of the public debt of the United States, authorized by law, including debts incurred for payment of pensions and bounties for services in suppressing insurrection or rebellion, shall not be questioned. But neither the United States nor any state shall assume or pay any debt or obligation incurred in aid of insurrection or rebellion against the United States, [or any claim for the loss or emancipation of any slave;] but all such debts, obligations, and claims shall be held illegal and void.

Section 5. The Congress shall have power to enforce, by appropriate legislation, the provisions of this article.

Amendment 15 (1870)

Section 1. The right of citizens of the United States to vote shall not be denied or abridged by the United States or any state on account of race, color, or previous condition of servitude.

Section 2. The Congress shall have power to enforce this article by appropriate legislation.

Amendment 16 (1913)

The Congress shall have power to lay and collect taxes on incomes, from whatever source derived, without apportionment among the several states, and without regard to any census or enumeration.

Amendment 17 (1913)

Section 1. The Senate of the United States shall be composed of two Senators from each state, elected by the people thereof, for six years; and each Senator shall have one vote. The electors in each state shall have the qualifications requisite for electors of the most numerous branch of the state legislatures.

Section 2. When vacancies happen in the representation of any state in the Senate, the executive authority of such state shall issue writs of election to fill such vacancies: *Provided* that the legislature of any state may empower the executive thereof to make temporary appointments until the people fill the vacancies by election as the legislature may direct.

[*Section 3.* This amendment shall not be so construed as to affect the election or term of any Senator chosen before it becomes valid as part of the Constitution.]

Amendment 18 (1919)

[*Section 1.* After one year from the ratification of this article the manufacture, sale, or transportation of intoxicating liquors within, the importation thereof into, or the exportation thereof from, the United States and all territory subject to the jurisdiction thereof for beverage purposes is hereby prohibited.

Section 2. The Congress and the several states shall have concurrent power to enforce this article by appropriate legislation.

Section 3. This article shall be inoperative unless it shall have been ratified as an amendment to the Constitution by the legislatures of the several states, as provided in the Constitution, within seven years from the date of the submission hereof to the states by the Congress.]

Amendment 19 (1920)

Section 1. The right of citizens of the United States to vote shall not be denied or abridged by the United States or by any state on account of sex.

Section 2. Congress shall have power to enforce this article by appropriate legislation.

Amendment 20 (1933)

Section 1. The terms of the President and Vice-President shall end at noon on the 20th day of January, and the terms of Senators and Representatives at noon on the 3d day of January, of the years in which such terms would have ended if this article had not been ratified; and the terms of their successors shall then begin.

Section 2. The Congress shall assemble at least once in every year, and such meeting shall begin at noon on the 3d day of January, unless they shall by law appoint a different day.

Section 3. If at the time fixed for the beginning of the term of the President, the President-elect shall have died, the Vice-President-elect shall become President. If a President shall not have been chosen before the time fixed for the beginning of his term, or if the President-elect shall have failed to qualify, then the Vice-President-elect shall act as President until a President shall have qualified; and the Congress may by law provide for the case wherein neither a President-elect nor a Vice-President-elect shall have qualified, declaring who shall then act as President, or the manner in which one who is to act shall be selected, and such person shall act accordingly until a President or Vice-President shall have qualified.

Section 4. The Congress may by law provide for the case of the death of any of the persons from whom the House of Representatives may choose a President whenever the right of choice shall have devolved upon them, and for the case of the death of any of the persons from whom the Senate may choose a Vice-President whenever the right of choice shall have devolved upon them.

[**Section 5.** Sections 1 and 2 shall take effect on the 15th day of October following the ratification of this article.

Section 6. This article shall be inoperative unless it shall have been ratified as an amendment to the Constitution by the legislatures of three-fourths of the several states within seven years from the date of its submission.]

Amendment 21 (1933)

Section 1. The eighteenth article of amendment to the Constitution of the United States is hereby repealed.

Section 2. The transportation or importation into any state, territory, or possession of the United States for delivery or use therein of intoxicating liquors, in violation of the laws thereof, is hereby prohibited.

[*Section 3.* This article shall be inoperative unless it shall have been ratified as an amendment to the Constitution by conventions in the several states, as provided in the Constitution, within seven years from the date of the submission hereof to the states by the Congress.]

Amendment 22 (1951)

Section 1. No person shall be elected to the office of the President more than twice, and no person who has held the office of President, or acted as President, for more than two years of a term to which some other person was elected President shall be elected to the office of the President more than once. [But this Article shall not apply to any person holding the office of President when this Article was proposed by the Congress, and shall not prevent any person who may be holding the office of President, or acting as President, during the term within which this Article becomes operative from holding the office of President or acting as President during the remainder of such term.]

[*Section 2.* This article shall be inoperative unless it shall have been ratified as an amendment to the Constitution by the legislatures of three-fourths of the several states within seven years from the date of its submission to the states by the Congress.]

Amendment 23 (1961)

Section 1. The District constituting the seat of government of the United States shall appoint in such manner as the Congress may direct:

A number of electors of President and Vice-President equal to the whole number of Senators and Representatives in Congress to which the District would be entitled if it were a state, but in no event more than the least populous state; they shall be in addition to those appointed by the states, but they shall be considered, for the purposes of the election of President and Vice-President, to be electors appointed by a state; and they shall meet in the District and perform such duties as provided by the twelfth article of amendment.

Section 2. The Congress shall have power to enforce this article by appropriate legislation.

The Federalist, Number 10

". . . the most common and durable source of factions has been the various and unequal distribution of property."

After the Constitutional Convention had forwarded the Constitution to the states for their consideration and then adjourned in September 1787, the prospects of ratification seemed dark indeed. Opinion was sharply divided between the Federalists, who favored a stronger central government, and the Anti-Federalists, who opposed any loss of state sovereignty. Speaking of the Anti-Federalists and their attitude toward the Constitution, John Pierce of Georgia declared, "Some will oppose it from pride, some from self-interest, some from ignorance, but the greater number will be of that class who will oppose it from a dread of its swallowing up the individuality of the States."

Arguments pro and con filled the newspapers and rang out heatedly in social gatherings during the closing months of 1787 and throughout the year 1788. In New York City, a series of eighty-five letters arguing in favor of the Constitution appeared in the newspapers. The letters, signed simply Publius, were actually the work of Alexander Hamilton, James Madison, and John Jay.

Although the essays were prepared primarily to persuade New York to ratify the Constitution, they came in time to be recognized as "the best commentary on the principles of government ever written." This statement, ironically enough, was made by Jefferson, one of the foremost opponents of the Federalist point of view.

Number 10, written by Madison, discusses the economic roots of the conflicting interests that give rise to factions (political parties) and the best means of controlling their activities, as well as the tyranny of the majority.

November 24, 1787

Among the numerous advantages promised by a well-constructed union, none deserves to be more accurately developed than its tendency to break and control the violence of faction. The friend of popular governments never finds himself so much alarmed for their character and fate as when he contemplates their propensity [inclination] to this dangerous vice. . . .

By a faction, I understand a number of citizens, whether amounting to a majority or minority of the whole, who are united and actuated [moved] by some common impulse of passion, or of interest, adverse to the rights of other citizens or to the permanent and aggregate [collective] interests of the community.

There are two methods of curing the mischiefs of faction: the one, by removing its causes; the other, by controlling its effects.

There are again two methods of removing the causes of faction: the one, by destroying the liberty which is essential to its existence; the other, by giving to every citizen the same opinions, the same passions, and the same interests.

It could never be more truly said than of the first remedy, that it was worse than the disease. Liberty is to faction what air is to fire, an ailment without which it instantly expires. But it could not be less folly to abolish liberty, which is essential to political life, because it nourishes faction, than it would be to wish the annihilation of air, which is essential to animal life, because it imparts to fire its destructive agency.

The second expedient is as impracticable as the first would be unwise. As long as the reason of man continues fallible [capable of error], and he is at liberty to exercise it, different opinions will be formed. As long as the connection subsists between his reason and his self-love, his opinions and his passions will have a reciprocal [mutually dependent] influence on each other; and the former will be objects to which the latter will attach themselves. The diversity in the faculties of men, from which the rights of property originate, is not less an insuperable [incapable of being overcome] obstacle to a uniformity of interests. The protection of these faculties is the first object of government. From the protection of different and unequal faculties of acquiring property, the possession of different degrees and kinds of property immediately results; and from the influence of these on the sentiments and views of the respective proprietors ensues a division of the society into different interests and parties.

The latent [hidden] causes of faction are thus sown in the nature of man; and we see them everywhere brought into different degrees of activity, according to the different circumstances of civil society. A zeal for different opinions concerning religion, concerning government, and many other points, as well of speculation [contemplation] as of practice; an attachment to different leaders ambitiously contending for pre-eminence and power, or to persons of other descriptions whose fortunes have been interesting to the human passions, have, in turn, divided mankind into parties, inflamed them with mutual animosity [spite], and rendered them much more disposed to vex and oppress each other, than to co-operate for their common good. So strong is this propensity of mankind to fall into mutual animosities, that where no substantial occasion presents itself, the most frivolous and fanciful distinctions have been sufficient to kindle their unfriendly passions and excite their most violent conflicts. But the most common and durable source of factions has been the various and unequal distribution of property. Those who hold and those who are without property have ever formed distinct interests in society. Those who are creditors and those who are debtors fall under a like discrimination [show similar marked differences]. A landed interest, a manufacturing interest, a mercantile interest, a moneyed interest, with many lesser interests, grow up of necessity in civilized nations, and divide them into different classes, actuated by different sentiments and views. The regulation of these various and interfering interests forms the principal task of modern legislation, and involves the spirit of party and faction in the necessary and ordinary operations of the government. . . .

It is in vain to say that enlightened statesmen will be able to adjust these clashing interests and render them all subservient to [disposed to serve] the public good. Enlightened statesmen will not always be at the helm; nor, in many cases, can such an adjustment be made at all, without taking into view indirect and remote considerations, which will rarely prevail over the immediate interest which one party may find in disregarding the rights of another or the good of the whole.

The inference to which we are brought is that the causes of faction cannot be removed, and that relief is only to be sought in the means of controlling its effects.

If a faction consists of less than a majority, relief is supplied by the republican principle, which enables the majority to defeat its sinister views by regular vote. It may clog the administration, it may convulse [shake up] the society; but it will be unable to execute and mask its violence under the forms of the Constitution. When a majority is included in a faction, the form of popular government, on the other hand, enables it to sacrifice to its ruling passion or interest both the public good and the rights of other citizens. To secure the public good, and private rights, against the danger of such a faction, and at the same time to preserve the spirit and the form of popular government, is then the great object to which our inquiries are directed. Let me add that it is the great *desideratum* [desired objective] by which alone this form of government can be rescued from the opprobrium [disgrace] under which it has so long labored, and be recommended to the esteem and adoption of mankind. . . .

A republic, by which I mean a government in which the scheme of representation takes place . . . and promises the cure for which we are seeking. Let us examine the points in which it varies from pure democracy, and we shall comprehend both the nature of the cure and the efficacy [effectiveness] which it must derive from the union.

The two great points of difference between a democracy and a republic are: First, the delegation of the government, in the latter, to a small number of citizens elected by the rest; secondly, the greater number of citizens, and greater sphere of country, over which the latter may be extended.

The effect of the first difference is, on the one hand, to refine and enlarge the public views, by passing them through the medium of a chosen body of citizens, whose wisdom may best discern the true interest of their country, and whose patriotism and love of justice will be least likely to sacrifice it to temporary or partial considerations. Under such a regulation, it may well happen that the public voice, pronounced by the representatives of the people, will be more consonant to [in harmony with] the public good than if pronounced by the people themselves, convened for the purpose. On the other hand, the effect may be inverted. Men of factious [dissenting] tempers, of local prejudices, or of sinister designs, may by intrigue, by corruption, or by other means, first obtain the suffrages [rights to vote], and then betray the interests of the people. The question resulting is, whether small or extensive republics are most favorable to the election of proper guardians of the public weal [well-being]; and it is clearly decided in favor of the latter by two obvious considerations.

In the first place, it is to be remarked that, however small the republic may be, the representatives must be raised to a certain number, in order to guard against the cabals [intrigues] of a few; and that, however large it may be, they must be limited to a certain number, in order to guard against the confusion of a multitude. Hence, the number of representatives in the two cases not being in proportion to that of the constituents, and being proportionally greatest in the small republic, it follows that if the proportion of fit characters be not less in the large than in the small republic, the former will present a greater option, and consequently a greater probability of a fit choice.

In the next place, as each representative will be chosen by a greater number of citizens in the large than in the small republic, it will be more difficult for unworthy candidates to practice with success the vicious arts, by which elections are too often carried; and the suffrages of the people, being more free, will be more likely to center in men who possess the most attractive merit and the most diffusive and established characters.

It must be confessed that in this, as in most other cases, there is a mean, on both sides of which inconveniences will be found to lie. By enlarging too much the number of electors, you render the representative too little acquainted with all their local circumstances and lesser interests; as by reducing it too much, you render him unduly attached to these, and too little fit to comprehend and pursue great and national objects. The federal Constitution forms a happy combination in this respect; the great and aggregate interests being referred to the national [legislature]; the local and particular to the state legislatures.

The other point of difference is the greater number of citizens and extent of territory which may be brought within the compass of republican than of democratic government; and it is this circumstance principally which renders factious combinations less to be dreaded in the former, than in the latter. The smaller the society, the fewer probably will be the distinct parties and interests composing it; the fewer the distinct parties and interests, the more frequently will a majority be found of the same party; and the smaller the number of individuals composing a majority, and the smaller the compass [area] within which they are placed, the more easily will they concert [agree] and execute their plans of oppression. Extend the sphere, and you take in a greater variety of parties and interests; you make it less probable that a majority of the whole will have a common motive to invade the rights of other citizens; or if such a common motive exists, it will be more difficult for all who feel it to discover their own strength, and to act in unison with each other. Besides other impediments [obstacles], it may be remarked that where there is a consciousness of unjust or dishonorable purposes, communication is always checked by distrust, in proportion to the number whose concurrence [agreement] is necessary.

Hence, it clearly appears that the same advantage which a republic has over a democracy, in controlling the effects of faction, is enjoyed by a large over a small republic—is enjoyed by the Union over the states composing it. Does the advantage consist in the substitution of representatives, whose enlightened views and virtuous sentiments render them superior to local prejudices, and to schemes of injustice? It will not be denied that the representation of the Union will be most likely to possess these requisite endowments [gifts of nature]. Does it consist in the greater security afforded by a greater variety of parties, against the event of any one party being able to outnumber and oppress the rest? In an equal degree, does the increased variety of parties, comprised within the Union, increase this security? Does it, in fine, consist in the greater obstacles opposed to the concert and accomplishment of the secret wishes of an unjust and interested majority? Here, again, the extent of the Union gives it the most palpable [obvious] advantage.

The influence of factious leaders may kindle a flame within their

WASHINGTON'S PROCLAMATION OF NEUTRALITY 99

particular states, but will be unable to spread a general conflagration through the other states. A religious sect may degenerate into a political faction in a part of the confederacy; but the variety of sects dispersed over the entire face of it must secure the national councils against any danger from that source. A rage for paper money, for an abolition of debts, for an equal division of property, or for any other improper and wicked project will be less apt to pervade the whole body of the Union than a particular member of it; in the same proportion as such a malady is more likely to taint a particular county or district than an entire state.

In the extent and proper structure of the Union, therefore, we behold a republican remedy for the diseases most incident [apt to occur] to republican government. And according to the degree of pleasure and pride we feel in being republicans, ought to be our zeal in cherishing the spirit and supporting the character of federalists.

George Washington's Proclamation of Neutrality

". . . the duty and interest of the United States require . . . a conduct friendly and impartial toward the belligerent powers . . ."

In 1789, revolution broke out in France. Fighting under the slogan, "Liberté, Egalité, et Fraternité," the revolutionists won control of the government. Once in power, they turned upon the former rulers, beheading thousands of the French nobility, among them King Louis XVI and Queen Marie Antoinette.

The French Revolution alarmed the monarchs and the ruling classes of other countries, and their efforts to prevent the revolution from spreading brought them into conflict with the new French government. By 1793 a number of countries, including England, were at war with France.

The European conflict plunged the United States into the most serious crisis it had faced in its four brief years under the Constitution. American sympathies were divided, with some citizens favoring France, others Great Britain. When both the British and the French interfered with American shipping, already overheated tempers rose to the boiling point.

As a further complication, back in 1778 the Continental Congress had signed a treaty in which it promised to aid France in the event of war. French sympathizers insisted that the American government live up to the terms of the treaty. Aid to France would, however, bring the United States into conflict with England.

Finally, after careful consideration and with the unanimous backing of his cabinet, President Washington issued the Proclamation of Neutrality. Congress then supported this position by enacting neutrality legislation.

April 22, 1793

WHEREAS it appears that a state of war exists between Austria, Prussia, Sardinia, Great Britain, and the United Netherlands on the one part and France on the other, and the duty and interest of the United States require that they should with sincerity and good faith adopt and pursue a conduct friendly and impartial toward the belligerent powers:

I have therefore thought fit by these presents to declare the disposition of the United States to observe the conduct aforesaid toward those powers respectively, and to exhort [advise] and warn the citizens of the United States carefully to avoid all acts and proceeding whatsoever which may in any manner tend to contravene [oppose] such disposition.

And I do hereby also make known that whosoever of the citizens of the United States shall render himself liable to punishment or forfeiture under the law of nations by committing or aiding or abetting hostilities against any of the said powers, or by carrying to any of them those articles which are deemed contraband ° by the modern usage of nations, will not receive the protection of the United States against such punishment or forfeiture; . . .

George Washington's Farewell Address

"It is our true policy to steer clear of permanent alliances with any portion of the foreign world. . . ."

In 1796, at the age of 64, George Washington could look back upon a long and distinguished career of public service. As Commander-in-Chief of the Continental Army, as Chairman of the Constitutional Convention, and as the first President of the United States, he had served his country with unswerving devotion. Now, with less than six months remaining of his second term as Chief Executive, he contemplated the future with mixed feelings. He was eager to return to his beloved Mount Vernon, where he hoped to spend the rest of his life. But he was deeply concerned about the nation he had helped to create. Could it weather the storms of political strife? Could it steer a straight and independent course and avoid being drawn into the troubled affairs of the more powerful nations in Europe?

With these problems on his mind, and with the assistance of Alexander Hamilton, President Washington prepared to put in writing his last words of advice to his fellow citizens. The "Farewell Address," as it was called, was never delivered as a speech. It appeared first in published form in a Philadelphia newspaper, the Daily American Advertiser. Although it

° **contraband:** those goods—generally arms, ammunition, and implements of war—which neutrals are forbidden by international law to supply to warring nations. If neutrals engage in this unlawful trade, belligerents can seize and confiscate these goods.

had little influence on domestic politics, Washington's "Farewell Address" helped to shape American foreign policy until
well into the twentieth century.

September 17, 1796

Friends and Fellow Citizens: . . .
   . . . I constantly hoped that it would have been much earlier in
my power . . . to return to that retirement from which I had been re-
luctantly drawn. The strength of my inclination to do this previous
to the last election had even led to the preparation of an address to
declare it [to] you; but mature reflection on the then perplexed and
critical posture [position] of our affairs with foreign nations and
the unanimous advice of persons entitled to my confidence impelled
me to abandon the idea. I rejoice . . . that in the present circumstances of our country you will not disapprove my determination to
retire. . . .
   Every day the increasing weight of years admonishes me more and
more that the shade of retirement is as necessary to me as it will
be welcome. . . . I have the consolation to believe that while choice
and prudence invite me to quit the political scene, patriotism does
not forbid it. . . .
   Here, perhaps, I ought to stop. But a solicitude [anxiety] for your
welfare which cannot end but with my life, and the apprehension of
danger natural to that solicitude, urge me on an occasion like the
present to offer to your solemn contemplation and to recommend to
your frequent review some sentiments which are the result of much
reflection, of no inconsiderable observation, and which appear to me
all important to the permanency of your felicity [happiness] as a
people. These will be offered to you with the more freedom as you
can only see in them the disinterested warnings of a parting friend,
who can possibly have no personal motive to bias his counsel. . . .
   Interwoven as is the love of liberty with every ligament of your
hearts, no recommendation of mine is necessary to fortify or confirm
the attachment.
   The unity of government which constitutes you one people is also
now dear to you. It is justly so, for it is a main pillar in the edifice of

your real independence, the support of your tranquillity at home, your peace abroad, of your safety, of your prosperity, of that very liberty which you so highly prize. . . .

The name of American, which belongs to you in your national capacity, must always exalt the just pride of patriotism more than any appellation [name] derived from local discriminations. With slight shades of difference, you have the same religion, manners, habits, and political principles. You have in a common cause fought and triumphed together. The independence and liberty you possess are the work of joint councils and joint efforts, of common dangers, sufferings, and successes. . . .

In this sense it is that your union ought to be considered as a main prop of your liberty, and that the love of the one ought to endear to you the preservation of the other. . . .

In contemplating the causes which may disturb our union, it occurs as matter of serious concern that any ground should have been furnished for characterizing parties by *geographical* discriminations— *Northern* and *Southern*, *Atlantic* and *Western*—whence designing men may endeavor to excite a belief that there is a real difference of local interests and views. One of the expedients [methods] of party to acquire influence within particular districts is to misrepresent the opinions and aims of other districts. You cannot shield yourselves too much against the jealousies and heartburnings which spring from these misrepresentations; they tend to render alien [unfriendly] to each other those who ought to be bound together by fraternal affection. . . .

I have already intimated to you the danger of parties in the state, with particular reference to the founding of them on geographical discriminations. Let me now take a more comprehensive view, and warn you in the most solemn manner against the baneful [destructive] effects of the spirit of party generally.

This spirit, unfortunately, is inseparable from our nature, having its root in the strongest passions of the human mind. It exists under different shapes in all governments, more or less stifled, controlled, or repressed; but in those of the popular form it is seen in its greatest rankness [most extreme form] and is truly their worst enemy. . . .

It serves always to distract the public councils and enfeeble the public administration. It agitates the community with ill-founded jealousies and false alarms; kindles the animosity of one part against another; foments [excites] occasionally riot and insurrection. It opens the door to foreign influence and corruption, which find a facilitated [easy] access to the government itself through the channels of party passion. Thus the policy and the will of one country are subjected to the policy and will of another.

There is an opinion that parties in free countries are useful checks upon the administration of the government, and serve to keep alive the spirit of liberty. This within certain limits is probably true; and in governments of a monarchical cast patriotism may look with indulgence, if not with favor, upon the spirit of party. But in those of the popular character, in governments purely elective, it is a spirit not to be encouraged. From their natural tendency it is certain there will always be enough of that spirit for every salutary [beneficial] purpose, and there being constant danger of excess, the effort ought to be by force of public opinion to mitigate [regulate] and assuage [lessen] it. A fire not to be quenched, it demands a uniform vigilance to prevent its bursting into a flame, lest, instead of warming, it should consume.

It is important, likewise, that the habits of thinking in a free country should inspire caution in those entrusted with its administration to confine themselves within their respective constitutional spheres, avoiding in the exercise of the powers of one department to encroach upon another. The spirit of encroachment tends to consolidate the powers of all the departments in one, and thus to create, whatever the form of government, a real despotism. A just estimate of that love of power and proneness [inclination] to abuse it which predominates in the human heart is sufficient to satisfy us of the truth of this position. The necessity of reciprocal checks in the exercise of political power, by dividing and distributing it into different depositories, and constituting [establishing] each the guardian of the public weal against invasions by the others, has been evinced by experiments ancient and modern, some of them in our country and under our own eyes. To preserve them must be as necessary as to institute them. If in the opinion of the people the distribution or modification of the constitutional powers be in any particular wrong, let it be corrected by an amendment in the way which the Constitution designates. But let there be no change by usurpation; for though this in one instance may be the instrument of good, it is the customary weapon by which free governments are destroyed. The precedent must always greatly overbalance in permanent evil any partial or transient benefit which the use can at any time yield.

Of all the dispositions and habits which lead to political prosperity, religion and morality are indispensable supports. In vain would that man claim the tribute of patriotism who should labor to subvert these great pillars of human happiness—these firmest props of the duties of men and citizens. The mere politician, equally with the pious man, ought to respect and to cherish them. A volume could not trace all their connections with private and public felicity. Let it simply be asked, Where is the security for property, for reputation, for life, if the sense of religious obligation desert the oaths which are the instruments of investigation in courts of justice? And let us with caution indulge the supposition that morality can be maintained without religion. Whatever may be conceded to the influence of refined education on minds of peculiar structure, reason and experience both forbid us to expect that national morality can prevail in exclusion of religious principle. . . .

Promote, then, as an object of primary importance, institutions for the general diffusion of knowledge. In proportion as the structure of a government gives force to public opinion, it is essential that public opinion should be enlightened.

As a very important source of strength and security, cherish public credit. One method of preserving it is to use it as sparingly as possible, avoiding occasions of expense by cultivating peace, but remembering also that timely disbursements to prepare for danger frequently prevent much greater disbursements to repel it; avoiding likewise the accumulation of debt, not only by shunning occasions of expense, but by vigorous exertions in time of peace to discharge the debts which unavoidable wars have occasioned, not ungenerously throwing upon posterity the burden which we ourselves ought to bear. . . .

Observe good faith and justice toward all nations. Cultivate peace and harmony with all. . . .

Against the insidious wiles [sly tricks] of foreign influence (I conjure [beg] you to believe me, fellow citizens) the jealousy [suspicion] of a free people ought to be constantly awake, since history and experience prove that foreign influence is one of the most baneful foes of republican government. But that jealousy, to be useful, must be impartial, else it becomes the instrument of the very influence to be avoided, instead of a defense against it. Excessive partiality for one foreign nation and excessive dislike for another cause those whom they actuate [incite] to see danger only on one side, and serve to veil and even second [support] the arts of influence on the other. Real patriots who may resist the intrigues of the favorite are liable to become suspected and odious [offensive], while its tools and dupes usurp the applause and confidence of the people to surrender their interests.

The great rule of conduct for us in regard to foreign nations is in extending our commercial relations to have with them as little political connection as possible. So far as we have already formed engagements let them be fulfilled with perfect good faith. Here let us stop.

Europe has a set of primary interests which to us have none or a very remote relation. Hence she must be engaged in frequent controversies, the causes of which are essentially foreign to our concerns. Hence, therefore, it must be unwise in us to implicate ourselves by artificial ties in the ordinary vicissitudes [changes] of her politics or the ordinary combinations and collisions of her friendships or enmities.

Our detached and distant situation invites and enables us to pursue a different course. If we remain one people, under an efficient government, the period is not far off when we may defy material injury from external annoyance; when we may take such an attitude as will cause the neutrality we may at any time resolve upon to be scrupulously respected; when belligerent nations, under the impossibility of making acquisitions upon us, will not lightly hazard . . . giving us provocation; when we may choose peace or war, as our interest, guided by justice, shall counsel.

Why forego the advantages of so peculiar a situation? Why quit our own to stand upon foreign ground? Why, by interweaving our destiny with that of any part of Europe, entangle our peace and prosperity in the toils of European ambition, rivalship, interest, humor, or caprice [change of mind]?

It is our true policy to steer clear of permanent alliances with any portion of the foreign world, so far, I mean, as we are now at liberty to do it; for let me not be understood as capable of patronizing infidelity to existing engagements. I hold the maxim no less applicable to public than to private affairs that honesty is always the best policy. I repeat, therefore, let those engagements be observed in their genuine sense. But in my opinion it is unnecessary and would be unwise to extend them.

Taking care always to keep ourselves by suitable establishments on a respectable defensive posture, we may safely trust to temporary alliances for extraordinary emergencies.

Harmony, liberal intercourse with all nations are recommended by policy, humanity, and interest. But even our commercial policy should hold an equal and impartial hand, neither seeking nor granting exclusive favors or preferences; consulting the natural course of things; diffusing and diversifying by gentle means the streams of commerce, but forcing nothing; establishing with powers so disposed, in order to give trade a stable course, to define the rights of our merchants, and to enable the government to support them, conventional rules of intercourse, the best that present circumstances and mutual opinion will permit, but temporary and liable to be from time to time abandoned or varied as experience and circumstances shall dictate; constantly keeping in view that it is folly in one nation to look for disinterested favors from another; that it must pay with a portion of its independence for whatever it may accept under that character; that by such acceptance it may place itself in the condition of having given equivalents for nominal favors, and yet of being reproached with ingratitude for not giving more. There can be no greater error than to expect or calculate [plan] upon real favors from nation to nation. It is an illusion which experience must cure, which a just pride ought to discard. . . .

Though in reviewing the incidents of my administration I am unconscious of intentional error, I am nevertheless too sensible of my defects not to think it probable that I may have committed many errors. Whatever they may be, I fervently beseech the Almighty to avert or mitigate the evils to which they may tend. I shall also carry with me the hope that my country will never cease to view them with indulgence, and that, after forty-five years of my life dedicated to its service with an upright zeal, the faults of incompetent abilities will be consigned to oblivion, as myself must soon be to the mansions of rest.

Relying on its kindness in this as in other things, and actuated by that fervent love toward it which is so natural to a man who views in it the native soil of himself and his progenitors [ancestors] for several generations, I anticipate with pleasing expectation that retreat in which I promise myself to realize without alloy the sweet enjoyment of partaking in the midst of my fellow citizens the benign influence of good laws under a free government—the ever-favorite object of my heart, and the happy reward, as I trust, of our mutual cares, labors, and dangers.

Thomas Jefferson's First Inaugural Address

". . . error of opinion may be tolerated where reason is left free to combat it."

On the morning of March 4, 1801, Thomas Jefferson prepared to take the inaugural oath and become the third President of the United States. His victory over the Federalists in the fall elections had filled his political opponents with dismay. In their view, the Republican principles that Jefferson cherished were radical and dangerous. Grimly, foreseeing only ruin ahead, they stood in silence as the new Chief Executive began to address his audience.

Jefferson's first inaugural address is one of the great speeches in political literature. Designed to reassure his political opponents, it proclaimed a deep faith in the ideals of democracy, in a government responsive to the will of the majority, but at the same time respectful of the rights of the minority. In this famous address, Jefferson advocated the principle that the government is best which governs least, and vigorously affirmed the principle of intellectual freedom— freedom of inquiry and freedom of expression.

The well-known isolationist phrase, "entangling alliances with none," appears in this document and not, as many believe, in Washington's Farewell Address.

March 4, 1801

Friends and Fellow Citizens: . . .

All . . . will bear in mind this sacred principle, that though the will of the majority is in all cases to prevail, that will to be rightful must be reasonable; that the minority possess their equal rights, which equal law must protect, and to violate would be oppression. Let us, then, fellow citizens, unite with one heart and one mind. Let us restore to social intercourse [dealings] that harmony and affection without which liberty and even life itself are but dreary things. And let us reflect that, having banished from our land that religious intolerance under which mankind so long bled and suffered, we have yet gained little if we countenance [allow] a political intolerance as despotic, as wicked, and capable of as bitter and bloody persecutions. . . . But every difference of opinion is not a difference of principle. We have called by different names brethren of the same principle. We are all Republicans; we are all Federalists. If there be any among us who would wish to dissolve this Union or to change its republican form, let them stand undisturbed as monuments of the safety with which error of opinion may be tolerated where reason is left free to combat it. I know, indeed, that some honest men fear that a republican government cannot be strong, that this government is not strong enough; but would the honest patriot, in the full tide of successful experiment, abandon a government which has so far kept us free and firm on the theoretic [hypothetical] and visionary fear that this government, the world's best hope, may by possibility want energy to preserve itself? I trust not. I believe this, on the contrary, the strongest government on earth. I believe it the only one where every man, at the call of the law, would fly to the standard of the law, and would meet invasions of the public order as his own personal concern. Sometimes it is said that man cannot be trusted with the government of himself. Can he, then, be trusted with the government of others? Or have we found angels in the forms of kings to govern him? Let history answer this question.

Let us, then, with courage and confidence pursue our own Federal and Republican principles, our attachment to union and representative government. Kindly separated by nature and a wide ocean from the exterminating havoc of one quarter of the globe; too high-minded to endure the degradations of the others; possessing a chosen country, with room enough for our descendants to the thousandth and thousandth generation; entertaining a due sense of our equal right to the use of our own faculties, to the acquisitions of our own industry, to honor and confidence from our fellow citizens, resulting not from birth, but from our actions and their sense of them; enlightened by a benign religion, professed, indeed, and practiced in various forms, yet all of them inculcating [implanting] honesty, truth, temperance, gratitude, and the love of man; acknowledging and adoring an overruling Providence, which by all its dispensations proves that it delights in the happiness of man here and his greater happiness hereafter—with all these blessings, what more is necessary to make us a happy and a prosperous people? Still one thing more, fellow citizens—a wise and frugal government, which shall restrain men from injuring one another, shall leave them otherwise free to regulate their own pursuits of industry and improvement, and shall not take from the mouth of labor the bread it has earned. This is the sum of good government, and this is necessary to close the circle of our felicities.

About to enter, fellow citizens, on the exercise of duties which comprehend [include] everything dear and valuable to you, it is proper you should understand what I deem the essential principles of our government and consequently those which ought to shape its administration. I will compress them within the narrowest compass they will bear, stating the general principle, but not all its limitations. Equal and exact justice to all men, of whatever state or persuasion religious or political; peace, commerce, and honest friendship with all nations, entangling alliances with none; the support of the state governments in all their rights, as the most competent administrations for our domestic concerns and the surest bulwarks [defenses] against anti-republican tendencies; the preservation of the general government in its whole constitutional vigor, as the sheet anchor [main support] of our peace at home and safety abroad; a jealous care of the right of election by the people—a mild and safe corrective of abuses which are lopped by the sword of revolution where peaceable remedies are unprovided; absolute acquiescence in the decisions of the majority, the vital principle of republics, from which [there] is no appeal but to force, the vital principle and immediate parent of despotism; a well-disciplined militia, our best reliance in peace and for the first moments of war, till regulars may relieve them; the supremacy of the civil over the military authority; economy in the public expense, that labor may be lightly burdened; the honest payment of our debts and sacred preservation of the public faith; encouragement of agriculture, and of commerce as its handmaid; the diffusion of information and arraignment [bringing up] of all abuses at the bar of the public reason; freedom of religion; freedom of the press; and freedom of person under the protection of the habeas corpus,° and trial by juries impartially selected. These principles form the bright constellation which has gone before us and guided our steps through an age of revolution and reformation. The wisdom of our sages and blood of our heroes have been devoted to their attainment. They should be the creed of our political faith, the text of civic instruction, the touchstone by which to try the services of those we trust; and should we wander from them in moments of error or of alarm, let us hasten to retrace our steps and to regain the road which alone leads to peace, liberty, and safety.

I repair, then, fellow citizens, to the post you have assigned me. With experience enough in subordinate offices to have seen the difficulties of this the greatest of all, I have learned to expect that it will rarely fall to the lot of imperfect man to retire from this station with the reputation and the favor which bring him into it. Without pretensions to that high confidence you reposed in our first and greatest revolutionary character [Washington] whose pre-eminent services had entitled him to the first place in his country's love and destined for him the fairest page in the volume of faithful history, I ask so much confidence only as may give firmness and effect to the legal administration of your affairs. I shall often go wrong through defect of judgment. When right, I shall often be thought wrong by those whose positions will not command a view of the whole ground. I ask your indulgence for my own errors, which will never be intentional, and your support against the errors of others, who may condemn what they would not if seen in all its parts. The approbation implied by your suffrage is a great consolation to me for the past, and my future solicitude will be to retain the good opinion of those who have bestowed it in advance, to conciliate that of others by doing them all the good in my power, and to be instrumental to the happiness and freedom of all.

° See note, page 20.

Relying, then, on the patronage of your good will, I advance with obedience to the work, ready to retire from it whenever you become sensible how much better choice it is in your power to make. And may that Infinite Power which rules the destinies of the universe lead our councils to what is best, and give them a favorable issue for your peace and prosperity.

John Marshall's Opinion in Marbury v. Madison

"It is emphatically the province and duty of the judicial department to say what the law is...."

The famous case of Marbury v. Madison, which began as a political controversy, ended as a sweeping victory for judicial review.

William Marbury was one of the "midnight judges" appointed by Federalist President John Adams shortly before his term expired on March 4, 1801. Madison, the new Secretary of State, acting on orders from Republican President Thomas Jefferson, refused to give Marbury his commission. Marbury and three other appointees then petitioned the Supreme Court for a writ of mandamus—a court order requiring a public official to perform his duties.

Chief Justice John Marshall, a Federalist, found himself on the horns of a dilemma. If he granted the writ of mandamus, the Republicans would disregard it. If he did not grant the writ, people might think that the Supreme Court was evading its responsibilities. Marshall escaped from this predicament by declaring that it was Secretary of State Madison's duty to deliver the commission to Marbury, but that the Supreme Court had no power to order Madison to do so. In defense of this position, Marshall pointed out that Section 13 of the Judiciary Act of 1789, which gave the Supreme Court power to issue such writs, was unconstitutional. Marshall argued that this section of the Judiciary Act was unconstitutional because it increased the original power of the Supreme Court, and this could be done, not by an act of Congress, but only by an amendment to the Constitution.

The case of Marbury v. Madison was the first in which the Supreme Court declared a law of Congress unconstitutional. In so doing, it established the principle of judicial review.

February 24, 1803

... The government of the United States has been emphatically termed a government of laws, and not of men. . . .

The powers of the legislature are defined and limited; and that those limits may not be mistaken, or forgotten, the Constitution is written. To what purpose are powers limited, and to what purpose is that limitation committed to writing, if these limits may, at any time, be passed by those intended to be restrained? . . . It is a proposition too plain to be contested that the Constitution controls any legislative act repugnant to it; or that the legislature may alter the Constitution by an ordinary act.

. . . a legislative act contrary to the Constitution is not law. . . .

It is emphatically the province [function] and duty of the judicial department to say what the law is. Those who apply the rule to particular cases must of necessity expound [explain in detail] and interpret that rule. If two laws conflict with each other, the courts must decide on the operation of each.

So if a law be in opposition to the Constitution; if both the law and the Constitution apply to a particular case, so that the court must either decide that case conformably to the law, disregarding the Constitution, or conformably to the Constitution, disregarding the law, the court must determine which of these conflicting rules governs the case. This is of the very essence of judicial duty.

If, then, the courts are to regard the Constitution, and the Constitution is superior to any ordinary act of the legislature, the Constitution, and not such ordinary act, must govern the case to which they both apply.

Those, then, who controvert [deny] the principle that the Constitution is to be considered in court as a paramount law, are reduced to the necessity of maintaining that courts must close their eyes on the Constitution and see only the law.

This doctrine would subvert the very foundation of all written constitutions. It would declare that an act which, according to the principles and theory of our government, is entirely void, is yet, in practice, completely obligatory [binding]. It would declare that if the legislature shall do what is expressly forbidden, such act, notwithstanding the express prohibition, is in reality effectual. It would be giving to the legislature a practical and real omnipotence with the same breath which professes to restrict their powers within narrow limits. It is prescribing [laying down] limits and declaring that those limits may be passed at pleasure.

That it thus reduces to nothing what we have deemed the greatest improvement on political institutions, a written constitution, would of itself be sufficient, in America, where written constitutions have been viewed with so much reverence, for rejecting the construction. But the peculiar expressions of the Constitution of the United States furnish additional arguments in favor of its rejection.

The judicial power of the United States is extended to all cases arising under the Constitution.

Could it be the intention of those who gave this power to say that in using it the Constitution should not be looked into? That a case arising under the Constitution should be decided without examining the instrument under which it arises?

This is too extravagant to be maintained. . . .

James Madison's War Message

"British cruisers have been ... violating the
American flag on the great highway of nations...."

On June 1, 1812, President James Madison sent a message
to Congress urging the legislators to declare war on Great
Britain. In this sobering message, the President advanced a
number of reasons for a declaration of war, among them the
need to restore peace to the frontier by putting an end to
Indian raids upon white settlements. Madison charged that
the British, from their forts and trading posts in Canada,
were furnishing the Indians with guns and powder and in-
citing them to attack American settlers.

The President devoted the greater part of his message,
however, to a discussion of the British seizure of American
seamen, of the British blockade of American ports, and of
Great Britain's violation of the right of a neutral nation to
the freedom of the high seas.

On June 18, Congress declared war.

June 1, 1812

To the Senate and House of Representatives of the United States:
I communicate to Congress certain documents, being a continuation of those heretofore laid before them on the subject of our affairs
with Great Britain....

The conduct of her government presents a series of acts hostile to
the United States as an independent and neutral nation.

British cruisers have been in the continued practice of violating
the American flag on the great highway of nations, and of seizing and
carrying off persons sailing under it, not in the exercise of a belligerent right [right of a nation at war] founded on the law of nations
against an enemy, but of a municipal prerogative over British sub-

jects.° British jurisdiction is thus extended to neutral vessels in a situation where no laws can operate but the law of nations and the laws of the country to which the vessels belong. . . .

The practice . . . is so far from affecting British subjects alone that, under the pretext of searching for these, thousands of American citizens, under the safeguard of public law and of their national flag, have been torn from their country and from everything dear to them; have been dragged on board ships of war of a foreign nation and exposed, under the severities of their discipline, to be exiled to the most distant and deadly climes, to risk their lives in the battles of their oppressors, and to be the melancholy instruments of taking away those of their own brethren.

Against this crying enormity [outrageous offense], which Great Britain would be so prompt to avenge if committed against herself, the United States have in vain exhausted remonstrances and expostulations [protests]. . . .

British cruisers have been in the practice also of violating the rights and the peace of our coasts. They hover over and harass our entering and departing commerce. . . . They have added the most lawless proceedings in our very harbors, and have wantonly spilt American blood within the sanctuary of our territorial jurisdiction. . . .

Under pretended blockades, without the presence of an adequate force and sometimes without the practicability of applying one, our commerce has been plundered in every sea, the great staples of our country have been cut off from their legitimate markets, and a destructive blow aimed at our agricultural and maritime interests. . . . And to render the outrage the more signal [evident] these mock blockades have been reiterated and enforced in the face of official communications from the British government declaring as the true definition of a legal blockade "that particular ports must be actually invested and previous warning given to vessels bound to them not to enter."

Not content with these occasional expedients for laying waste our neutral trade, the Cabinet of Britain resorted at length to the sweeping system of blockades, under the name of orders in council,°

° *prerogative over British subjects:* Madison here refers to the British policy based on the principle popularly expressed in the saying, "Once an Englishman, always an Englishman."
° The British Orders in Council forbade American vessels to enter any ports under Napoleon's control, either in Europe, the West Indies, or India.

which has been molded and managed as might best suit its political views, its commercial jealousies, or the avidity [eagerness] of British cruisers. . . .

It has become, indeed, sufficiently certain that the commerce of the United States is to be sacrificed, not as interfering with the belligerent rights of Great Britain; not as supplying the wants of her enemies, which she herself supplies; but as interfering with the monopoly which she covets for her own commerce and navigation. . . .

In reviewing the conduct of Great Britain toward the United States our attention is necessarily drawn to the warfare just renewed by the savages on one of our extensive frontiers—a warfare which is known to spare neither age nor sex and to be distinguished by features peculiarly shocking to humanity. It is difficult to account for the activity and combinations which have for some time been developing themselves among tribes in constant intercourse [dealings] with British traders and garrisons without connecting their hostility with that influence and without recollecting the authenticated [proved] examples of such interpositions heretofore furnished by the officers and agents of that government.°

Such is the spectacle of injuries and indignities which have been heaped on our country, and such the crisis which its unexampled forbearance [unusual patience] and conciliatory efforts have not been able to avert.

Our moderation and conciliation have had no other effect than to encourage perseverance and to enlarge pretensions. We behold our seafaring citizens still the daily victims of lawless violence, committed on the great common and highway of nations, even within sight of the country which owes them protection. We behold our vessels, freighted with the products of our soil and industry, or returning with the honest proceeds of them, wrested from their lawful destinations, confiscated by prize courts ° no longer the organs of public law but the instruments of arbitrary edicts [decrees issued at will], and their unfortunate crews dispersed and lost, or forced or inveigled [lured] in British ports into British fleets, while arguments are employed in

° This reference is to the Battle of Tippecanoe where the Americans under General William Henry Harrison defeated the Indians in 1811. Madison is charging that the British had stirred up the Indians against the Americans and had supplied them with arms.

° *prize court:* a court having jurisdiction to decide the disposition of ships captured at sea in time of war.

support of these aggressions which have no foundation but in a principle equally supporting a claim to regulate our external commerce in all cases whatsoever.

We behold, in fine [in brief], on the side of Great Britain a state of war against the United States, and on the side of the United States a state of peace toward Great Britain.

Whether the United States shall continue passive under these progressive usurpations [continued seizures] and these accumulating wrongs, or ... [oppose] force to force in defense of their national rights ... is a solemn question which the Constitution wisely confides to the legislative department of the government. In recommending it to their early deliberations I am happy in the assurance that the decision will be worthy [of] the enlightened and patriotic councils of a virtuous, a free, and a powerful nation. ...

John Marshall's Opinion in Trustees of Dartmouth College v. Woodward

"A corporation is an artificial being, invisible, intangible, and existing only in contemplation of law."

In 1819, in the case of Trustees of Dartmouth College v. Woodward, Chief Justice John Marshall delivered an opinion that has been called the "Magna Carta of the American corporation." This famous case involved an attempt to violate a contract.

Dartmouth College was established during colonial days under a royal charter granted by the British government. In 1816, the New Hampshire Republicans, after winning a majority of seats in the state legislature, passed a law altering the original charter, or contract. The new law took control out of the hands of the old private Board of Trustees, who were Federalists, and placed it under the control of the state, now dominated by the Republicans.

The Board of Trustees, charging that this violation of the charter was unconstitutional, sued to have the original charter restored. The state court of New Hampshire upheld the action of the legislature. But when the case reached the Supreme Court, Marshall ruled that the New Hampshire law was unconstitutional on the grounds that a charter granted to a private corporation is a contract and is protected by the contract clause in the Constitution of the United States.

By protecting corporations against interference by the states which created them, Marshall encouraged the growth of the corporate form of business.

February 2, 1819

. . . The American people have said, in the Constitution of the United States, that "no state shall pass any bill of attainder,° ex post facto ° law, or law impairing the obligation of contracts." In the same instrument they have also said "that the judicial power shall extend to all cases in law and equity ° arising under the Constitution." On the judges of this Court, then, is imposed the high and solemn duty of protecting, from even legislative violation, those contracts which the Constitution of our country has placed beyond legislative control; and, however irksome the task may be, this is a duty from which we dare not shrink. . . .

It can require no argument to prove that the circumstances of this case constitute a contract. An application is made to the Crown for a charter to incorporate a religious and literary institution. In the application it is stated that large contributions have been made for

---

° **bill of attainder:** a legislative measure that punishes a person without permitting him to have a trial in court.

° **ex post facto law:** a law passed "after the deed"; a law that imposes a penalty for an act that was legal at the time it was committed.

° **equity:** a system of rules and principles that is applied when a fair and just settlement of a case cannot be reached under the regular written law.

the object, which will be conferred on the corporation as soon as it shall be created. The charter is granted, and on its faith the property is conveyed. Surely in this transaction every ingredient of a complete and legitimate contract is to be found.

The points for consideration are:

1. Is this contract protected by the Constitution of the United States?

2. Is it impaired by the acts under which the defendant holds? . . .

1. On the first point. . . . A corporation is an artificial being, invisible, intangible, and existing only in contemplation of law. Being the mere creature of law, it possesses only those properties which the charter of its creation confers upon it, either expressly or as incidental to its very existence. These are such as are supposed best calculated to effect the object for which it was created. Among the most important are immortality, and, if the expression may be allowed, individuality; properties, by which a perpetual succession of many persons are considered as the same, and may act as a single individual. They enable a corporation to manage its own affairs, and to hold property. . . . It is chiefly for the purpose of clothing bodies of men in succession with these qualities and capacities that corporations were invented and are in use. By these means, a perpetual succession of individuals are capable of acting for the promotion of the particular object, like one immortal being. . . .

From this review of the charter, it appears that Dartmouth College is an eleemosynary [charitable] institution, incorporated for the purpose of perpetuating the application of the bounty of the donors to the specified objects of that bounty; that its trustees or governors were originally named by the founder, and invested with the power of perpetuating themselves; that they are not public officers, nor is it a civil institution, participating in the administration of government; but a charity school, or a seminary of education, incorporated for the preservation of its property, and the perpetual application of that property to the objects of its creation. . . .

This is plainly a contract to which the donors, the trustees, and the Crown (to whose rights and obligations New Hampshire succeeds) were the original parties. It is a contract made on a valuable consideration. It is a contract for the security and disposition of property. It is a contract on the faith of which real [land] and personal [all property except land] estate has been conveyed to the corporation. It is, then, a contract within the letter of the Constitution, and within its spirit also. . . .

The opinion of the Court, after mature deliberation, is, that this is a contract, the obligation of which cannot be impaired without violating the Constitution of the United States. This opinion appears to us to be equally supported by reason and by the former decisions of this Court.

2. We next proceed to the inquiry whether its obligation has been impaired by those acts of the legislature of New Hampshire to which the special verdict refers.

From the review of this charter which has been taken it appears that the whole power of governing the college . . . was vested in the trustees. On the part of the Crown it was expressly stipulated that this corporation, thus constituted, should continue forever; and that the number of trustees should forever consist of twelve, and no more. By this contract the Crown was bound, and could have made no violent alteration in its essential terms without impairing its obligation.

By the Revolution, the duties as well as the powers of government devolved on [passed into the hands of] the people of New Hampshire. . . . It is too clear to require the support of argument that all contracts and rights respecting property remained unchanged by the Revolution. The obligations, then, which were created by the charter to Dartmouth College were the same in the new that they had been in the old government. The power of the government was also the same. A repeal of this charter at any time prior to the adoption of the present Constitution of the United States would have been an extraordinary and unprecedented act of power, but one which could have been contested only by the restrictions upon the legislature to be found in the constitution of the state. But the Constitution of the United States has imposed this additional limitation, that the legislature of a state shall pass no act "impairing the obligation of contracts."

It has been already stated that the act "to amend the charter and enlarge and improve the corporation of Dartmouth College" increases the number of trustees to twenty-one, gives the appointment of the additional members to the executive of the state, and creates a board of overseers, to consist of twenty-five persons, of whom twenty-one are also appointed by the executive of New Hampshire, who have power to inspect and control the most important acts of the trustees.

On the effect of this law, two opinions cannot be entertained. Between acting directly and acting through the agency of trustees and overseers no essential difference is perceived. The whole power of governing the college is transformed from trustees appointed according to the will of the founder, expressed in the charter, to the executive of New Hampshire. The management and application of the funds of this eleemosynary institution, which are placed by the donors in the hands of trustees named in the charter, and empowered to perpetuate themselves, are placed by this act [New Hampshire law] under the control of the government of the state. The will of the state is substituted for the will of the donors in every essential operation of the college. This is not an immaterial change. . . . The charter of 1769 exists no longer. It is reorganized . . . in such a manner as to convert a literary institution, molded according to the will of its founders and placed under the control of private literary men, into a machine entirely subservient to the will of government. This may be for the advantage of this college in particular, and may be for the advantage of literature in general; but it is not according to the will of the donors, and is subversive of that contract on the faith of which their property was given. . . .

It results from this opinion, that the acts of the legislature of New Hampshire, which are stated in the special verdict found in this cause, are repugnant to the Constitution of the United States; and that the judgment on this special verdict ought to have been for the plaintiffs. The judgment of the state court must, therefore, be reversed. . . .

John Marshall's Opinion in McCulloch v. Maryland

"...the government of the Union ...
is supreme within its sphere of action."

The Second Bank of the United States was a powerful financial institution with branches in a number of cities, including Baltimore, Maryland. State banks, finding it difficult to compete with the national bank, urged their legislatures to take action against it. The Maryland legislators responded by passing a law imposing a heavy tax on bank notes issued by banks not chartered by the state. McCulloch, the cashier of the Baltimore branch of the Bank of the United States, refused to pay the tax.

The case of McCulloch v. Maryland ended in the Supreme Court, which decided in favor of McCulloch. Speaking for the Court, Chief Justice Marshall ruled that Maryland's attempt to tax the Bank of the United States was unconstitutional because, in his words, "the power to tax involves the power to destroy."

Marshall's ruling in this famous case freed federal agencies from the threat of state taxation. By reaffirming the principle of a loose construction of the Constitution, Marshall greatly strengthened the power of the national government.

March 6, 1819

... The government of the Union ... is emphatically and truly a government of the people. In form and in substance it emanates from them, its powers are granted by them, and are to be exercised directly on them, and for their benefit.

This government is acknowledged by all to be one of enumerated powers. . . . That principle is now universally admitted. But the question respecting the extent of the powers actually granted is perpetually arising, and will probably continue to arise, as long as our system shall exist. In discussing these questions, the conflicting powers of the state and general governments must be brought into view, and the supremacy of their respective laws, when they are in opposition, must be settled.

If any one proposition could command the universal assent of mankind, we might expect it would be this: that the government of the Union, though limited in its powers, is supreme within its sphere of action. This would seem to result necessarily from its nature. It is the government of all; its powers are delegated by all; it represents all, and acts for all. Though any one state may be willing to control its operations, no state is willing to allow others to control them. The nation, on those subjects on which it can act, must necessarily bind its component parts. But this question is not left to mere reason: the people have, in express terms, decided it by saying, "this Constitution and the laws of the United States, which shall be made in pursuance thereof," "shall be the supreme law of the land," and by requiring that the members of the state legislatures, and the officers of the executive and judicial departments of the states, shall take the oath of fidelity to it.

The government of the United States, then, though limited in its powers, is supreme; and its laws, when made in pursuance of the Constitution, form the supreme law of the land, "anything in the Constitution or laws of any state to the contrary notwithstanding." . . .

Although among the enumerated powers of government we do not find the word "bank" or "incorporation," we find the great powers to lay and collect taxes; to borrow money; to regulate commerce; to declare and conduct a war; and to raise and support armies and navies. The sword and the purse, all the external relations, and no inconsiderable portion of the industry of the nation, are entrusted to its government. . . .

It is not denied that the powers given to the government imply the ordinary means of execution. That, for example, of raising revenue and applying it to national purposes is admitted to imply the power of conveying money from place to place, as the exigencies of the nation may require, and of employing the usual means of conveyance. But it is denied that the government has its choice of means, or that it may employ the most convenient means, if to employ them it be necessary to erect a corporation. . . .

The government which has a right to do an act, and has imposed on it the duty of performing that act, must, according to the dictates of reason, be allowed to select the means; and those who contend that it may not select any appropriate means, that one particular mode of effecting the object is excepted, take upon themselves the burden of establishing that exception. . . .

But the Constitution of the United States has not left the right of Congress to employ the necessary means, for the execution of the powers conferred on the government, to general reasoning. To its enumeration of powers is added that of making "all laws which shall be necessary and proper, for carrying into execution the foregoing powers, and all other powers vested by this Constitution, in the government of the United States, or in any department thereof." . . .

The result of the most careful and attentive consideration bestowed upon this clause is that if it does not enlarge, it cannot be construed to restrain, the powers of Congress, or to impair the right of the legislature to exercise its best judgment in the selection of measures to carry into execution the Constitutional powers of the government. If no other motive for its insertion can be suggested, a sufficient one is found in the desire to remove all doubts respecting the right to legislate on that vast mass of incidental powers which must be involved in the Constitution, if that instrument be not a splendid bauble [toy].

We admit, as all must admit, that the powers of the government are limited, and that its limits are not to be transcended. But we think the sound construction of the Constitution must allow . . . the national legislature that discretion, with respect to the means by which the powers it confers are to be carried into execution, which will enable that body to perform the high duties assigned to it, in the manner most beneficial to the people. Let the end be legitimate, let it be within the scope of the Constitution, and all means which are appropriate, which are plainly adapted to that end, which are not prohibited, but consist [consistent] with the letter and spirit of the Constitution, are constitutional. . . .

After the most deliberate consideration, it is the unanimous and decided opinion of this Court, that the act to incorporate the Bank of the United States is a law made in pursuance of the Constitution, and is a part of the supreme law of the land. . . .

It being the opinion of the Court, that the act incorporating the bank is constitutional; and that the power of establishing a branch in the state of Maryland might be properly exercised by the bank itself, we proceed to inquire:

Whether the state of Maryland may, without violating the Constitution, tax that branch?

That the power of taxation is one of vital importance; that it is retained by the states; that it is not abridged by the grant of a similar power to the government of the Union; that it is to be concurrently exercised by the two governments: are truths which have never been denied. . . .

That the power to tax involves the power to destroy; that the power to destroy may defeat and render useless the power to create; that there is a plain repugnance [contradiction], in conferring on one government a power to control the Constitutional measures of another, which other, with respect to those very measures, is declared to be supreme over that which exerts the control, are propositions not to be denied. . . .

If the states may tax one instrument, employed by the government in the execution of its powers, they may tax any and every other instrument. They may tax the mail; they may tax the mint; they may tax patent rights; they may tax the papers of the customhouse; they may tax judicial process; they may tax all the means employed by the government, to an excess which would defeat all the ends of government. This was not intended by the American people. They did not design to make their government dependent on the states. . . .

The question is, in truth, a question of supremacy; and if the right of the states to tax the means employed by the general government be conceded, the declaration that the Constitution, and the laws made in pursuance thereof, shall be the supreme law of the land, is empty and unmeaning declamation. . . .

But when a state taxes the operations of the government of the United States, it acts upon institutions created, not by their own constituents, but by people over whom they claim no control. It acts upon the measures of a government created by others as well as themselves, for the benefit of others in common with themselves. The difference is that which always exists, and always must exist, between the action of the whole on a part, and the action of a part on the whole—between the laws of a government declared to be supreme, and those of a government which, when in opposition to those laws, is not supreme. . . .

The Court has bestowed on this subject its most deliberate consideration. The result is a conviction that the states have no power, by taxation or otherwise, to retard, impede, burden, or in any manner control, the operations of the Constitutional laws enacted by Congress to carry into execution the powers vested in the general government. This is, we think, the unavoidable consequence of that supremacy which the Constitution has declared. We are unanimously of [the] opinion that the law passed by the legislature of Maryland, imposing a tax on the Bank of the United States, is unconstitutional and void. . . .

The Monroe Doctrine

"... the American continents ... are henceforth not to be considered as subjects for future colonization by any European powers. . . ."

The Monroe Doctrine is neither a law of Congress nor a part of the United States Constitution. It is a declaration made by President James Monroe as a part of his annual State of the Union message to Congress.

This declaration, unquestionably one of the most influential in American history, was prompted by Monroe's fear that the Holy Alliance of Russia, Prussia, and Austria might attempt to restore the newly established independent states of Latin America to their former colonial status, and that Russia might attempt further to expand its control from Alaska southward along the Pacific Coast. Influenced by his Secretary of State, John Quincy Adams, the President announced in bold and unmistakable terms that the Western

Hemisphere was closed to further European colonization and political intervention.

From 1823 to the present, the Monroe Doctrine has remained one of the cornerstones of American foreign policy.

December 2, 1823

...At the proposal of the Russian Imperial Government, made through the minister of the Emperor residing here, a full power and instructions have been transmitted to the minister of the United States at St. Petersburg to arrange by amicable negotiations the respective rights and interests of the two nations on the northwest coast of this continent. A similar proposal had been made by His Imperial Majesty to the government of Great Britain, which has likewise been acceded to. The government of the United States has been desirous by this friendly proceeding of manifesting the great value which they have invariably attached to the friendship of the Emperor and their solicitude to cultivate the best understanding with his government. In the discussions to which this interest has given rise and in the arrangements by which they may terminate the occasion has been judged proper for asserting, as a principle in which the rights and interests of the United States are involved, that the American continents, by the free and independent condition which they have assumed and maintain, are henceforth not to be considered as subjects for future colonization by any European powers....

The citizens of the United States cherish sentiments the most friendly in favor of the liberty and happiness of their fellow men on that side of the Atlantic [in Europe]. In the wars of the European powers in matters relating to themselves we have never taken any part, nor does it comport with our policy to do so. It is only when our rights are invaded or seriously menaced that we resent injuries or make preparation for our defense. With the movements in this hemisphere we are of necessity more immediately connected, and by causes which must be obvious to all enlightened and impartial observers. The political system of the allied powers [Holy Alliance] is essentially different in this respect from that of America. This difference proceeds from that which exists in their respective governments;

and to the defense of our own, which has been achieved by the loss of so much blood and treasure, and matured by the wisdom of their most enlightened citizens, and under which we have enjoyed unexampled felicity, this whole nation is devoted. We owe it, therefore, to candor and to the amicable relations existing between the United States and those powers to declare that we should consider any attempt on their part to extend their system to any portion of this hemisphere as dangerous to our peace and safety. With the existing colonies or dependencies of any European power, we have not interfered and shall not interfere. But with the governments who have declared their independence and maintained it, and whose independence we have, on great consideration and on just principles, acknowledged, we could not view any interposition for the purpose of oppressing them, or controlling in any other manner their destiny, by any European power in any other light than as the manifestation of an unfriendly disposition toward the United States. In the war between those new governments and Spain, we declared our neutrality at the time of their recognition, and to this we have adhered, and shall continue to adhere, provided no change shall occur which, in the judgment of the competent authorities of this government, shall make a corresponding change on the part of the United States indispensable to their security.

The late events in Spain and Portugal show that Europe is still unsettled. Of this important fact no stronger proof can be adduced [offered] than that the allied powers should have thought it proper, on any principle satisfactory to themselves, to have interposed by force in the internal concerns of Spain. To what extent such interposition may be carried, on the same principle, is a question in which all independent powers whose governments differ from theirs are interested, even those most remote, and surely none more so than the United States. Our policy in regard to Europe, which was adopted at an early stage of the wars which have so long agitated that quarter of the globe, nevertheless remains the same, which is, not to interfere in the internal concerns of any of its powers; to consider the government *de facto* ° as the legitimate government for us; to cultivate friendly relations with it, and to preserve those relations by a frank, firm, and manly policy, meeting in all instances the just claims of

° **de facto government:** a government which is in actual control of a country, although it may not have been given diplomatic recognition by other nations.

every power, submitting to injuries from none. But in regard to those continents [North and South America] circumstances are eminently and conspicuously different. It is impossible that the allied powers should extend their political system to any portion of either continent without endangering our peace and happiness; nor can anyone believe that our southern brethren [Latin America], if left to themselves, would adopt it of their own accord. It is equally impossible, therefore, that we should behold such interposition in any form with indifference. If we look to the comparative strength and resources of Spain and those new governments, and their distance from each other, it must be obvious that she can never subdue them. It is still the true policy of the United States to leave the parties to themselves, in the hope that other powers will pursue the same course. . . .

John Marshall's Opinion in Gibbons v. Ogden

". . . the act of Congress . . . is supreme; and the law of the state . . . must yield to it."

Shortly after Robert Fulton staged the successful demonstration of his steamboat, the Clermont, on the Hudson River in 1807, the New York state legislature gave him and his partner, Robert Livingston, exclusive rights to operate vessels driven by steam on the waterways of New York. Some years later, Fulton and Livingston agreed, in exchange for monetary considerations, to allow Aaron Ogden to operate steamboats between New Jersey and New York.

In the meantime, Thomas Gibbons had obtained a coasting license from the United States government. Operating under this license, he, too, began to run steamboats between New Jersey and New York.

Ogden appealed to the New York courts to stop Gibbons from competing with him, claiming his rights were superior to those of Gibbons. Ogden won in the lower courts, but lost when the case reached the Supreme Court in 1824.

The case of Gibbons v. Ogden is one of the most far-reaching in American history. Marshall's interpretation of the commerce clause established the precedent for later federal regulation of interstate transportation and communication. It opened the door to the development of a single, nation-wide market unhampered by state barriers. Moreover, an opposition to monopoly and the support of free enterprise are implicit in the decision. For these reasons, Marshall's ruling in this famous case has been described as the "Emancipation Proclamation of American Commerce."

March 2, 1824

...The words [in the Constitution] are: "Congress shall have power to regulate commerce with foreign nations, and among the several states, and with the Indian tribes." The subject to be regulated is commerce; and our Constitution being ... one of enumeration, it becomes necessary to settle the meaning of the word....

Commerce, undoubtedly, is traffic, but it is something more—it is intercourse [business dealings]. It describes the commercial intercourse between nations, and parts of nations, in all its branches, and is regulated by prescribing rules for carrying on that intercourse. The mind can scarcely conceive a system for regulating commerce between nations which shall exclude all laws concerning navigation, which shall be silent on the admission of the vessels of the one nation into the ports of the other, and be confined to prescribing rules for the conduct of individuals, in the actual employment of buying and selling, or of barter.

If commerce does not include navigation, the government of the Union has no direct power over that subject, and can make no law prescribing what shall constitute American vessels, or requiring that they shall be navigated by American seamen. Yet this power has been exercised from the commencement of the government, has been exercised with the consent of all, and has been understood by all to be a commercial regulation. All America understands, and has uniformly understood, the word "commerce" to comprehend navigation. It was so understood, and must have been so understood, when the Constitution was framed. The power over commerce, including navigation, was one of the primary objects for which the people of America adopted their government, and must have been contemplated in forming it. The convention [Constitutional Convention] must have used the word in that sense, because all have understood it in that sense; and the attempt to restrict it comes too late. . . .

The word used in the Constitution, then, comprehends, and has been always understood to comprehend, navigation within its meaning; and a power to regulate navigation is as expressly granted as if that term had been added to the word "commerce." To what commerce does this power extend? The Constitution informs us, to commerce "with foreign nations, and among the several states, and with the Indian tribes." It has, we believe, been universally admitted that these words comprehend every species of commercial intercourse between the United States and foreign nations. No sort of trade can be carried on between this country and any other to which this power does not extend. . . .

This principle is, if possible, still more clear when applied to commerce "among the several states." They either join each other, in which case they are separated by a mathematical line, or they are remote from each other, in which case other states lie between them. What is commerce "among" them; and how is it to be conducted? Can a trading expedition between two adjoining states commence and terminate outside of each? And if the trading intercourse be between two states remote from each other, must it not commence in one, terminate in the other, and probably pass through a third? Commerce among the states must, of necessity, be commerce with the states. In the regulation of trade with the Indian tribes, the action of the law, especially when the Constitution was made, was chiefly within a state. . . .

The power of Congress, then, comprehends navigation within the limits of every state in the Union, so far as that navigation may be, in any manner, connected with "commerce with foreign nations, or among the several states, or with the Indian tribes." It may, of consequence, pass the jurisdictional line of New York, and act upon the very waters to which the prohibition now under consideration applies. . . .

Since, however, in exercising the power of regulating their own purely internal affairs, whether of trading or police, the states may sometimes enact laws the validity of which depends on their interfering with, and being contrary to, an act of Congress passed in pursuance of [putting into effect] the Constitution, the Court will enter upon the inquiry, whether the laws of New York, as expounded by the highest tribunal of that state, have, in their application to this case, come into collision with an act of Congress, and deprived a citizen of a right to which that act entitles him. Should this collision exist, it will be immaterial whether those laws were passed in virtue of a concurrent power "to regulate commerce with foreign nations and among the several states," or in virtue of a power to regulate their domestic trade and police. In one case and the other the acts of New York must yield to the law of Congress; and the decision sustaining the privilege they confer against a right given by a law of the Union must be erroneous. This opinion has been frequently expressed in this Court, and is founded as well on the nature of the government as on the words of the Constitution. In argument, however, it has been contended that, if a law passed by a state in the exercise of its acknowledged sovereignty comes into conflict with a law passed by Congress in pursuance of the Constitution, they affect the subject, and each other, like equal opposing powers. But the framers of our Constitution foresaw this state of things, and provided for it by declaring the supremacy not only of itself but of the laws made in pursuance of it. The nullity ° of any act inconsistent with the Constitution is produced by the declaration that the Constitution is supreme law. . . . In every such case the act of Congress, or the treaty, is supreme; and the law of the state . . . must yield to it.

° *nullity:* total absence of legal effect.

Daniel Webster's Reply to Robert Hayne

*"... Liberty and Union, now and forever,
one and inseparable!"*

Even before 1830, it was obvious that the "Era of Good Feelings" was deteriorating into an era of hard feelings. As early as 1819–1820, the debate over the admission of Missouri into the Union had generated bitter feelings and divided the country. During the 1820's, the tariff issue had created sharp differences of opinion. Now, in 1830, a debate over the public land policy led to the more fundamental question of the nature of the Union itself.

In the closing days of 1829, Senator Samuel A. Foot of Connecticut introduced a resolution calling for a temporary restriction on the sale of public lands. As the debate gathered momentum, Senators from the South and the West found themselves aligned against their colleagues from the North. Before long, less and less was being said about public lands and more and more about the nature of the Union created by the Constitution.

On January 19, Senator Robert Y. Hayne of South Carolina, in a vigorous defense of the principle of states' rights, argued that "the very life of our system is the independence of the states. . . ." The following day, Senator Daniel Webster of Massachusetts rose to challenge this argument, and for more than a week these two men debated the origin and nature of the Constitution and the Union. Webster's speech of January 26–27 is considered one of the most eloquent ever delivered on the floor of the United States Senate.

January 26-27, *1830*

... This leads us to inquire into the origin of this government and the source of its power. Whose agent is it? Is it the creature of the state legislatures, or the creature of the people? ... It is, sir, the people's Constitution, the people's government, made for the people, made by the people, and answerable to the people. The people of the United States have declared that this Constitution shall be supreme law. We must either admit the proposition or deny their authority. The states are, unquestionably, sovereign, so far as their sovereignty is not affected by this supreme law. But the state legislatures, as political bodies, however sovereign, are yet not sovereign over the people. So far as the people have given power to the general government, so far the grant is unquestionably good, and the government holds of the people and not of the state governments. . . .

The people, then, sir, erected this government. They gave it a Constitution; and in that Constitution they have enumerated the powers which they bestow on it. They have made it a limited government. They have defined its authority. They have restrained it to the exercise of such powers as are granted; and all others, they declare, are reserved to the states or the people. But, sir, they have not stopped here. If they had, they would have accomplished but half their work. No definition can be so clear as to avoid possibility of doubt; no limitation so precise as to exclude all uncertainty. Who then shall construe this grant of the people? Who shall interpret their will, where it may be supposed they have left it doubtful? With whom do they repose this ultimate right of deciding on the powers of the government? Sir, they have settled all this in the fullest manner. They have left it with the government itself, in its appropriate branches. Sir, the very chief end, the main design, for which the whole Constitution was framed and adopted, was to establish a government that should not be obliged to act through state agency, or depend on state opinion and state discretion. The people had had quite enough of that kind of government under the Confederacy. Under that system, the legal action, the application of law to individuals belonged exclusively to the states. Congress could only recommend; their acts were not of binding force, till the states had adopted and sanctioned them. Are we in that condition still? Are we yet at the mercy of state discretion and state construction? Sir, if we are, then vain will be our attempt to maintain the Constitution under which we sit. But, sir, the people have wisely provided, in the Constitution itself, a proper, suitable mode and tribunal for settling questions of constitutional law. There are in the Constitution grants of power to Congress and restrictions on those powers. There are, also, prohibitions on the states. Some authority must, therefore, necessarily exist, having the ultimate jurisdiction to fix and ascertain the interpretation of these grants, restrictions, and prohibitions. The Constitution has, itself, pointed out, ordained, and established that authority. How has it accomplished this great and essential end? By declaring, sir, that "the Constitution, and the laws of the United States made in pursuance thereof, shall be the supreme law of the land, anything in the constitution or laws of any state to the contrary notwithstanding."

This, sir, was the first great step. By this, the supremacy of the Constitution and laws of the United States is declared. The people so will it. No state law is to be valid which comes in conflict with the Constitution or any law of the United States. But who shall decide this question of interference? To whom lies the last appeal? This, sir, the Constitution itself decides also, by declaring "that the judicial power shall extend to all cases arising under the Constitution and laws of the United States." These two provisions, sir, cover the whole ground. They are, in truth, the keystone of the arch. With these, it is a Constitution; without them it is a Confederacy. In pursuance of these clear and express provisions, Congress established, at its very first session, in the Judicial Act, a mode for carrying them into full effect and for bringing all questions of constitutional power to the final decision of the Supreme Court. It then, sir, became a government. It then had the means of self-protection; and, but for this, it would, in all probability, have been now among things which are past. Having constituted the government, and declared its powers, the people have further said: that since somebody must decide on the extent of these powers, the government shall itself decide; subject, always, like other popular governments, to its responsibility to the people. . . .

If, sir, the people, in these respects, had done otherwise than they have done, their Constitution could neither have been preserved, nor would it have been worth preserving. And, if its plain provisions shall now be disregarded, and these new doctrines interpolated in it, it will become as feeble and helpless a being as its enemies, whether early or more recent, could possibly desire. It will exist in every state, but as a poor dependent on state permission. It must borrow leave to be; and will be no longer than state pleasure, or state discretion, sees fit to grant the indulgence and to prolong its poor existence.

But, sir, although there are fears, there are hopes, also. The people have preserved this, their own chosen Constitution, for forty years, and have seen their happiness, prosperity, and renown grow with its growth, and strengthen with its strength. They are now, generally, strongly attached to it. Overthrown by direct assault, it cannot be; evaded, undermined, nullified, it will not be, if we, and those who shall succeed us here, as agents and representatives of the people, shall conscientiously and vigilantly discharge the two great branches of our public trust, faithfully to preserve, and wisely to administer it.

I have thus stated the reasons of my dissent to the [states' rights] doctrines which have been advanced and maintained. I am conscious, sir, of having detained you and the Senate much too long. I was drawn into the debate with no previous deliberation, such as is suited to the discussion of so grave and important a subject. But it is a subject of which my heart is full, and I have not been willing to suppress the utterance of its spontaneous sentiments. I cannot, even now, persuade myself to relinquish it, without expressing, once more, my deep conviction, that, since it respects [concerns] nothing less than the union of the states, it is of most vital and essential importance to the public happiness. I profess, sir, in my career, hitherto, to have kept steadily in view the prosperity and honor of the whole country and the preservation of our federal Union.

It is to that Union we owe our safety at home, and our consideration and dignity abroad. It is to that Union that we are chiefly indebted for whatever makes us most proud of our country. That Union we reached only by the discipline of our virtues in the severe school of adversity. It had its origin in the necessities of disordered finance, prostrate commerce, and ruined credit.° Under its benign influence, these great interests immediately awoke, as from the dead, and sprang forth with newness of life. Every year of its duration has teemed with fresh proofs of its utility and its blessings; and, although our territory

° Webster is here referring to the so-called "critical period" of 1783–1789.

has stretched out wider and wider, and our population spread farther and farther, they have not outrun its protection or its benefits. It has been to us all a copious fountain of national, social, and personal happiness.

I have not allowed myself, sir, to look beyond the Union, to see what might lie hidden in the dark recess behind.

I have not coolly weighed the chances of preserving liberty, when the bonds that unite us together shall be broken asunder. I have not accustomed myself to hang over the precipice of disunion, to see whether, with my short sight, I can fathom the depth of the abyss below; nor could I regard him as a safe counselor, in the affairs of this government, whose thoughts should be mainly bent on considering, not how the Union should be best preserved, but how tolerable might be the condition of the people when it shall be broken up and destroyed. While the Union lasts, we have high, exciting, gratifying prospects spread out before us, for us and our children. Beyond that, I seek not to penetrate the veil. God grant that, in my day, at least, that curtain may not rise. God grant that, on my vision, never may be opened what lies behind.

When my eyes shall be turned to behold, for the last time, the sun in heaven, may I not see him shining on the broken and dishonored fragments of a once glorious Union; on states dissevered, discordant, belligerent; on a land rent with civil feuds, or drenched, it may be, in fraternal blood! Let their last feeble and lingering glance, rather, behold the gorgeous ensign of the republic, now known and honored throughout the earth, still full high advanced, its arms and trophies streaming in their original luster, not a stripe erased or polluted, nor a single star obscured, bearing for its motto no such miserable interrogatory as, *What is all this worth?* Nor those other words of delusion and folly, *Liberty first, and Union afterwards*: but everywhere, spread all over in characters of living light, blazing on all its ample folds, as they float over the sea and over the land, and in every wind under the whole heavens, that other sentiment, dear to every true American heart—Liberty *and* Union, now and forever, one and inseparable!

Andrew Jackson's Veto of the Bank Bill

*"... when the laws undertake ... to make the rich richer ...
humble members of society ... have a right to complain...."*

The Second Bank of the United States was chartered in 1816 for a period of twenty years. From the beginning, it aroused strong opposition on the ground that it was a monopoly and, as such, concentrated great economic power in the hands of a small group of privileged men.

By 1832, opposition had become so strong that the friends of the Bank decided to make a political issue of the matter, even though the charter still had four years to run. A bill calling for the renewal of the charter successfully passed both houses of Congress, but when it reached the President's desk, Andrew Jackson vetoed it. In his veto message, Jackson bluntly charged that the bank was undemocratic, unconstitutional, and, as a monopoly controlled in part by foreigners, harmful to the best interests of the nation.

July 10, 1832

... The present corporate body ... enjoys an exclusive privilege of banking under the authority of the general government, a monopoly °of its favor and support, and, as a necessary consequence, almost a monopoly of the foreign and domestic exchange. The powers, privileges, and favors bestowed upon it in the original charter, by increasing the value of the stock far above its par value,° operated as a gratuity [gift] of many millions to the stockholders....

The act before me proposes another gratuity to the holders of the same stock, and in many cases to the same men, of at least seven mil-

° *monopoly:* exclusive control over the supply of a commodity or service, free from competition.
° *par value:* value stated on the face of the certificate.

lions more. . . . It is not our own citizens only who are to receive the bounty of our government. More than eight millions of the stock of this bank are held by foreigners. By this act the American Republic proposes virtually to make them a present of some millions of dollars. For these gratuities to foreigners and to some of our own opulent citizens the act secures no equivalent [equal exchange] whatever. They are the certain gains of the present stockholders under the operation of this act, after making full allowance for the payment of the bonus [gift]. . . .

Every monopoly and all exclusive privileges are granted at the expense of the public, which ought to receive a fair equivalent. The many millions which this act proposes to bestow on the stockholders of the existing bank must come directly or indirectly out of the earnings of the American people. It is due . . . them, therefore, if their government sell monopolies and exclusive privileges, that they should at least exact for them as much as they are worth in open market. . . .

It is not conceivable how the present stockholders [of the bank] can have any claim to the special favor of the government. The present corporation has enjoyed its monopoly during the period stipulated in the original contract. If we must have such a corporation, why should not the government sell out the whole stock and thus secure to the people the full market value of the privileges granted? Why should not Congress create and sell twenty-eight millions of stock, incorporating the purchases with all the powers and privileges secured in this act and putting the premium [value above par] upon the sales into the Treasury?

But this act does not permit competition in the purchase of this monopoly. It seems to be predicated on the erroneous idea that the present stockholders have a prescriptive [established by law] right not only to the favor but to the bounty of government. It appears that more than a fourth part of the stock is held by foreigners and the residue is held by a few hundred of our own citizens, chiefly of the richest class. For their benefit does this act exclude the whole American people from competition in the purchase of this monopoly and dispose of it for many millions less than it is worth. This seems the less excusable because some of our citizens not now stockholders petitioned that the door of competition might be opened, and offered to take a charter on terms much more favorable to the government and country.

But this proposition, although made by men whose aggregate wealth is believed to be equal to all the private stock in the existing bank, has been set aside, and the bounty of our government is proposed to be again bestowed on the few who have been fortunate enough to secure the stock and at this moment wield the power of the existing institution. I cannot perceive the justice or policy of this course. If our government must sell monopolies, it would seem to be its duty to take nothing less than their full value, and if gratuities must be made once in fifteen or twenty years, let them not be bestowed on the subjects of a foreign government nor upon a designated and favored class of men in our own country. It is but justice and good policy as far as the nature of the case will admit, to confine our favors to our own fellow citizens, and let each in his turn enjoy an opportunity to profit by our bounty. In the bearings of the act before me upon these points I find ample reasons why it should not become a law. . . .

If the opinion of the Supreme Court ° covered the whole ground of this act, it ought not to control the co-ordinate authorities of this government. The Congress, the Executive, and the Court must each for itself be guided by its own opinion of the Constitution. Each public officer who takes an oath to support the Constitution swears that he will support it as he understands it, and not as it is understood by others. It is as much the duty of the House of Representatives, of the Senate, and of the President to decide upon the constitutionality of any bill or resolution which may be presented to them for passage or approval as it is of the supreme judges when it may be brought before them for judicial decision. The opinion of the judges has no more authority over Congress than the opinion of Congress has over the judges, and on that point the President is independent of both. The authority of the Supreme Court must not, therefore, be permitted to control the Congress or the Executive when acting in their legislative capacities, but to have only such influence as the force of their reasoning may deserve. . . .

It is to be regretted that the rich and powerful too often bend the acts of government to their selfish purposes. Distinctions in society

° Jackson is referring to the opinion of Chief Justice John Marshall in the case of *McCulloch* v. *Maryland*, in which the Second Bank of the United States was held to be constitutional. Jackson is saying here that he does not consider this ruling binding on him as President.

will always exist under every just government. Equality of talents, of education, or of wealth cannot be produced by human institutions. In the full enjoyment of the gifts of Heaven and the fruits of superior industry, economy, and virtue, every man is equally entitled to protection by law; but when the laws undertake to add to these natural and just advantages artificial distinctions, to grant titles, gratuities, and exclusive privileges, to make the rich richer and the potent more powerful, the humble members of society—the farmers, mechanics, and laborers—who have neither the time nor the means of securing like favors to themselves, have a right to complain of the injustice of their government. There are no necessary evils in government. Its evils exist only in its abuses. If it would confine itself to equal protection, and, as Heaven does its rains, shower its favors alike on the high and the low, the rich and the poor, it would be an unqualified blessing. In the act before me there seems to be a wide and unnecessary departure from these just principles.

Nor is our government to be maintained or our Union preserved by invasions of the rights and powers of the several states. In thus attempting to make our general government strong, we make it weak. Its true strength consists in leaving individuals and states as much as possible to themselves—in making itself felt, not in its power, but in its beneficence; not in its control, but in its protection; not in binding the states more closely to the center, but leaving each to move unobstructed in its proper orbit.

Experience should teach us wisdom. Most of the difficulties our government now encounters and most of the dangers which impend over [threaten] our union have sprung from an abandonment of the legitimate objects of government by our national legislation, and the adoption of such principles as are embodied in this act. Many of our rich men have not been content with equal protection and equal benefits, but have besought us to make them richer by act of Congress. By attempting to gratify their desires we have in the results of our legislation arrayed section against section, interest against interest, and man against man, in a fearful commotion which threatens to shake the foundations of our union. It is time to pause in our career to review our principles, and if possible revive that devoted patriotism and spirit of compromise which distinguished the sages of the Revolution and the fathers of our Union. . . .

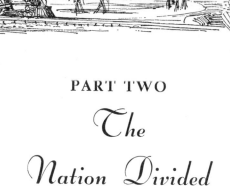

PART TWO

The
Nation Divided

Abraham Lincoln was seventeen years old when Jefferson died in 1826. Jefferson, the elderly statesman, had lived to see the nation born. Lincoln, the youth, lived to see the Union tested by fire and sword in one of the most tragic conflicts in history.

Lincoln also lived to see revolutionary changes in the economic life of the nation. When he was born in a log cabin in 1809, nine out of ten Americans were living on farms, and the frontier had not yet reached the Mississippi River. When he died in 1865, the Industrial Revolution was in full swing, and the factory chimney was replacing the farmhouse as the symbol of the nation's economy.

William Lloyd Garrison's "The Liberator"

*"I will be as harsh as truth and
as uncompromising as justice."*

On January 1, 1831, citizens of Boston read the first issue of a weekly newspaper, The Liberator, in which, in burning words on the opening page, William Lloyd Garrison declared uncompromising war against the institution of slavery. "On this subject," Garrison cried, "I do not wish to think, or speak, or write with moderation."

William Lloyd Garrison meant what he said. For more than thirty years, from 1831 to 1865, he fought with passionate conviction against human bondage, demanding immediate abolition of slavery. His extreme views antagonized many people. Deserted by many of his former friends, persecuted by many of his fellow citizens, and even forced on one occasion to seek safety in a Boston jail from an angry mob, Garrison continued through the pages of The Liberator to crusade for the cause in which he believed so deeply.

The Liberator never attained a large circulation, but its influence was enormous. Inspired, at least in part, by Garrison's words and his example, thousands of men and women rallied to the anti-slavery movement.

January 1, 1831

... During my recent tour for the purpose of exciting the minds of the people by a series of discourses on the subject of slavery, every place that I visited gave fresh evidence of the fact that a greater revolution in public sentiment was to be effected in the free states—*and particularly in New England*—than ... [in] the South. I found con-

144

tempt more bitter, opposition more active, detraction [slander] more relentless, prejudice more stubborn, and apathy more frozen, than among slaveowners themselves. Of course, there were individual exceptions to the contrary. This state of things afflicted, but did not dishearten me. I determined, at every hazard, to lift up the standard of emancipation in the eyes of the nation, *within sight of Bunker Hill and in the birthplace of liberty.* That standard is now unfurled; and long may it float, unhurt by the spoliations [robberies] of time or the missiles of a desperate foe—yea, till every chain be broken, and every bondman set free! Let Southern oppressors tremble—let their secret abettors [supporters] tremble—let their Northern apologists [defenders] tremble—let all the enemies of the persecuted blacks tremble. . . .

In defending the great cause of human rights, I wish to derive the assistance of all religions and of all parties.

Assenting to the "self-evident truth" maintained in the American Declaration of Independence, "that all men are created equal, and endowed by their Creator with certain inalienable rights—among which are life, liberty, and the pursuit of happiness," I shall strenuously contend for the immediate enfranchisement [freeing] of our slave population. . . .

I am aware that many object to the severity of my language; but is there not cause for severity? I *will be* as harsh as truth and as uncompromising as justice. On this subject, I do not wish to think, or speak, or write, with moderation. No! No! Tell a man whose house is on fire, to give a moderate alarm; tell him to moderately rescue his wife from the hands of a ravisher; tell the mother to gradually extricate her babe from the fire into which it has fallen—but urge me not to use moderation in a cause like the present. I am in earnest—I will not equivocate [evade the truth]—I will not excuse—I will not retreat a single inch—AND I WILL BE HEARD. The apathy of the people is enough to make every statue leap from its pedestal, and to hasten the resurrection of the dead.

It is pretended that I am retarding the cause of emancipation by the coarseness of my invective [violent abuse] and the precipitancy [great haste] of my measures. *The charge is not true.* On this question my influence—humble as it is—is felt at this moment to a considerable extent, and shall be felt in coming years—not perniciously, but beneficially—not as a curse, but as a blessing; and posterity will bear testimony that I was right. I desire to thank God that he enables me to disregard "the fear of man which bringeth a snare," and to speak his truth in its simplicity and power. . . .

Dorothea Dix's Memorial to the Legislature of Massachusetts

"I come to present the strong claims of suffering humanity."

In 1836, ill health forced Dorothea Lynde Dix to close the boarding school she had been running in her grandmother's home in Boston. A trip to England, in the course of which she met and talked with a number of leading humanitarians, aroused her compassion for the poor and the oppressed.

It was a visit to the East Cambridge jail, however, that launched Miss Dix on the career she followed for the rest of her life. Horrified by what she saw, and in spite of her delicate health, she began to visit other jails, poorhouses, and institutions for the mentally disordered throughout the Commonwealth of Massachusetts. During the next eighteen months, she filled notebook after notebook with records of horrors almost beyond belief.

In 1843, armed with her supporting evidence, Miss Dix presented a "memorial" to the Massachusetts legislature in which she pleaded for the immediate correction of the abuses. The legislators, shocked into action, responded with the passage of laws to improve conditions.

Regarded by many as "the most useful and distinguished woman that America had produced," Dorothea Dix's lasting monument was the improved treatment of the poor, the imprisoned, and the mentally diseased in the United States and Europe.

January 1843

Gentlemen: I respectfully ask to present this memorial [statement of facts]. . . .

About two years . . . [ago] leisure afforded opportunity and duty prompted me to visit several prisons and almshouses [poorhouses] in the vicinity of this metropolis. I found, near Boston, in the jails and asylums for the poor, a numerous class brought into unsuitable connection with criminals and the general mass of paupers. I refer to idiots and insane persons, dwelling in circumstances not only adverse to their own physical and moral improvement, but productive of extreme disadvantages to all other persons brought into association with them. . . .

I come to present the strong claims of suffering humanity. I come to place before the legislature of Massachusetts the condition of the miserable, the desolate, the outcast. I come as the advocate [one who pleads a cause] of helpless, forgotten, insane, and idiotic men and women; of beings sunk to a condition from which the most unconcerned would start with real horror; of beings wretched in our prisons, and more wretched in our almshouses. . . .

Men of Massachusetts, I beg, I implore, I demand pity and protection for these of my suffering, outraged sex.° Fathers, husbands, brothers, I would supplicate . . . for this boon; but what do I say? I dishonor you, divest you at once of Christianity and humanity, does this appeal imply distrust. If it comes burdened with a doubt of your righteousness in this legislation, then blot it out; while I declare confidence in your honor, not less than your humanity. Here you will put away the cold, calculating spirit of selfishness and self-seeking; lay off the armor of local strife and political opposition; here and now, for once, forgetful of the earthly and perishable, come up to these halls and consecrate them with one heart and one mind to works of righteousness and just judgment. . . .

Injustice is also done to the *convicts:* it is certainly very wrong that they should be doomed day after day and night after night to listen

---

° *my suffering, outraged sex:* Several preceding paragraphs, not included here, described in detail the conditions under which women were imprisoned.

to the ravings of madmen and madwomen. This is a kind of punishment that is not recognized by our statutes, and is what the criminal ought not to be called upon to undergo. The confinement of the criminal and of the insane in the same building is subversive of that good order and discipline which should be observed in every well-regulated prison. I do most sincerely hope that more permanent provision will be made for the pauper insane by the state, either to restore Worcester Insane Asylum to what it was originally designed to be or else make some just appropriation for the benefit of this very unfortunate class of our "fellow beings."

Gentlemen, I commit to you this sacred cause. Your action upon this subject will affect the present and future condition of hundreds and of thousands. In this legislation, as in all things, may you exercise that "wisdom which is the breath of the power of God."

Respectfully submitted,
D. L. DIX

James Polk's Message on War with Mexico

"... war exists, and, notwithstanding all our efforts to avoid it, exists by the act of Mexico herself...."

At noon on Monday, May 11, 1846, President James Polk sent a message to Congress in which he declared that "now, after reiterated menaces, Mexico has passed the boundary of the United States, has invaded our territory and shed American blood upon the American soil." Two days later, Congress responded to Polk's war message with the declaration that "by the act of the Republic of Mexico, a state of war exists between that government and the United States."

Polk's justification for declaring war on Mexico immediately became a matter of heated argument. In the Spot Resolutions, which he introduced in the House of Representatives, Abraham Lincoln, then a young Congressman from Illinois, questioned whether the "spot" where American blood had been shed—the area between the Rio Grande and the Nueces River—was really United States territory. Other Congressmen, although ready to agree that the territory was at the time claimed by both countries, argued that Mexico had deliberately sent troops into the disputed area with the intent of provoking a conflict. But the argument, which continues to the present day, was academic, for with Polk's message and the subsequent action by Congress, the two countries were at war.

May 11, 1846

To the Senate and House of Representatives:

The existing state of the relations between the United States and Mexico renders it proper that I should bring the subject to the consideration of Congress. . . .

In my message at the commencement of the present session I informed you that upon the earnest appeal both of the Congress and convention of Texas I had ordered an efficient military force to take a position "between the Nueces and the Del Norte [Rio Grande]." This had become necessary to meet a threatened invasion of Texas by the Mexican forces, for which extensive military preparations had been made. The invasion was threatened solely because Texas had determined, in accordance with a solemn resolution of the Congress of the United States, to annex herself to our Union, and under these circumstances it was plainly our duty to extend our protection over her citizens and soil.

This force was concentrated at Corpus Christi, and remained there until after I had received such information from Mexico as rendered it probable, if not certain, that the Mexican government would refuse to receive our envoy.

Meantime, Texas, by the final action of our Congress, had become an integral part of our Union. The Congress of Texas, by its act of December 19, 1836, had declared the Rio del Norte to be the boundary of that republic. Its jurisdiction had been extended and exercised beyond the Nueces. The country between that river and the Del Norte had been represented in the Congress and in the convention of Texas, had thus taken part in the act of annexation itself, and is now included within one of our Congressional districts. Our own Congress had, moreover, with great unanimity [agreement], by the act approved December 31, 1845, recognized the country beyond the Nueces as a part of our territory by including it within our own revenue system, and a revenue officer to reside within that district has been appointed by and with the advice and consent of the Senate. It became, therefore, of urgent necessity to provide for the defense of that portion of our country. Accordingly, on the thirteenth of January last, instructions were issued to the general in command of these troops to occupy the left bank of the Del Norte. This river, which is the southwestern boundary of the state of Texas, is an exposed frontier. From this quarter invasion was threatened. . . .

The movement of the troops to the Del Norte was made by the commanding general under positive instructions to abstain from all aggressive acts toward Mexico or Mexican citizens and to regard the relations between that republic and the United States as peaceful unless she should declare war or commit acts of hostility indicative of a state of war. He was specially directed to protect private property. . . .

The Mexican forces at Matamoras assumed a belligerent attitude, and on the twelfth of April, General Ampudia, then in command, notified General Taylor to break up his camp within twenty-four hours and to retire beyond the Nueces River, and in the event of his failure to comply with these demands announced that arms, and arms alone, must decide the question. But no open act of hostility was committed until the twenty-fourth of April. On that day General Arista, who had succeeded to the command of the Mexican forces, communicated to General Taylor that "he considered hostilities commenced and should prosecute them." A party of dragoons [mounted infantrymen] of sixty-three men and officers were on the same day dispatched from the American camp up the Rio del Norte, on its left bank, to ascertain whether the Mexican troops had crossed or were preparing to cross the river, "became engaged with a large body of these troops, and after a short affair, in which some 16 were killed and wounded, appear to have been surrounded and compelled to surrender.". . .

The grievous wrongs perpetrated by Mexico upon our citizens through a long period of years remain unredressed [uncorrected], and solemn treaties pledging her public faith for this redress have been disregarded. . . .

The cup of forbearance had been exhausted even before the recent information from the frontier of the Del Norte.

But now, after reiterated menaces, Mexico has passed the boundary of the United States, has invaded our territory and shed American blood upon the American soil. She has proclaimed that hostilities have commenced and that the two nations are now at war.

As war exists, and, notwithstanding all our efforts to avoid it, exists by the act of Mexico herself, we are called upon by every consideration of duty and patriotism to vindicate with decision the honor, the rights, and the interests of our country. . . .

In further vindication of our rights and defense of our territory, I invoke the prompt action of Congress to recognize the existence of the war, and to place at the disposition of the Executive the means of prosecuting the war with vigor, and thus hastening the restoration of peace. . . .

The Seneca Falls Declaration and Resolutions on Woman's Rights

"... all men and women are created equal ..."

In 1848, stimulated and inspired by the idealism of Jacksonian democracy, Lucretia Mott and Elizabeth Cady Stanton took the initiative in organizing the first women's rights convention in history.

At the time, women had legal rights hardly better than those of children. Women could not vote. They could not

compete with men in the professions of medicine, law, and
the ministry. In many states, when women married, control
over the property they owned passed to their husbands.

On July 19, 1848, the women, assembled in convention at
Seneca Falls, New York, adopted a series of resolutions. In
ringing words, and appealing to the principles embodied in
the Declaration of Independence, they announced their determination to fight for full equality with men.

July 19, 1848

When, in the course of human events, it becomes necessary for one
portion of the family of man to assume among the people of the
earth a position different from that which they have hitherto occupied, but one to which the laws of nature and of nature's God entitle
them, a decent respect to the opinions of mankind requires that they
should declare the causes that impel them to such a course.

We hold these truths to be self-evident: that all men and women
are created equal; that they are endowed by their Creator with certain
inalienable rights; that among these are life, liberty, and the pursuit
of happiness; that to secure these rights governments are instituted,
deriving their just powers from the consent of the governed. Whenever any form of government becomes destructive of these ends, it is
the right of those who suffer from it to refuse allegiance to it, and
to insist upon the institution of a new government, laying its foundation on such principles, and organizing its powers in such form, as to
them shall seem most likely to effect their safety and happiness.
Prudence, indeed, will dictate that governments long established
should not be changed for light and transient causes; and accordingly
all experience has shown that mankind are more disposed to suffer
while evils are sufferable, than to right themselves by abolishing the
forms to which they are accustomed. But when a long train of abuses
and usurpations pursuing invariably the same object evinces a design
to reduce them under absolute despotism, it is their duty to throw
off such government, and to provide new guards for their future security. Such has been the patient sufferance [suffering] of the women
under this government, and such is now the necessity which con-

strains them to demand the equal station to which they are entitled.

The history of mankind is a history of repeated injuries and usurpations on the part of man toward woman, having in direct object the establishment of an absolute tyranny over her. To prove this, let facts be submitted to a candid world.

Having deprived her of this first right of a citizen, the elective franchise [right to vote], thereby leaving her without representation in the halls of legislation, he has oppressed her on all sides.

He has made her, if married, in the eye of the law, civilly dead. . . .

Now, in view of this entire disfranchisement [loss of right to vote] of one half of the people of this country, their social and religious degradation—in view of the unjust laws above mentioned, and because women do feel themselves aggrieved, oppressed, and fraudulently deprived of their most sacred rights, we insist that they have immediate admission to all the rights and privileges which belong to them as citizens of the United States.

In entering upon the great work before us, we anticipate no small amount of misconception, misrepresentation, and ridicule; but we shall use every instrumentality [means] within our power to effect our object. We shall employ agents, circulate tracts [pamphlets], petition the state and national legislatures, and endeavor to enlist the pulpit and the press in our behalf. We hope this convention will be followed by a series of conventions embracing every part of the country.

RESOLUTIONS

Resolved, That all laws which prevent woman from occupying such a station in society as her conscience shall dictate, or which place her in a position inferior to that of man, are contrary to the great precept of nature, and, therefore, of no force or authority.

Resolved, That woman is man's equal—was intended to be so by the Creator, and the highest good of the race demands that she should be recognized as such. . . .

Resolved, That woman has too long rested satisfied in the circumscribed [narrow] limits which corrupt customs and a perverted [misdirected] application of the Scriptures have marked out for her, and that it is time she should move in the enlarged sphere which her great Creator has assigned her.

Resolved, That it is the duty of the women of this country to secure to themselves their sacred right to the elective franchise.

Resolved, That the equality of human rights results necessarily from the fact of the identity [sameness of essential character] of the race in capabilities and responsibilities.

Resolved, That the speedy success of our cause depends upon the zealous and untiring efforts of both men and women, for the overthrow of the monopoly of the pulpit, and for the securing to women an equal participation with men in the various trades, professions, and commerce.

Resolved, therefore, That, being invested by the Creator with the same capabilities, and the same consciousness of responsibility for their exercise, it is demonstrably the right and duty of woman, equally with man, to promote every righteous cause by every righteous means; and especially in regard to the great subjects of morals and religion, it is self-evidently her right to participate with her brother in teaching them, both in private and in public, by writing and by speaking, by any instrumentalities proper to be used, and in any assemblies proper to be held. . . .

Horace Mann's Twelfth Annual Report to the Massachusetts Board of Education

"Education . . . is the great equalizer of the conditions of men. . . ."

In 1837, at the age of forty-one, Horace Mann turned his back on a profitable law practice and a promising career in politics to become the first secretary of the Massachusetts Board of Education, a newly created organization. He devoted the rest of his life to a crusade for free public education.

In the twelve annual reports which he prepared for the Massachusetts Board of Education; in the Common School

Journal, which he founded and edited for ten years; and through numerous lectures he delivered wherever he could gather an audience, he developed a philosophy of education based on the principle that the tax-supported public school is "the well-spring of freedom and a ladder of opportunity."

Horace Mann was one of the most outstanding of a number of leaders who laid the foundations of a system of free public education in the United States. His unflagging efforts earned for him the proud title of "the Father of American public schools."

1848

... Our means of education are the grand machinery by which the "raw material" of human nature can be worked up into inventors and discoverers, into skilled artisans [workers] and scientific farmers, into scholars and jurists, into the founders of benevolent institutions, and the great expounders of ethical and theological science.° By means of early education, those embryos of talent may be quickened, which will solve the difficult problems of political and economical law; and by them, too, the genius may be kindled which will blaze forth in the poets of humanity. Our schools, far more than they have done, may supply the presidents and professors of colleges, and superintendents of public instruction, all over the land; and send, not only into our sister states, but across the Atlantic, the men of practical science, to superintend the construction of the great works of art. Here, too, may those judicial powers be developed and invigorated, which will make legal principles so clear and convincing as to prevent appeals to force; and should the clouds of war ever lower [threaten] our country, some hero may be found—the nursling of our schools, and ready to become the leader of our armies—that best of all heroes, who will secure the glories of a peace, unstained by the magnificent murders of the battlefield. . . .

Vast and overshadowing private fortunes are among the greatest dangers to which the happiness of the people in a republic can be subjected. Such fortunes would create a feudalism of a new kind;

° *great expounders . . . science:* philosophers.

but one more oppressive and unrelenting than that of the Middle Ages. . . .

Now, surely, nothing but universal education can counterwork [oppose] this tendency to the domination of capital ° and the servility of labor. If one class possesses all the wealth and the education, while the residue of society is ignorant and poor, it matters not by what name the relation between them may be called: the latter, in fact and in truth, will be the servile dependents and subjects of the former. But if education be equally diffused, it will draw property after it by the strongest of all attractions; for such a thing never did happen, and never can happen, as that an intelligent and practical body of men should be permanently poor. Property and labor in different classes are essentially antagonistic; but property and labor in the same class are essentially fraternal. The people of Massachusetts have, in some degree, appreciated the truth that the unexampled prosperity of the state—its comfort, its competence, its general intelligence and virtue—is attributable to the education, more or less perfect, which all its people have received; but are they sensible of a fact equally important—namely, that it is to this same education that two thirds of the people are indebted for not being today the vassals of as severe a tyranny, in the form of capital, as the lower classes of Europe are bound to in the form of brute force?

Education, then, beyond all other devices of human origin, is the great equalizer of the conditions of men—the balance-wheel of the social machinery. I do not here mean that it so elevates the moral nature as to make men disdain and abhor the oppression of their fellow men. . . . But I mean that it gives each man the independence and the means by which he can resist the selfishness of other men. It does better than to disarm the poor of their hostility toward the rich: it prevents being poor. . . .

Now, so far as these natural and yet undeveloped resources of the earth are hereafter to be brought to light, and made the ministering servants of human welfare; we suppose that they are to be brought to light by the exercise of the human faculties—in the same way that all the scientific and mechanical improvements of past times have been brought to light—that is, by education. And the greater the proportion of minds in any community which are educated, and the more

---

° *capital:* The term refers here to capitalists who use their accumulated wealth (monev or property) in private business enterprises.

thorough and complete the education which is given them, the more rapidly through the sublime stages of progress will that community advance in all the means of enjoyment and elevation; and the more will it outstrip and outshine its less educated neighbors. The advance-guard of education and intelligence will gather the virgin wealth of whatever region they explore as a result of their knowledge, just as the Portuguese reaped the great harvest of the riches of India as their reward for discovering the new route to India. . . .

John C. Calhoun's Speech on the Compromise of 1850

". . . the responsibility of saving the Union rests on the North. . . ."

By 1850, the controversy over slavery and related issues had brought the North and the South to the brink of war. Senator Henry Clay, whose earlier efforts to reconcile the differences between the two sections of the country had won him the proud title of "the Great Compromiser," now undertook once more to find a middle ground on which both North and South could stand. Clay's proposals initiated one of the most critical and tense debates in American history.

On March 4, Senator John C. Calhoun, his once powerful voice shattered by the disease that shortly led to his death, sat grim and silent while a colleague read his speech condemning the compromise proposals. The Union cannot be saved by compromise, Calhoun insisted, but only "by a full and final settlement, on the principle of justice, of all the questions at issue between the two sections." And if the North cannot agree to accept this solution, let it "say so, and let the states we both represent agree to separate and part in peace."

Calhoun, who had devoted his life to the Southern cause, did not live to see the outcome of the great debate. He died

on March 31, nearly six months before Congress finally
adopted the Compromise of 1850 and more than ten years
before the North and the South, abandoning all thought of
further compromise, plunged into armed conflict.

March 4, 1850

I have, Senators, believed from the first that the agitation of the
subject of slavery would, if not prevented by some timely and effective measure, end in disunion. Entertaining this opinion, I have, on
all proper occasions, endeavored to call the attention of both . . . great
parties which divide the country to adopt some measure to prevent
so great a disaster, but without success. The agitation has been permitted to proceed, with almost no attempt to resist it, until it has
reached a point when it can no longer be disguised or denied that
the Union is in danger. You have thus had forced upon you the greatest and the gravest question that can ever come under your consideration: How can the Union be preserved?

To give a satisfactory answer to this mighty question, it is indispensable to have an accurate and thorough knowledge of the nature
and the character of the cause by which the Union is endangered.
Without such knowledge it is impossible to pronounce, with any certainty, by what measure it can be saved; just as it would be impossible for a physician to pronounce, in the case of some dangerous disease, with any certainty, by what remedy the patient could be saved,
without similar knowledge of the nature and character of the cause
which produced it. The first question, then, presented for consideration in the investigation I propose to make in order to obtain such
knowledge, is: What is it that has endangered the Union?

To this question there can be but one answer: that the immediate
cause is the almost universal discontent which pervades all the states
composing the Southern section of the Union. This widely extended
discontent is not of recent origin. It commenced with the agitation
of the slavery question, and has been increasing ever since. The next
question, going one step further back, is: What has caused this widely
diffused and almost universal discontent?

It is a great mistake to suppose, as is [done] by some, that it originated with demagogues,° who excited the discontent with the intention of aiding their personal advancement, or with the disappointed
ambition of certain politicians, who resorted to it as the means of
retrieving their fortunes. On the contrary, all the great political influences of the section were arrayed [lined up] against excitement, and
exerted to the utmost to keep the people quiet. The great mass of the
people of the South were divided, as in the other section, into Whigs
and Democrats. The leaders and the presses of both parties in the
South were very solicitous [anxious] to prevent excitement and to
preserve quiet; because it was seen that the effects of the former would
necessarily tend to weaken, if not destroy, the political ties which
united them with their respective parties in the other section. Those
who know the strength of party ties will readily appreciate the im-
mense force which this cause exerted against agitation, and in favor
of preserving quiet. But, great as it was, it was not sufficient to prevent the widespread discontent which now pervades the section. No.
Some cause, far deeper and more powerful than the one supposed,
must exist to account for discontent so wide and deep. The question
then recurs: What is the cause of this discontent? It will be found
in the belief of the people of the Southern states, as prevalent as the
discontent itself, that they cannot remain, as things now are, consistently with honor and safety, in the Union. The next question to be
considered is: What has caused this belief?

One of the causes is, undoubtedly, to be traced to the long-contin-
ued agitation of the slave question on the part of the North, and the
many aggressions which they have made on the rights of the South
during the time. . . .

There is another lying back of it, with which this is intimately connected, that may be regarded as the great and primary cause. This is
to be found in the fact that the equilibrium between the two sections,
in the government as it stood when the Constitution was ratified and
the government put in action, has been destroyed. At that time there
was nearly a perfect equilibrium between the two, which afforded ample means to each to protect itself against the aggression of the other;
but, as it now stands . . . the North has acquired a decided ascendancy
[controlling influence] over every department of this government, and

---

° *demagogues:* leaders or orators who seek to use social discontent to create
trouble for the government or to gain political influence.

through it a control over all the powers of the system. A single section governed by the will of the numerical majority, has now, in fact, the control of the government and the entire powers of the system. . . .

As, then, the North has the absolute control over the government, it is manifest that on all questions between it and the South, where there is a diversity of interests, the interest of the latter will be sacrificed to the former, however oppressive the effects may be; as the South possesses no means by which it can resist, through the action of the government. But if there was no question of vital importance to the South, in reference to which there was a diversity of views between the two sections, this state of things might be endured without the hazard of destruction to the South. But such is not the fact. There is a question of vital importance to the Southern section, in reference to which the views and feelings of the two sections are as opposite and hostile as they can possibly be.

I refer to the relation between the two races in the Southern section, which constitutes a vital portion of her social organization. Every portion of the North entertains views and feelings more or less hostile to it. Those most opposed and hostile regard it as a sin and consider themselves under the most sacred obligation to use every effort to destroy it. Indeed, to the extent that they conceive that they have power, they regard themselves as implicated in the sin, and responsible for not suppressing it by the use of all and every means. Those less opposed and hostile regard it as a crime—an offense against humanity, as they call it; and although not so fanatical [extremely partisan], feel themselves bound to use all efforts to effect the same object; while those who are least opposed and hostile regard it as a blot and a stain on the character of what they call the Nation, and feel themselves accordingly bound to give it no countenance or support. On the contrary, the Southern section regards the relation as one which cannot be destroyed without subjecting the two races to the greatest calamity; and the section to poverty, desolation, and wretchedness; and accordingly they feel bound, by every consideration of interest and safety, to defend it. . . .

. . . all the elements in favor of agitation are stronger now than they were in 1835, when it first commenced. . . . Unless something decisive is done . . . what is to stop this agitation before the great and final object at which it aims—the abolition of slavery in the states—

is consummated [gained]? Is it, then, not certain that if something is
not done to arrest it, the South will be forced to choose between abolition and secession? . . .

It is a great mistake to suppose that disunion can be effected by a
single blow. The cords which bound these states together in one common Union are far too numerous and powerful for that. Disunion
must be the work of time. It is only through a long process, and suc-
cessively, that the cords can be snapped, until the whole fabric falls
asunder. Already the agitation of the slavery question has snapped
some of the most important, and has greatly weakened all the others,
as I shall proceed to show.

The cords that bind the states together are not only many, but various in character. Some are spiritual or ecclesiastical; some political;
others social. Some appertain [are related] to the benefit conferred
by the Union, and others to the feeling of duty and obligation.

The strongest of those of a spiritual and ecclesiastical nature con-
sisted in the unity of the great religious denominations, all of which
originally embraced the whole Union. . . . The ties which held each
denomination together formed a strong cord to hold the whole Union together; but, powerful as they were, they have not been able to
resist the explosive effect of slavery agitation. . . .

The strongest cord of a political character consists of the many
and powerful ties that have held together the two great parties which
have, with some modifications, existed from the beginning of the government. They both extended to every portion of the Union, and
strongly contributed to hold all its parts together. But this powerful
cord has fared no better than the spiritual. It resisted for a long time
the explosive tendency of the agitation, but has finally snapped under its force—if not entirely, in a great measure. Nor is there one of
the remaining cords which has not been greatly weakened. To this
extent the Union has already been destroyed by agitation, in the
only way it can be, sundering and weakening the cords which bind it
together.

If the agitation goes on, the same force, acting with increased in-
tensity, as has been shown, will finally snap every cord, when nothing
will be left to hold the states together except force. But, surely, that
can, with no propriety of language, be called a Union, when the only
means by which the weaker is held connected with the stronger portion is force. It may, indeed, keep them connected; but the connec-

tion will partake much more of the character of subjugation, on the part of the weaker to the stronger, than the union of free, independent, and sovereign states in one confederation, as they stood in the early stages of the government, and which only is worthy of the sacred name of Union.

Having now, Senators, explained what it is that endangers the Union, and traced it to its cause, and explained its nature and character, the question again recurs: How can the Union be saved? To this I answer: There is but one way by which it can be, and that is, by adopting such measures as will satisfy the states belonging to the Southern section, that they can remain in the Union consistently with their honor and their safety. There is, again, only one way by which this can be effected, and that is by removing the causes by which this belief has been produced. Do this, and discontent will cease, harmony and kind feelings between the sections will be restored, and every apprehension of danger to the Union removed. The question, then, is: How can this be done? But, before I undertake to answer this question, I propose to show by what [means] the Union cannot be saved.

It cannot, then, be saved by eulogies on the Union, however splendid or numerous. The cry of "Union, Union, the glorious Union!" can no more prevent disunion than the cry of "Health, health, glorious health!" on the part of the physician, can save a patient lying dangerously ill. So long as the Union, instead of being regarded as a protector, is regarded in the opposite character, by not much less than a majority of the states, it will be in vain to attempt to conciliate them by pronouncing eulogies on it.

Besides, this cry of Union comes commonly from those whom we cannot believe to be sincere. It usually comes from our assailants. But we cannot believe them to be sincere; for, if they loved the Union, they would necessarily be devoted to the Constitution. It made the Union, and to destroy the Constitution would be to destroy the Union. But the only reliable and certain evidence of devotion to the Constitution is to abstain, on the one hand, from violating it, and to repel, on the other, all attempts to violate it. It is only by faithfully performing these high duties that the Constitution can be preserved, and with it the Union.

But how stands the profession of devotion to the Union by our assailants, when brought to this test? Have they abstained from violating the Constitution? Let the many acts passed by the Northern states to set aside and annul the clause of the Constitution providing for the delivery up of fugitive slaves answer. I cite this, not that it is the only instance (for there are many others), but because the violation in this particular [instance] is too notorious and palpable to be denied. Again, have they stood forth faithfully to repel violations of the Constitution? Let their course in reference to the agitation of the slavery question, which was commenced and has been carried on for fifteen years, avowedly [openly declared] for the purpose of abolishing slavery in the states—an object all acknowledged to be unconstitutional—answer. Let them show a single instance during this long period in which they have denounced the agitators or their attempts to effect what is admitted to be unconstitutional, or a single measure which they have brought forward for that purpose. How can we, with all these facts before us, believe that they are sincere in their profession of devotion to the Union, or avoid believing their profession is but intended to increase the vigor of their assaults and to weaken the force of our resistance?

Nor can we regard the profession of devotion to the Union, on the part of those who are not our assailants, as sincere, when they pronounce eulogies upon the Union, evidently with the intent of charging us with disunion, without uttering one word of denunciation against our assailants. If friends of the Union, their course should be to unite with us in repelling these assaults, and denouncing the authors as enemies of the Union. Why they avoid this and pursue the course they do, it is for them to explain.

Nor can the Union be saved by invoking the name of the illustrious Southerner whose mortal remains repose on the western bank of the Potomac. He [Washington] was one of us—a slaveholder and a planter. We have studied his history, and find nothing in it to justify submission to wrong. On the contrary, his great fame rests on the solid foundation that, while he was careful to avoid doing wrong to others, he was prompt and decided in repelling wrong. I trust that, in this respect, we profited by his example.

Nor can we find anything in his history to deter us from seceding from the Union, should it fail to fulfill the objects for which it was instituted, by being permanently and hopelessly converted into the means of oppressing instead of protecting us. On the contrary, we find much in his example to encourage us, should we be forced to the extremity of deciding between submission and disunion. . . .

Having now shown what cannot save the Union, I return to the question with which I commenced: How can the Union be saved? There is but one way by which it can with any certainty; and that is, by a full and final settlement, on the principle of justice, of all the questions at issue between the two sections. The South asks for justice, simple justice, and less she ought not to take. She has no compromise to offer but the Constitution; and no concession or surrender to make. She has already surrendered so much that she has little left to surrender. Such a settlement would go to the root of the evil, and remove all cause of discontent, by satisfying the South so that she could remain honorably and safely in the Union, and thereby restore the harmony and fraternal feeling between the sections, which existed anterior to [before] the Missouri agitation. Nothing else can, with any certainty, finally and forever settle the questions at issue, terminate agitation, and save the Union.

But can this be done? Yes, easily; not by the weaker party, for it can of itself do nothing, not even protect itself, but by the stronger. The North has only to will it to accomplish it, to do justice by conceding to the South an equal right in the acquired territory, and to do her duty by causing the stipulations relative to fugitive slaves to be faithfully fulfilled, to cease the agitation of the slave question, and to provide for the insertion of a provision in the Constitution, by an amendment, which will restore to the South, in substance, the power she possessed of protecting herself before the equilibrium between the sections was destroyed by the action of this government.° There will be no difficulty in devising [forming] such a provision, one that will protect the South, and which, at the same time, will improve and strengthen the government, instead of impairing and weakening it.

But will the North agree to this? It is for her to answer the question. But, I will say, she cannot refuse, if she has half the love of the Union which she professes to have, or without justly exposing herself

---

° The amendment to which Calhoun is referring is one that would incorporate his idea of the *concurrent majority*. According to this plan the South, as a section, would have the power to veto legislation which it considered harmful to its economic interests. This would be accomplished by having *two* elected presidents, one representing each section, but each having the power of veto.

to the charge that her love of power and aggrandizement is far greater than her love of the Union. At all events, the responsibility of saving the Union rests on the North, and not on the South. The South cannot save it by any act of hers, and the North may save it without any sacrifice whatever, unless to do justice and to perform her duties under the Constitution should be regarded by her as a sacrifice.

It is time, Senators, that there should be an open and manly avowal on all sides, as to what is intended to be done. If the question is not now settled, it is uncertain whether it ever can hereafter be; and we, as the representatives of the states of this Union, regarded as governments, should come to a distinct understanding as to our respective views, in order to ascertain whether the great questions at issue can be settled or not. If you, who represent the stronger portion, cannot agree to settle them on the broad principle of justice and duty, say so; and let the states we both represent agree to separate and part in peace. If you are unwilling we should part in peace, tell us so; and we shall know what to do when you reduce the question to submission or resistance. If you remain silent, you will compel us to infer by your acts what you intend. In that case, California will become the test question. If you admit her, under all the difficulties that oppose her admission, you compel us to infer that you intend to exclude us from the whole of the acquired territories, with the intention of destroying irretrievably the equilibrium between the two sections. We would be blind not to perceive in that case that your real objects are power and aggrandizement, and infatuated [foolish] not to act accordingly.

I have now, Senators, done my duty in expressing my opinions fully, freely, and candidly, on this solemn occasion. In doing so, I have been governed by the motives which have governed me in all the stages of the agitation of the slavery question since its commencement. I have exerted myself, during the whole period, to arrest it, with the intention of saving the Union, if it could be done; and if it could not, to save the section where it has pleased Providence to cast my lot, and which I sincerely believe has justice and the Constitution on its side. Having faithfully done my duty to the best of my ability, both to the Union and my section, throughout this agitation, I shall have the consolation, let what will come, that I am free from all responsibility.

Roger B. Taney's Opinion in Dred Scott v. Sandford

"... neither Dred Scott ... nor any of his family, were made free by being carried into this territory. ..."

The Dred Scott decision was the first since the famous case of Marbury v. Madison (1803) in which the Supreme Court declared an act of Congress unconstitutional.

Dred Scott, a Negro slave, had been taken from Missouri, a slave state, into Minnesota Territory, where slavery was prohibited by the Missouri Compromise of 1820. Later, after he was taken back to Missouri, he started a suit in the courts to obtain his freedom. He based his case on the fact that he had become free the moment he entered territory where slavery was prohibited.

When the case reached the Supreme Court, Chief Justice Taney declared that slaves were not citizens and had no right to sue in either a state or a federal court. This could have ended the case, but seven of the nine Judges, including Chief Justice Taney, went on to rule that Congress had no power to prohibit slavery in the Territories of the United States, and that the Missouri Compromise of 1820 was therefore unconstitutional.

March 6, 1857

Chief Justice Taney: ...

The plaintiff ... was, with his wife and children, held as slaves by the defendant, in the state of Missouri, and he brought this action in the Circuit Court of the United States for that district, to assert [claim] the title of himself and his family to freedom.

The declaration is ... that he and the defendant are citizens of different states; that is, that he is a citizen of Missouri, and the defendant a citizen of New York.°

The defendant pleaded ... that the plaintiff was not a citizen of the state of Missouri, as alleged [declared] in his declaration, being a Negro of African descent whose ancestors were of pure African blood, and who were brought into this country and sold as slaves. ...

The question is simply this: Can a Negro, whose ancestors were imported into this country, and sold as slaves, become a member of the political community formed and brought into existence by the Constitution of the United States, and as such become entitled to all the rights and privileges and immunities guaranteed by that instrument to the citizen? One of which rights is the privilege of suing in a court of the United States in the cases specified in the Constitution. ...

The words "people of the United States" and "citizens" are synonymous terms, and mean the same thing. They both describe the political body who, according to our republican institutions, form the sovereignty, and who hold the power and conduct the government through their representatives. They are what we familiarly call the "sovereign people," and every citizen is one of this people, and a constituent member of this sovereignty. The question before us is, whether the class of persons described in the plea ... compose a portion of this people, and are constituent members of this sovereignty. We think they are not, and that they are not included, and were not intended to be included, under the word "citizens" in the Constitution, and can, therefore, claim none of the rights and privileges which that instrument provides for and secures to citizens of the United States. On the contrary, they were at that time considered as a subordinate and inferior class of beings, who had been subjugated by the dominant race, and whether emancipated or not, yet remained subject to their authority. ...

The question then arises, whether the provisions of the Constitution, in relation to the personal rights and privileges to which the citizen of a state should be entitled, embraced [included] the Negro African race, at that time in this country, or who might afterward

° This case was being brought under the Diversity of Citizenship Clause (Article III, Section 2) of the United States Constitution, which gives a citizen of one state the right to sue a citizen of another state in the federal courts.

be imported, who had then [been] or should afterward be made free in any state; and to put it in the power of a single state to make him a citizen of the United States, and endow him with the full rights of citizenship in every other state without their consent. Does the Constitution of the United States act upon him whenever he shall be made free under the laws of a state, and raised there to the rank of a citizen, and immediately clothe him with all the privileges of a citizen in every other state, and in its own courts?

The Court thinks . . . the plaintiff . . . could not be a citizen of the state of Missouri, within the meaning of the Constitution of the United States, and, consequently, was not entitled to sue in its courts.

It is true, every person, and every class and description of persons, who were at the time of the adoption of the Constitution recognized as citizens in the several states, became also citizens of this new political body; but none other; it was formed by them, and for them and their posterity, but for no one else. And the personal rights and privileges guaranteed to citizens of this new sovereignty were intended to embrace those only who were then members of the several state communities, or who should afterward, by birthright or otherwise, become members, according to the provisions of the Constitution and the principles on which it was founded. . . .

It becomes necessary, therefore, to determine who were citizens of the several states when the Constitution was adopted. . . .

In the opinion of the Court, the legislation and histories of the times, and the language used in the Declaration of Independence, show that neither the class of persons who had been imported as slaves, nor their descendants, whether they had become free or not, were then acknowledged as a part of the people, nor intended to be included in the general words used in that memorable instrument. . . .

They had for more than a century before been regarded as beings of an inferior order and altogether unfit to associate with the white race, either in social or political relations; and so far inferior that they had no rights which the white man was bound to respect; and that the Negro might justly and lawfully be reduced to slavery for his benefit. He was bought and sold and treated as an ordinary article of merchandise and traffic [trade] whenever a profit could be made by it. This opinion was at that time fixed and universal in the civilized portion of the white race. It was regarded as an axiom [established principle] in morals as well as in politics, which no one thought of disputing, or supposed to be open to dispute; and men in every grade and position in society daily and habitually acted upon it in their private pursuits [occupations], as well as in matters of public concern. . . .

A Negro of the African race was regarded . . . as an article of property and held and bought and sold as such in every one of the thirteen colonies which united in the Declaration of Independence and afterward formed the Constitution of the United States. . . .

The legislation of the different colonies furnished positive and indisputable proof of this fact. . . .

The language of the Declaration of Independence is equally conclusive: . . .

"We hold these truths to be self-evident: that all men are created equal; that they are endowed by their Creator with certain inalienable rights; that among these are life, liberty, and the pursuit of happiness; that to secure these rights, governments are instituted, deriving their just powers from the consent of the governed."

The general words above quoted would seem to embrace the whole human family, and if they were used in a similar instrument at this day would be so understood. But it is too clear for dispute that the enslaved African race were not intended to be included and formed no part of the people who framed and adopted this declaration. . . .

Yet the men who framed this declaration were great men—high in literary acquirements—high in their sense of honor, and incapable of asserting principles inconsistent with those on which they were acting. They perfectly understood the meaning of the language they used and how it would be understood by others; and they knew that it would not in any part of the civilized world be supposed to embrace the Negro race, which, by common consent, had been excluded from civilized governments and the family of nations and doomed to slavery. They spoke and acted according to the then established doctrine and principles and in the ordinary language of the day, and no one misunderstood them. The unhappy black race were separated from the white by indelible marks, and laws long before established, and were never thought of or spoken of except as property and when the claims of the owner or the profit of the trader were supposed to need protection.

This state of public opinion had undergone no change when the

Constitution was adopted, as is equally evident from its provisions and language. . . .

But there are two clauses in the Constitution which point directly and specifically to the Negro race as a separate class of persons, and show clearly that they were not regarded as a portion of the people or citizens of the government then formed.

One of these clauses reserves to each of the thirteen states the right to import slaves until the year 1808, if it thinks it proper. And the importation which it thus sanctions was unquestionably of persons of the race of which we are speaking, as the traffic in slaves in the United States had always been confined to them. And by the other provision the states pledge themselves to each other to maintain the right of property of the master, by delivering up to him any slave who may have escaped from his service, and be found within their respective territories. . . .

The legislation of the states . . . shows, in a manner not to be mistaken, the inferior and subject condition of that race at the time the Constitution was adopted, and long afterward, throughout the thirteen states by which that instrument was framed. . . .

Upon a full and careful consideration of the subject, the Court is of [the] opinion that, upon the facts stated . . . Dred Scott was not a citizen of Missouri within the meaning of the Constitution of the United States, and not entitled as such to sue in its courts; and, consequently, that the Circuit Court had no jurisdiction of the case. . . .

We proceed, therefore, to inquire whether the facts relied on by the plaintiff entitled him to his freedom. . . .

In considering this part of the controversy, two questions arise: 1. Was he, together with his family, free in Missouri by reason of the stay in the territory of the United States hereinbefore mentioned? And 2. If they were not, is Scott himself free by reason of his removal to Rock Island, in the state of Illinois, as stated in the above admissions [statements]?

We proceed to examine the first question.

The Act of Congress, upon which the plaintiff relies [the Missouri Compromise of 1820], declares that slavery and involuntary servitude, except as a punishment for crime, shall be forever prohibited in all that part of the territory ceded by France, under the name of Louisiana, which lies north of thirty-six degrees thirty minutes north latitude, and not included within the limits of Missouri. And the difficulty which meets us at the threshold of this part of the inquiry is, whether Congress was authorized to pass this law under any of the powers granted to it by the Constitution; for if the authority is not given by that instrument, it is the duty of this Court to declare it void and inoperative, and incapable of conferring freedom upon anyone who is held as a slave under the laws of any one of the states.

The counsel for the plaintiff has laid much stress upon that article in the Constitution which confers on Congress the power "to dispose of and make all needful rules and regulations respecting the territory or other property belonging to the United States"; but, in the judgment of the Court, that provision has no bearing on the present controversy, and the power there given, whatever it may be, is confined, and was intended to be confined, to the territory which at that time belonged to, or was claimed by, the United States, and was within their boundaries as settled by the treaty with Great Britain, and can have no influence upon a territory afterward acquired from a foreign government. . . .

The power of Congress over the person or property of a citizen can never be a mere discretionary power under our Constitution and form of government. The powers of the government and the rights and privileges of the citizen are regulated and plainly defined by the Constitution itself. And when the territory becomes a part of the United States, the federal government enters into possession in the character impressed upon it by those who created it. It enters upon it with its powers over the citizen strictly defined, and limited by the Constitution, from which it derives its own existence, and by virtue of which alone it continues to exist and act as a government and sovereignty. It has no power of any kind beyond it; and it cannot, when it enters a territory of the United States, put off its character, and assume discretionary or despotic powers which the Constitution has denied to it. It cannot create for itself a new character separated from the citizens of the United States, and the duties it owes them under the provisions of the Constitution. The territory being a part of the United States, the government and the citizen both enter it under the authority of the Constitution, with their respective rights defined and marked out; and the federal government can exercise no power over his person or property, beyond what that instrument confers, nor lawfully deny any right which it has reserved. . . .

The rights of private property have been guarded with equal care.

Thus the rights of property are united with the rights of person, and placed on the same ground by the Fifth Amendment to the Constitution. . . . An act of Congress which deprives a person of the United States of his liberty or property merely because he came himself or brought his property into a particular territory of the United States, and who had committed no offense against the laws, could hardly be dignified with the name of due process of law. . . .

And this prohibition is not confined to the states, but the words are general, and extend to the whole territory over which the Constitution gives it power to legislate, including those portions of it remaining under territorial government, as well as that covered by states. It is a total absence of power everywhere within the dominion of the United States, and places the citizens of a territory, so far as these rights are concerned, on the same footing with citizens of the states, and guards them as firmly and plainly against any inroads which the general government might attempt, under the plea of implied or incidental [not expressly stated] powers. And if Congress itself cannot do this—if it is beyond the powers conferred on the federal government—it will be admitted, we presume, that it could not authorize a territorial government to exercise them. It could confer no power on any local government, established by its authority, to violate the provisions of the Constitution. . . .

If the Constitution recognizes the right of property of the master in a slave, and makes no distinction between that description of property and other property owned by a citizen, no tribunal, acting under the authority of the United States, whether it be legislative, executive, or judicial, has a right to draw such a distinction, or deny to it the benefit of the provisions and guarantees which have been provided for the protection of private property against the encroachments of the government. . . .

The right of property in a slave is distinctly and expressly affirmed in the Constitution. The right to traffic in it, like an ordinary article of merchandise and property, was guaranteed to the citizens of the United States, in every state that might desire it, for twenty years. And the government in express terms is pledged to protect it in all future time, if the slave escapes from his owner. . . . And no word can be found in the Constitution which gives Congress a greater power over slave property, or which entitles property of that kind to less protection than property of any other description. The only power conferred is the power coupled with the duty of guarding and protecting the owner in his rights.

Upon these considerations, it is the opinion of the Court that the Act of Congress which prohibited a citizen from holding and owning property of this kind in the territory of the United States north of the line therein mentioned, is not warranted by the Constitution, and is, therefore, void; and that neither Dred Scott himself, nor any of his family, were made free by being carried into this territory; even if they had been carried there by the owner, with the intention of becoming a permanent resident. . . .

Upon the whole, therefore, it is the judgment of this Court, that it appears by the record before us that the plaintiff . . . is not a citizen of Missouri, in the sense in which that word is used in the Constitution; and that the Circuit Court of the United States, for that reason, had no jurisdiction in the case, and could give no judgment in it. . . .

Abraham Lincoln's First Inaugural Address

*"We are not enemies, but friends.
We must not be enemies."*

On March 4, 1861, newly elected President Lincoln, having just taken the oath of office, stepped forward to deliver his inaugural address. There was an awkward moment as he stood with his manuscript in one hand, his tall hat in the other, uncertain about what to do. Then Senator Douglas, his former rival for high office, stepped forward and took the hat, thereby freeing the President from his embarrassing predicament.

Lincoln spoke to a divided nation. By March 4, seven Southern states had seceded from the Union and the Confederacy had already been organized. In North and South alike, people waited anxiously to hear how the new Chief Executive proposed to deal with the gravest crisis in the nation's history.

Repeating earlier pledges not to interfere with slavery in the states where it already existed, Lincoln went on to warn that he intended to maintain the Union that he had solemnly sworn to "preserve, protect, and defend."

March 4, 1861

Fellow Citizens of the United States: In compliance with a custom as old as the government itself, I appear before you to address you briefly, and to take in your presence the oath prescribed by the Constitution of the United States to be taken by the President "before he enters on the execution of his office.". . .

Apprehension seems to exist among the people of the Southern states that by the accession of a Republican administration their property and their peace and personal security are to be endangered. There has never been any reasonable cause for such apprehension. Indeed, the most ample evidence to the contrary has all the while existed and been open to their inspection. It is found in nearly all the published speeches of him who now addresses you. I do but quote from one of those speeches when I declare that "I have no purpose, directly or indirectly, to interfere with the institution of slavery in the states where it exists. I believe I have no lawful right to do so, and I have no inclination to do so.". . .

I now reiterate these sentiments. . . .

I take the official oath today with no mental reservations. . . .

A disruption of the Federal Union, heretofore only menaced, is now formidably attempted.

I hold that, in contemplation of universal law and of the Constitution, the Union of these states is perpetual. . . . It is safe to assert that no government proper ever had a provision in its organic [functional] law for its own termination. Continue to execute all the express provisions of our national Constitution, and the Union will endure forever. . . .

Again if the United States be not a government proper, but an association of states in the nature of contract merely, can it as a contract be peaceably unmade by less than all the parties who made it? One party to a contract may violate it—break it, so to speak; but does it not require all to lawfully rescind [unmake] it? . . .

It follows . . . that no state upon its own mere motion can lawfully get out of the Union; that resolves [resolutions] and ordinances to that effect are legally void [without power]; and that acts of violence, within any state or states, against the authority of the United States, are insurrectionary [rebellious] or revolutionary, according to circumstances.

I, therefore, consider that, in view of the Constitution and the laws, the Union is unbroken; and to the extent of my ability I shall take care, as the Constitution itself expressly enjoins upon me [charges me], that the laws of the Union be faithfully executed in all the states. Doing this I deem to be only a simple duty on my part; and I shall perform it so far as practicable, unless my rightful masters, the American people, shall withhold the requisite means, or in some authoritative manner direct the contrary. I trust this will not be regarded as a menace, but only as the declared purpose of the Union that it will constitutionally defend and maintain itself.

In doing this there needs to be no bloodshed or violence; and there shall be none, unless it be forced upon the national authority. The power confided to me will be used to hold, occupy, and possess the property and places belonging to the government, and to collect the duties and imposts; but beyond what may be necessary for these objects, there will be no invasion, no using of force against or among the people anywhere. . . .

The mails, unless repelled, will continue to be furnished in all parts of the Union. So far as possible, the people everywhere shall have that sense of perfect security which is most favorable to calm thought and reflection. . . .

That there are persons in one section or another who seek to destroy the Union at all events, and are glad of any pretext to do it, I will neither affirm nor deny; but if there be such, I need address no word to them. To those, however, who really love the Union may I not speak?

Before entering upon so grave a matter as the destruction of our national fabric [structure], with all its benefits, its memories, and its hopes, would it not be wise to ascertain precisely why we do it? Will you hazard so desperate a step while there is any possibility that any portion of the ills you fly from have no real existence? Will you, while the certain ills you fly to are greater than all the real ones you fly from —will you risk the commission of so fearful a mistake?

All profess to be content in the Union if all constitutional rights can be maintained. Is it true, then, that any right, plainly written in the Constitution, has been denied? I think not. Happily the human mind is so constituted that no party can reach to the audacity of doing this. Think, if you can, of a single instance in which a plainly written provision of the Constitution has ever been denied. If by the mere force of numbers a majority should deprive a minority of any clearly written constitutional right, it might, in a moral point of view, justify revolution—[it] certainly would if such a right were a vital one. But such is not our case. All the vital rights of minorities and of individuals are so plainly assured to them by affirmations and negations, guarantees and prohibitions, in the Constitution, that controversies never arise concerning them. But no organic law can ever be framed with a provision specifically applicable to every question which may occur in practical administration. No foresight can anticipate, nor any document of reasonable length contain, express provisions for all possible questions. Shall fugitives from labor be surrendered by national or by state authority? The Constitution does not expressly say. *May* Congress prohibit slavery in the territories? The Constitution does not expressly say. *Must* Congress protect slavery in the territories? The Constitution does not expressly say.

From questions of this class spring all our constitutional controversies, and we divide . . . them into majorities and minorities. If the minority will not acquiesce, the majority must, or the government must cease. There is no other alternative; for continuing the government is acquiescence on one side or the other.

If a minority in such case will secede rather than acquiesce, they make a precedent which in turn will divide and ruin them; for a minority of their own will secede from them whenever a majority refuses to be controlled by such minority. For instance, why may not any portion of a new confederacy a year or two hence arbitrarily secede again, precisely as portions of the present Union now claim to secede from it? All who cherish disunion sentiments are now being educated to the exact temper [frame of mind] of doing this. . . .

Plainly, the central idea of secession is the essence of anarchy [breaking up of law and order]. A majority held in restraint by constitutional checks and limitations, and always changing easily with deliberate changes of popular opinions and sentiments, is the only true sovereign of a free people. Whoever rejects it does, of necessity, fly to anarchy or to despotism. Unanimity is impossible; the rule of a minority, as a permanent arrangement, is wholly inadmissible; so that, rejecting the majority principle, anarchy or despotism in some form is all that is left.

I do not forget the position assumed by some, that constitutional questions are to be decided by the Supreme Court; nor do I deny that such decisions must be binding, in any case, upon the parties to a suit, as to the object of that suit, while they are also entitled to a very high respect and consideration in all parallel cases by all other departments of the government. And, while it is obviously possible that such decision may be erroneous in any given case, still the evil effect following it, being limited to that particular case, with the chance that it may be overruled and never become a precedent for other cases, can better be borne than could the evils of a different practice. At the same time, the candid citizen must confess that if the policy of the government, upon vital questions affecting the whole people, is to be irrevocably fixed by decisions of the Supreme Court, the instant they are made, in ordinary litigation [process of law] between parties in personal actions, the people will have ceased to be their own rulers, having to that extent practically resigned the government into the hands of that eminent tribunal.° Nor is there in this view any assault upon the Court or the judges. It is a duty from which they may not shrink to decide cases properly brought before them, and it is no fault of theirs if others seek to turn their decisions to political purposes.

One section of our country believes slavery is right, and ought to be extended, while the other believes it is wrong, and ought not to be extended. This is the only substantial dispute. The fugitive slave clause of the Constitution and the law for the suppression of the foreign slave trade are each as well enforced, perhaps, as any law can ever be in a community where the moral sense of the people imperfectly supports the law itself. The great body of the people abide by the dry

° Lincoln is referring here to the Dred Scott case, and he is criticizing the decision of the Supreme Court.

legal obligation in both cases, and a few break over [disobey] in each. This, I think, cannot be perfectly cured; and it would be worse in both cases after the separation of the sections than before. The foreign slave trade, now imperfectly suppressed, would be ultimately revived, without restriction, in one section, while fugitive slaves, now only partially surrendered, would not be surrendered at all by the other.

Physically speaking, we cannot separate. We cannot remove our respective sections from each other, nor build an impassable wall between them. A husband and wife may be divorced and go out of the presence and beyond the reach of each other; but the different parts of our country cannot do this. They cannot but remain face to face, and intercourse [dealings], either amicable or hostile, must continue between them. Is it possible, then, to make that intercourse more advantageous or more satisfactory after separation than before? Can aliens make treaties easier than friends can make laws? Can treaties be more faithfully enforced between aliens than laws can among friends? Suppose you go to war, you cannot fight always; and when, after much loss on both sides, and no gain on either, you cease fighting, the identical old questions as to terms of intercourse are again upon you.

This country, with its institutions, belongs to the people who inhabit it. Whenever they shall grow weary of the existing government, they can exercise their constitutional right of amending it, or their revolutionary right to dismember or overthrow it. I cannot be ignorant of the fact that many worthy and patriotic citizens are desirous of having the national Constitution amended. While I make no recommendation of amendments, I fully recognize the rightful authority of the people over the whole subject, to be exercised in either of the modes [ways] prescribed in the instrument itself [the Constitution], and I should, under existing circumstances, favor rather than oppose a fair opportunity being afforded the people to act upon it. . . .

Why should there not be a patient confidence in the ultimate justice of the people? Is there any better or equal hope in the world? In our present differences, is either party without faith of being in the right? If the Almighty Ruler of nations, with His eternal truth and justice, be on your side of the North, or on yours of the South, that truth and that justice will surely prevail by the judgment of this great tribunal of the American people.

By the frame of the government under which we live, this same people have wisely given their public servants but little power for mischief; and have, with equal wisdom, provided for the return of that little to their own hands at very short intervals. While the people retain their virtue and vigilance, no administration, by any extreme . . . wickedness or folly, can very seriously injure the government in the short space of four years.

My countrymen, one and all, think calmly and well upon this whole subject. Nothing valuable can be lost by taking time. If there be an object to hurry any of you in hot haste to a step which you would never take deliberately, that object will be frustrated by taking time; but no good object can be frustrated by it. Such of you as are now dissatisfied still have the old Constitution unimpaired, and, on the sensitive point, the laws of your own framing under it; while the new administration will have no immediate power, if it would, to change either. If it were admitted that you who are dissatisfied hold the right side in the dispute, there still is no single good reason for precipitate action. Intelligence, patriotism, Christianity, and a firm reliance on Him Who has never yet forsaken this favored land, are still competent to adjust in the best way all our present difficulty.

In your hands, my dissatisfied fellow countrymen, and not in mine, is the momentous issue of civil war. The government will not assail you. You can have no conflict without being yourselves the aggressors. You have no oath registered in heaven to destroy the government, while I shall have the most solemn one to "preserve, protect, and defend" it.

I am loath [unwilling] to close. We are not enemies, but friends. We must not be enemies. Though passion may have strained, it must not break, our bonds of affection. The mystic chords of memory, stretching from every battlefield and patriot grave to every living heart and hearthstone all over this broad land, will yet swell the chorus of the Union when again touched, as surely they will be, by the better angels of our nature.

The Homestead Act

"... any person who is the head of a family ... and is a citizen of the United States ... shall ... be entitled to ... one quarter-section ... of ... public lands. ..."

In the spring of 1862, Congress, living up to a campaign promise made by the Republican party in the election of 1860, adopted a new and generous government land policy. The Homestead Act, as it was called, authorized the government to give 160 acres of its public land to any homesteader who paid a registration fee of ten dollars and lived on his homestead for at least five years. By 1865, the government had given away 2,500,000 acres of land to some 15,000 homesteaders. After the end of the War Between the North and the South, settlers in growing numbers poured into the West to take advantage of the gift of free land.

May 20, 1862

Be it enacted, That any person who is the head of a family, or who has arrived at the age of twenty-one years, and is a citizen of the United States, or who shall have filed his declaration of intention to become such, as required by the naturalization laws of the United States, and who has never borne arms against the United States government or given aid and comfort to its enemies, shall ... be entitled to enter one quarter-section or a less quantity of unappropriated public lands, upon which said person may have filed a pre-emption claim.° ...

That the person applying for the benefit of this act shall, upon application to the register of the land office in which he or she is about to make such entry, make affidavit ° before the said register or receiver that he or she is the head of a family, or is twenty-one or more

---

° *pre-emption claim:* the right under federal law to settle on public land and then to purchase it before anyone else can do so.

° *affidavit:* a sworn statement in writing.

years of age, or shall have performed service in the Army or Navy of
the United States, and that he [or she] has never borne arms against
the government of the United States or given aid and comfort to its
enemies, and that such application is made for his or her exclusive
use and benefit, and that said entry is made for the purpose of actual
settlement and cultivation, and not, either directly or indirectly, for
the use or benefit of any other person or persons whomsoever; and
upon filing the said affidavit with the register or receiver, and on payment of ten dollars, he or she shall thereupon be permitted to enter
the quantity of land specified: *Provided however* that no certificate
shall be given or patent issued therefor until the expiration of five
years from the date of such entry; and if, at the expiration of such
time, or at any time within two years thereafter, the person making
such entry ... shall prove by two credible witnesses that he ... [has]
resided upon or cultivated the same for the term of five years immediately succeeding the time of filing the affidavit aforesaid, and shall
make affidavit that no part of said land has been alienated [trans-
ferred to another], and that he has borne true allegiance to the government of the United States; then, in such case, he ... if at that
time a citizen of the United States, shall be entitled to a patent, as
in other cases provided for by law: *And provided, further,* that in
case of the death of both father and mother, leaving an infant child
or children under twenty-one years of age, the right and fee [estate]
shall inure to the benefit of [belong to] said infant child or children. . . .

The Morrill Act

*"... there be granted to the several states ... an amount
of public land ... [for] the endowment, support, and
maintenance of at least one college. ..."*

The Morrill Act, adopted by Congress in 1862, proved to
be one of the most important laws ever passed in the United
States in support of education. It was designed to encourage
each state to organize "at least one college" devoted primarily

but not exclusively to agricultural and industrial education. The encouragement was provided in the form of large grants of public land. The law authorized the states to sell this land, invest the money, and use the income from the investments to construct and maintain state colleges.

July 2, 1862

Be it enacted by the Senate and House of Representatives of the United States of America in Congress assembled: That there be granted to the several states . . . an amount of public land . . . equal to thirty thousand acres for each senator and representative in Congress to which the states are respectively entitled by the apportionment under the census of eighteen hundred and sixty: Provided, that no mineral lands shall be selected or purchased under the provisions of this act.

Section 2. And be it further enacted: That the land aforesaid, after being surveyed, shall be apportioned to the several states in sections or subdivisions of sections, not less than one-quarter of a section; and whenever there are public lands in a state subject to sale at private entry at one dollar and twenty-five cents per acre, the quantity to which said state shall be entitled shall be selected from such lands within the limits of such state, and the Secretary of the Interior is hereby directed to issue to each of the states in which there is not the quantity of public lands subject to sale at private entry at one dollar and twenty-five cents per acre, to which said state may be entitled under the provisions of this act, land scrip ° to the amount in acres for the deficiency of its distributive share: said scrip to be sold by said states and the proceeds thereof applied to the uses and purposes prescribed in this act, and for no other use or purpose whatsoever. . . .

Section 4. And be it further enacted: That all moneys derived from the sale of the lands . . . and from the sale of land scrip . . . shall be invested in stocks of the United States, or of the states, or some other safe stocks, yielding not less than five per centum upon the par value

° **land scrip:** a certificate entitling the possessor to ownership of a specific quantity of public land.

of said stocks; and that the moneys so invested shall constitute a perpetual fund, the capital of which shall remain forever undiminished ... and the interest of which shall be inviolably appropriated, by each state which may take and claim the benefit of this act, to the endowment, support, and maintenance of at least one college where the leading object shall be, without excluding other scientific and classical studies, and including military tactics, to teach such branches of learning as are related to agriculture and mechanic arts, in such manner as the legislatures of the state may respectively prescribe, in order to promote the liberal and practical education of the industrial classes in the several pursuits and professions in life. . . .

No state while in a condition of rebellion or insurrection against the government of the United States shall be entitled to the benefit of this act. . . .

The Emancipation Proclamation

". . . all persons held as slaves within any state . . . in rebellion against the United States, shall be . . . forever free. . . ."

For more than three hours on New Year's Day, 1863, President Lincoln shook hands and exchanged greetings with guests at the annual Presidential reception in the White House. Then he slipped away to his private office where, in the presence of a few friends, he prepared to sign his name to the Emancipation Proclamation. Pen in hand, he leaned forward to write his name, and then, pausing a moment, said, "I never, in my life, felt more certain that I was doing right. . . ." With this, he wrote his name in bold letters across the bottom of the document.

The Emancipation Proclamation did not, of course, bring an end to human bondage in the United States. It was completely silent about slavery in the border states, and mere words on paper could not free the slaves still within the areas controlled by the Confederacy. But the Proclamation did transform the war, which up to then had been fought primarily to preserve the Union, into a crusade against slavery and, in so doing, ended the threat of foreign intervention on the side of the Confederacy.

January 1, 1863

BY THE PRESIDENT OF THE UNITED STATES OF AMERICA

A Proclamation

WHEREAS on the twenty-second day of September, A.D. 1862, a proclamation was issued by the President of the United States, containing, among other things, the following, to wit:

"That on the first day of January, A.D. 1863, all persons held as slaves within any state or designated part of a state, the people whereof shall then be in rebellion against the United States, shall be then, thenceforward, and forever free; and the executive government of the United States, including the military and naval authority thereof, will recognize and maintain the freedom of such persons and will do no act or acts to repress such persons or any of them, in any efforts they may make for their actual freedom.

"That the Executive will on the first day of January aforesaid, by proclamation, designate the states and parts of states, if any, in which the people thereof, respectively, shall then be in rebellion against the United States; and the fact that any state or the people thereof shall on that day be in good faith represented in the Congress of the United States by members chosen thereto at elections wherein a majority of the qualified voters of such states shall have participated shall, in the absence of strong countervailing [opposing] testimony, be deemed conclusive evidence that such state and the people thereof are not then in rebellion against the United States."

Now, therefore, I, Abraham Lincoln, President of the United States, by virtue of the power in me vested as Commander-in-Chief of the Army and Navy of the United States in time of actual armed rebellion against the authority and government of the United States, and as a fit and necessary war measure for suppressing said rebellion, do, on this first day of January, A.D. 1863, and in accordance with my purpose so to do, publicly proclaimed for the full period of one hundred days from the first day above mentioned, order and designate as the states and parts of states wherein the people thereof, respectively, are this day in rebellion against the United States the following, to wit:

Arkansas, Texas, Louisiana (except the parishes of St. Bernard, Plaquemines, Jefferson, St. John, St. Charles, St. James, Ascension, Assumption, Terrebonne, Lafourche, St. Mary, St. Martin, and Orleans, including the city of New Orleans), Mississippi, Alabama, Florida, Georgia, South Carolina, North Carolina, and Virginia (except the forty-eight counties designated as West Virginia, and also the counties of Berkeley, Accomac, Northampton, Elizabeth City, York, Princess Anne, and Norfolk, including the cities of Norfolk and Portsmouth), and which excepted parts are for the present left precisely as if this proclamation were not issued.

And by virtue of the power and for the purpose aforesaid, I do order and declare that all persons held as slaves within said designated states and parts of states are, and henceforward shall be, free; and that the executive government of the United States, including the military and naval authorities thereof, will recognize and maintain the freedom of said persons.

And I hereby enjoin upon the people so declared to be free to abstain from all violence, unless in necessary self-defense; and I recommend to them that, in all cases when allowed, they labor faithfully for reasonable wages.

And I further declare and make known that such persons of suitable condition will be received into the armed service of the United States to garrison forts, positions, stations, and other places, and to man vessels of all sorts in said service.

And upon this act, sincerely believed to be an act of justice, warranted by the Constitution upon military necessity, I invoke the considerate judgment of mankind and the gracious favor of Almighty God.

Abraham Lincoln's Gettysburg Address

"... government of the people, by the people, for the people, shall not perish from the earth."

On November 19, 1863, thousands of men and women, including many of America's most distinguished leaders, gathered to dedicate the national cemetery at Gettysburg. Edward Everett, one of the country's greatest orators, delivered the major address, which lasted for about two hours. Then President Lincoln, who had been asked to make a few "dedicatory remarks," slowly rose to his feet and began to speak, glancing down now and then at the sheet of paper he held in one hand. In less than three minutes he finished. The crowd applauded politely, but Lincoln left with the feeling that his speech had been "a flat failure."

The next day, Edward Everett sent a note to the President. "I should be glad," Everett wrote, "if I could flatter myself that I came as near to the central idea of the occasion in two hours as you did in two minutes." In his reply to Everett, Lincoln said: "In our respective parts yesterday, you could not have been excused to make a short address, nor I a long one. I am pleased to know that, in your judgment, the little I did say was not entirely a failure."

November 19, 1863

Four score and seven years ago our fathers brought forth on this continent a new nation, conceived in liberty, and dedicated to the proposition that all men are created equal.

Now we are engaged in a great civil war, testing whether that nation, or any nation so conceived and so dedicated, can long endure. We are met on a great battlefield of that war. We have come to dedicate a portion of that field as a final resting place for those who here gave their lives that that nation might live. It is alogether fitting and proper that we should do this.

But, in a larger sense, we cannot dedicate—we cannot consecrate—we cannot hallow—this ground. The brave men, living and dead, who struggled here, have consecrated it far above our poor power to add or detract. The world will little note nor long remember what we say here, but it can never forget what they did here. It is for us, the living, rather, to be dedicated here to the unfinished work which they who fought here have thus far so nobly advanced. It is rather for us to be here dedicated to the great task remaining before us—that from these honored dead we take increased devotion to that cause for which they gave the last full measure of devotion; that we here highly resolve that these dead shall not have died in vain; that this nation, under God, shall have a new birth of freedom; and that government of the people, by the people, for the people, shall not perish from the earth.

Abraham Lincoln's Second Inaugural Address

*"With malice toward none, with charity for all . . .
let us . . . bind up the nation's wounds. . . ."*

The cannon were still roaring and men from the North and the South were still fighting and dying when, on March 4, 1865, Abraham Lincoln, with his right hand on the Bible, took the oath of office and began his second term as President of the United States. But it was evident that the long and tragic war was drawing to a close, and in his second inaugural address Lincoln outlined the policy he intended to follow in regard to the South once the fighting ceased. In deeply moving language, Lincoln appealed for mercy and understanding and a united effort to achieve "a just and lasting peace among ourselves and with all nations."

March 4, 1865

Fellow countrymen: At this second appearing to take the oath of the Presidential office there is less occasion for an extended address than there was at the first. Then a statement somewhat in detail of a course to be pursued seemed fitting and proper. Now, at the expiration of four years, during which public declarations have been constantly called forth on every point and phase of the great contest which still absorbs the attention and engrosses the energies of the nation, little that is new could be presented. The progress of our arms, upon which all else chiefly depends, is as well known to the public as to myself, and it is, I trust, reasonably satisfactory and encouraging to all. With high hope for the future, no prediction in regard to it is ventured.

On the occasion corresponding to this four years ago all thoughts were anxiously directed to an impending civil war. All dreaded it, all sought to avert it. While the inaugural address was being delivered from this place, devoted altogether to *saving* the Union without war, insurgent [rebellious] agents were in the city seeking to *destroy* it without war—seeking to dissolve the Union and divide effects [possessions] by negotiation [arranging of terms]. Both parties deprecated war, but one of them would *make* war rather than let the nation survive, and the other would *accept* war rather than let it perish, and the war came.

One eighth of the whole population was colored slaves, not distributed generally over the Union, but localized in the southern part of it. These slaves constituted a peculiar and powerful interest. All knew that this interest was somehow the cause of the war. To strengthen, perpetuate, and extend this interest was the object for which the insurgents would rend the Union even by war, while the government claimed no right to do more than to restrict the territorial enlargement of it. Neither party expected for the war the magnitude or the duration which it has already attained. Neither anticipated that the *cause* of the conflict might cease with or even before the conflict itself should cease. Each looked for an easier triumph, and a result less fundamental and astounding. Both read the same Bible and pray to the same God, and each invokes His aid against the other. It may seem strange that any men should dare to ask a just God's assistance in wringing their bread from the sweat of other men's faces, but let us judge not, that we be not judged. The prayers of both could not be answered. That of neither has been answered fully. The Almighty has His own purposes. "Woe unto the world because of offenses; for it must needs be that offenses come, but woe to that man by whom the offense cometh." If we shall suppose that American slavery is one of those offenses which, in the providence of God, must needs come, but which, having continued through His appointed time, He now wills to remove, and that He gives to both North and South this terrible war as the woe due to those by whom the offense came, shall we discern therein any departure from those divine attributes which the believers in a living God always ascribe to Him? Fondly do we hope, fervently do we pray, that this mighty scourge [curse] of war may speedily pass away. Yet, if God wills that it continue until all the wealth piled by the bondsman's two hundred and fifty years of unrequited [unpaid] toil shall be sunk, and until every drop of blood drawn with the lash shall be paid by another drawn with the sword, as was said three thousand years ago, so still it must be said, "The judgments of the Lord are true and righteous altogether."

With malice toward none, with charity for all, with firmness in the right as God gives us to see the right, let us strive on to finish the work we are in, to bind up the nation's wounds, to care for him who shall have borne the battle and for his widow and his orphan, to do all which may achieve and cherish a just and lasting peace among ourselves and with all nations.

PART THREE
The
Nation Reunited

Theodore Roosevelt was six years old in 1865 when Lincoln was killed by an assassin's bullet. During Roosevelt's boyhood, the United States was still a predominantly agricultural country. Before he died in 1919, the United States had become one of the leading industrial powers of the world. During his rich and full life Roosevelt saw the reunited nation grow from thirty-six to forty-eight states, expand overseas, and fight a great war "to make the world safe for democracy."

Morrison R. Waite's Opinion in Munn v. Illinois

*"When ... one devotes his property to a use in which
the public has an interest, he ... must submit to be
controlled by the public for the common good. ..."*

The situation that led to the far-reaching decision in Munn
v. Illinois developed during the early 1870's when the legislatures of a number of midwestern states passed laws, collec-
tively known as the "Granger Laws," designed to regulate the
rates charged by railroads and grain elevators. Munn and
Scott, who owned a grain elevator in Chicago, refused to obey
the Illinois law on the ground that it deprived them of private property without due process of law and thus violated the
Fourteenth Amendment.

When the case reached the Supreme Court, the Court
ruled that state legislatures could regulate business "affected
with a public interest." This rule became a precedent for
the subsequent regulation of all forms of public transportation and communications, meat packing and food processing,
the production and sale of gas and electricity, and numerous
other activities involving the health, safety, welfare, and
morals of the people.

1877

The question to be determined in this case is whether ... Illinois
can ... fix by law the maximum of charges for the storage of grain in
warehouses at Chicago and other places in the state. ...

When one becomes a member of society, he necessarily parts with
some rights or privileges which, as an individual not affected by his
relations to others, he might retain. "A body politic," as aptly defined

in the preamble of the constitution of Massachusetts, "is a social compact by which the whole people covenants [agrees] with each citizen, and each citizen with the whole people, that all shall be governed by certain laws for the common good." This does not confer power upon the whole people to control rights which are purely and exclusively private . . . but it does authorize the establishment of laws requiring each citizen to so conduct himself and so use his own property as not unnecessarily to injure another. This is the very essence of government. . . . From this source come the police powers. . . . Under these powers the government regulates the conduct of its citizens one toward another, and the manner in which each shall use his own property, when such regulation becomes necessary for the public good. In their exercise it has been customary in England from time immemorial, and in this country from its first colonization, to regulate ferries, common carriers [those engaged in public transportation] . . . millers . . . etc., and in so doing to fix a maximum of charge to be made for services rendered. . . . To this day, statutes are to be found in many of the states upon some or all these subjects; and we think it has never yet been successfully contended that such legislation came within any of the constitutional prohibitions against interference with private property. . . .

From this it is apparent that, down to the time of the adoption of the Fourteenth Amendment, it was not supposed that statutes regulating the use, or even the price of the use, of private property necessarily deprived an owner of his property without due process of law. Under some circumstances they may, but not under all. . . .

Property does become clothed with a public interest when used in a manner to make it of public consequence, and affect the community at large. When, therefore, one devotes his property to a use in which the public has an interest, he, in effect, grants to the public an interest in that use, and must submit to be controlled by the public for the common good, to the extent of the interest he has thus created. He may withdraw his grant by discontinuing the use; but, so long as he maintains the use, he must submit to the control. . . .

From the same source comes the power to regulate the charges of common carriers. . . .

Common carriers exercise a sort of public office, and have duties to perform in which the public is interested. . . . Their business is therefore "affected with a public interest." . . .

But we need not go further. Enough has already been said to show that, when private property is devoted to a public use, it is subject to public regulation. It remains only to ascertain whether the warehouses of these plaintiffs in error,° and the business which is carried on there, come within the operation of this principle. . . .

In this connection it must also be borne in mind that, although in 1874 there were in Chicago fourteen warehouses adapted to this particular business, and owned by about thirty persons, nine business firms controlled them, and that the prices charged and received for storage were such "as have been from year to year agreed upon and established by the different elevators or warehouses in the city of Chicago, and which rates have been annually published in one or more newspapers printed in said city, in the month of January in each year, as the established rates for the year then next ensuing such publication." Thus it is apparent that all the elevating facilities through which these vast productions "of seven or eight great states of the West" must pass on the way "to four or five of the states on the seashore" may be a "virtual" monopoly.°

Under such circumstances it is difficult to see why, if the common carrier, or the miller . . . pursues a public employment and exercises "a sort of public office," these plaintiffs in error do not. They stand, to use again the language of their counsel, in the very "gateway of commerce," and take toll from all who pass. Their business most certainly "tends to a common charge and is become a thing of public interest and use." . . . Certainly, if any business can be clothed "with a public interest . . ." this has been. It may not be made so by the operation of the constitution of Illinois or this statute, but it is by the facts. . . .

For us the question is one of power, not of expediency. If no state of circumstances could justify such a statute, then we may declare this one void, because in excess of the legislative power of the state. But if it could we must presume it did. Of the propriety of legislative

<hr/>

° *plaintiff in error:* a term used at this time to refer to those who were appealing to the Court on a Writ of Error. Munn, having lost in the lower courts, was appealing to the Supreme Court on the ground that his loss was based on legal errors.

° *virtual monopoly:* An actual or real monopoly represents exclusive control over the supply of a commodity or service, free from competition. A virtual monopoly is one which has the effect of a monopoly but which, on appearance, does not seem to be a monopoly.

interference within the scope of legislative power, the legislature is the exclusive judge.

Neither is it a matter of any moment that no precedent can be found for a statute precisely like this. It is conceded that the business is one of recent origin, that its growth has been rapid, and that it is already of great importance. And it must be conceded that it is a business in which the whole public has a direct and positive interest. It presents, therefore, a case for the application of a long-known and well-established principle in social science, and this statute simply extends the law so as to meet this new development of commercial progress. There is no attempt to compel these owners to grant the public an interest in their property, but to decline their obligations, if they use it in this particular manner.

It matters not in this case that these plaintiffs in error had built their warehouses and established their business before the regulations complained of were adopted. What they did was from the beginning subject to the power of the body politic to require them to conform to such regulations as might be established by the proper authorities for the common good. They entered upon their business and provided themselves with the means to carry it on subject to this condition. If they did not wish to submit themselves to such interference, they should not have clothed the public with an interest in their concerns. The same principle applies to them that does to the proprietor of a hackney carriage, and as to him it has never been supposed that he was exempt from regulating statutes or ordinances because he had purchased his horses and carriage and established his business before the statute or the ordinance was adopted.

It is insisted, however, that the owner of property is entitled to a reasonable compensation for its use, even though it be clothed with a public interest, and that what is reasonable is a judicial and not a legislative question.°

As has already been shown, the practice has been otherwise. In countries where the common law ° prevails, it has been customary from time immemorial for the legislature to declare what shall be a reasonable compensation under such circumstances, or perhaps more properly speaking, to fix a maximum beyond which any charge

---

° *legislative question:* a matter for the state legislatures, not for the courts.

° *the common law:* generally refers to the law based on customs and judicial decisions. Statutory laws are those enacted by the legislatures.

made would be unreasonable.... The controlling fact is the power to regulate at all. If that exists, the right to establish the maximum charge, as one of the means of regulation, is implied....

We know that this is a power which may be abused; but that is no argument against its existence. For protection against abuses by legislatures the people must resort to the polls, not to the courts....

The warehouses of these plaintiffs in error are situated and their business carried on exclusively within the limits of the state of Illinois. They are used as instruments by those engaged in state as well as those engaged in interstate commerce.... Incidentally they may become connected with interstate commerce, but not necessarily so. Their regulation is a thing of domestic concern and, certainly, until Congress acts in reference to their interstate relations, the state may exercise all the powers of government over them, even though in so doing it may indirectly operate upon commerce outside its immediate jurisdiction....

The Pendleton Act

"... offices ... shall be filled ...
from among those graded highest
... [in] competitive examinations."

The Pendleton Act of 1883, sometimes called the "Magna Carta of Civil Service Reform," was born out of the tragic death of President James A. Garfield. On July 2, 1881, in the Washington railroad station, a mentally unbalanced office seeker, angered because he had not been appointed to the position he wanted, shot and mortally wounded the President.

Pressure to reform the "spoils system," under which party loyalty was the test for public office, had been building up for a number of years. The assassination of President Garfield shocked the nation into a clearer awareness of the evils and inefficiency of the "spoils system," and Congress responded to the widespread demand for reform with the passage of the Pendleton Civil Service Act.

January 16, 1883

Be it enacted... That the President is authorized to appoint, by and with the advice and consent of the Senate, three persons, not more than two of whom shall be adherents of the same party, as Civil Service Commissioners, and said three commissioners shall constitute the United States Civil Service Commission. Said commissioners shall hold no other official place under the United States.

Section 2. That it shall be the duty of said commissioners: ... To aid the President, as he may request, in preparing suitable rules for carrying this act into effect, and ... said rules shall provide and declare, as nearly as the conditions of good administration will warrant, as follows:

First, for open, competitive examinations for testing the fitness of applicants for the public service now classified ° or to be classified hereunder. Such examinations shall be practical in their character, and so far as may be shall relate to those matters which will fairly test the relative capacity and fitness of the persons examined to discharge the duties of the service into which they seek to be appointed.

Second, that all the offices, places, and employments so arranged or to be arranged in classes shall be filled by selections according to grade from among those graded highest as the results of such competitive examinations.

Third, appointments to the public service aforesaid in the departments at Washington shall be apportioned among the several states and Territories and the District of Columbia upon the basis of population as ascertained at the last preceding census. ...

Fourth, that there shall be a period of probation [trial] before any absolute appointment or employment aforesaid.

Fifth, that no person in the public service is for that reason under any obligations to contribute to any political fund, or to render any political service, and that he will not be removed or otherwise prejudiced for refusing to do so.

Sixth, that no person in said service has any right to use his official

° *classified:* those federal positions for which civil service examinations had to be taken.

authority or influence to coerce the political action of any person or body. . . .

Section 8. That no person habitually using intoxicating beverages to excess shall be appointed to, or retained in, any office, appointment, or employment to which the provisions of this act are applicable.

Section 9. That whenever there are already two or more members of a family in the public service in the grades covered by this act, no other member of such family shall be eligible to appointment to any of said grades.

Section 10. That no recommendation of any person who shall apply for office or place under the provisions of this act which may be given by any Senator or member of the House of Representatives, except as to the character or residence of the applicant, shall be received or considered by any person concerned in making any examination or appointment under this act.

Section 11. That no Senator, or Representative, or Territorial Delegate of the Congress, or Senator, Representative, or Delegate elect, or any officer or employee of either of said houses, and no executive, judicial, military, or naval officer of the United States, and no clerk or employee of any department, branch, or bureau of the executive, judicial, or military or naval service of the United States, shall, directly or indirectly, solicit or receive, or be in any manner concerned in soliciting or receiving, any assessment, subscription, or contribution for any political purpose whatever, from any officer, clerk, or employee of the United States, or any department, branch, or bureau thereof, or from any person receiving any salary or compensation from moneys derived from the Treasury of the United States. . . .

The Interstate Commerce Act

*"All charges made for any service . . . in the
transportation of passengers or property . . .
shall be reasonable and just. . . ."*

In 1886, the Supreme Court ruled in the case of the Wabash, St. Louis and Pacific Railway Company v. Illinois that state legislatures had no power to regulate traffic that moved across state boundaries. Since railroads were guilty of a number of unfair practices, and since the states could no longer regulate these practices, it was obvious that if anything were to be done, the federal government would have to act.

The Interstate Commerce Act, adopted by Congress in 1887, established a number of significant precedents. It marked the first attempt by the federal government to regulate railroad transportation; it created the first federal regulatory commission in American history; and it proved to be a turning point in the relations between government and business.

February 4, 1887

Be it enacted: . . . That the provisions of this act shall apply to any common carrier or common carriers engaged in the transportation of passengers or property wholly by railroad, or partly by railroad and partly by water when both are used, under a common control, management, or arrangement, for a continuous carriage or shipment, from one state or territory of the United States, or the District of Columbia, to any other state or territory of the United States, or the District of Columbia, or from any place in the United States to an adjacent foreign country, or from any place in the United States through a foreign country to any other place in the United States. . . .

The term "railroad" as used in this act shall include all bridges and ferries used or operated in connection with any railroad, and also all the road in use by any corporation operating a railroad, whether owned or operated under a contract, agreement, or lease; and the term "transportation" shall include all instrumentalities of shipment or carriage.

All charges made for any service rendered or to be rendered in the transportation of passengers or property as aforesaid, or in connection therewith, or for the receiving, delivering, storage, or handling of such property, shall be reasonable and just; and every unjust and unreasonable charge for such service is prohibited and declared to be unlawful.

Section 2. That if any common carrier subject to the provisions of this act shall, directly or indirectly, by any special rate, rebate,° drawback, or other device, charge, demand, collect, or receive from any person or persons a greater or less compensation for any service rendered, or to be rendered, in the transportation of passengers or property, subject to the provisions of this act, than it charges, demands, collects, or receives from any other person or persons for doing for him or them a like and contemporaneous service in the transportation of a like kind of traffic under substantially similar circumstances and conditions, such common carrier shall be deemed [considered] guilty of unjust discrimination, which is hereby prohibited and declared to be unlawful.

Section 3. That it shall be unlawful for any common carrier subject to the provisions of this act to make or give any undue or unreasonable preference or advantage to any particular person, company, firm, corporation, or locality....

Every common carrier subject to the provisions of this act shall, according to their respective powers, afford all reasonable, proper, and equal facilities for the interchange of traffic between their respective lines, and for the receiving, forwarding, and delivering of passengers and property to and from their several lines and those connecting therewith, and shall not discriminate in their rates and charges between such connecting lines; but this shall not be construed as requiring any such common carrier to give the use of its tracks or terminal facilities to another carrier engaged in like business.

Section 4. That it shall be unlawful for any common carrier subject to the provisions of this act to charge or receive any greater com-

° *rebate:* the return of part of the original amount paid.

pensation in the aggregate for the transportation of passengers or
of like kind of property, under substantially similar circumstances and
conditions, for a shorter than for a longer distance over the same line,
in the same direction, the shorter being included within the longer
distance. . . .

Section 5. That it shall be unlawful for any common carrier subject to the provisions of this act to enter into any contract, agreement, or combination with any other common carrier or carriers for
the pooling of freights of different and competing railroads, or to
divide between them the aggregate or net [amount over and above
expenses] proceeds of the earnings of such railroads, or any portion
thereof; and in any case of an agreement for the pooling of freights
as aforesaid, each day of its continuance shall be deemed a separate
offense.

Section 6. That every common carrier subject to the provisions
of this act shall print and keep for public inspection schedules show-
ing the rates and fares and charges for the transportation of passengers and property. . . . Copies for the use of the public shall be kept
in every depot or station upon any such railroad, in such places and
in such form that they can be conveniently inspected. . . .

No advance shall be made in the rates, fares, and charges which
have been established and published as aforesaid by any common carrier in compliance with the requirements of this section, except after
ten days' public notice, which shall plainly state the changes proposed to be made in the schedule then in force, and the time when
the increased rates, fares, or charges will go into effect. . . .

Every common carrier subject to the provisions of this act shall file,
with the Commission hereinafter provided for, copies of its schedules
of rates, fares, and charges which have been established and published
in compliance with the requirements of this section, and shall
promptly notify said Commission of all changes made in the same.
Every such common carrier shall also file with said Commission
copies of all contracts, agreements, or arrangements with other common carriers in relation to any traffic affected by the provisions of
this act to which it may be a party. . . .

Section 9. That any person or persons claiming to be damaged
by any common carrier subject to the provisions of this act may either make complaint to the Commission . . . hereinafter provided for,
or may bring suit in his or their own behalf for the recovery of the

damages for which such common carrier may be liable under the provisions of this act, in any district or circuit court of the United States of competent [legally qualified] jurisdiction. . . .

Section 10. That any common carrier subject to the provisions of this act, or, whenever such common carrier is a corporation, any director or officer thereof . . . [who] shall be guilty of any infraction of this act, or shall aid or abet . . . [such infraction], shall be deemed guilty of a misdemeanor, and shall, upon conviction thereof in any district court of the United States . . . be subject to a fine . . . not to exceed five thousand dollars for each offense.

Section 11. That a Commission is hereby created and established to be known as the Interstate Commerce Commission, which shall be composed of five Commissioners, who shall be appointed by the President, by and with the advice and consent of the Senate. The Commissioners . . . shall be appointed for terms of six years. . . . Any Commissioner may be removed by the President for inefficiency, neglect of duty, or malfeasance [misconduct] in office. Not more than three of the Commissioners shall be appointed from the same political party. No person in the employ of or holding any official relation to any common carrier subject to the provisions of this act, or owning stock or bonds thereof, or who is in any manner pecuniarily [in a manner relating to money] interested therein, shall enter upon the duties of or hold such office. Said Commissioners shall not engage in any other business, vocation, or employment. . . .

Section 12. That the Commission hereby created shall have authority to inquire into the management of the business of all common carriers subject to the provisions of this act, and shall keep itself informed as to the manner and method in which the same is conducted, and shall have the right to obtain from such common carriers full and complete information necessary to enable the Commission to perform the duties and carry out the objects for which it was created; and for the purposes of this act the Commission shall have power to require the attendance and testimony of witnesses and the production of all books, papers, tariffs, contracts, agreements, and documents relating to any matter under investigation. . . .

Section 13. That any person, firm, corporation, or association, or any mercantile, agricultural, or manufacturing society, or any body politic [group organized for government] or municipal organization complaining of anything done or omitted to be done by any common carrier subject to the provisions of this act in contravention [violation] of the provisions thereof, may apply to said Commission by petition, which shall briefly state the facts; whereupon a statement of the charges thus made shall be forwarded by the Commission to such common carrier, who shall be called upon to satisfy the complaint or to answer the same in writing within a reasonable time, to be specified by the Commission. . . .

Said Commission shall in like manner investigate any complaint forwarded by the railroad commissioner or railroad commission of any state or territory, at the request of such commissioner or commission, and may institute any inquiry on its own motion [application] in the same manner and to the same effect as though complaint had been made. . . .

Section 16. That whenever any common carrier . . . shall violate or refuse or neglect to obey any lawful order or requirement of the Commission in this act named, it shall be the duty of the Commission, and lawful for any company or person interested in such order or requirement, to apply . . . by petition to the circuit court of the United States . . . alleging such violation or disobedience, as the case may be; and the said court shall have power to hear and determine the matter, on such short notice to the common carrier complained of as the court shall deem reasonable. . . .

Section 20. That the Commission is hereby authorized to require annual reports from all common carriers subject to the provisions of this act, fix the time and prescribe the manner in which such reports shall be made, and to require from such carriers specific answers to all questions upon which the Commission may need information. Such reports shall also contain such information in relation to rates or regulations concerning fares or freights, or agreements, arrangements, or contracts with other common carriers, as the Commission may require. . . .

The Dawes Act

"... to provide for the allotment of lands ... to Indians ... and to extend the protection of the laws ... over the Indians. ..."

In 1887, with the passage of the Dawes Act, Congress made its first major attack upon the problem of assimilating the Indians into the main stream of American life. The men who wrote the law looked forward to a time when the Indians would abandon their tribal way of life, leave the reservations on which they were then living, and take their place in society with all the rights and privileges of American citizens.

February 8, 1887

An act to provide for the allotment of lands in severalty [in one's own right] to Indians on the various reservations, and to extend the protection of the laws of the United States and the territories over the Indians, and for other purposes.

Be it enacted: That in all cases where any tribe or band of Indians has been, or shall hereafter be, located upon any reservation created for their use ... the President of the United States ... is authorized, whenever in his opinion any reservation ... is advantageous for agriculture and grazing purposes, to cause said reservation, or any part thereof, to be surveyed, or re-surveyed if necessary, and to allot the lands in said reservation in severalty to any Indian located thereon in quantities as follows:

To each head of a family, one-quarter of a section;

To each single person over eighteen years of age, one-eighth of a section;

To each orphan child under eighteen years of age, one-eighth of a section; and

To each other single person under eighteen years ... one-sixteenth of a section. ...

Section 5. That upon the approval of the allotments provided for in this act by the Secretary of the Interior, he shall . . . declare that the United States does and will hold the land thus allotted, for the period of twenty-five years, in trust for the sole use and benefit of the Indian to whom such allotment shall have been made . . . and that at the expiration of said period the United States will convey the same by patent [legal document] to said Indian, or his heirs . . . free of all charge. . . .

Section 6. That upon the completion of said allotments and the patenting of the lands to said allottees, each and every member of the respective bands or tribes of Indians to whom allotments have been made shall have the benefit of and be subject to the laws, both civil and criminal, of the state or territory in which they may reside. . . . And every Indian born within the territorial limits of the United States to whom allotments shall have been made under the provisions of this act, or under any law or treaty, and every Indian born within the territorial limits of the United States who has voluntarily taken up, within said limits, his residence separate and apart from any tribe of Indians therein, and has adopted the habits of civilized life, is hereby declared to be a citizen of the United States, and is entitled to all the rights, privileges, and immunities of such citizens. . . .

The Sherman Antitrust Act

"Every contract, combination in the form of trust or otherwise, or conspiracy, in restraint of trade or commerce . . . is hereby declared to be illegal."

The Sherman Antitrust Act of 1890 was a milestone in the economic life of the country. With the passage of this law, Congress for the first time undertook to make rules for the conduct of big business.

During the 1870's and the 1880's, a number of giant industries—oil, sugar refining, steel, and others—became so powerful that they were able to eliminate most of the competition, secure a monopoly of the business in which they were engaged, and charge whatever prices they wished. Consumers and smaller competing businesses complained bitterly and demanded that the government step in to restore freedom of enterprise.

When it drafted the Sherman Antitrust Act, Congress failed to define such terms as "trust," "combination," "conspiracy," and "monopolization." As a result, the law proved difficult to enforce. It did, however, establish a precedent for later and more effective legislation.

July 2, 1890

An act to protect trade and commerce against unlawful restraints and monopolies [exclusive controls]. . . .

Be it enacted:

Section 1. Every contract, combination in the form of trust ° or otherwise, or conspiracy, in restraint of trade or commerce among the several states, or with foreign nations, is hereby declared to be illegal. Every person who shall make any such contract or engage in any such combination or conspiracy, shall be deemed guilty of a misdemeanor, and, on conviction thereof, shall be punished by fine not exceeding five thousand dollars,° or by imprisonment not exceeding one year, or by both said punishments . . . [at] the discretion of the Court.°

Section 2. Every person who shall monopolize, or attempt to monopolize, or combine or conspire with any other person or persons, to monopolize any part of the trade or commerce among the several

° **trust:** a form of business organization in which the stockholders of a number of corporations turned their shares of stock over to trustees and in return received trust certificates on which dividends were paid out of the profits of the trust. With control of the voting stock in their hands, the trustees could run several corporations as a single giant business enterprise and, in this way, exercise monopoly control of an entire industry.

° **fine not exceeding $5,000:** By an act of 1955 the fine is now $50,000 for each offense.

° In 1937, the Miller-Tydings law was passed, amending Section 1 of the Sherman Act. Under this new legislation, price-fixing agreements of nationally advertised articles are permitted between manufacturers and distributors in those states having Fair Trade laws.

states, or with foreign nations, shall be deemed guilty of a misdemeanor, and, on conviction thereof, shall be punished by fine not exceeding five thousand dollars, or by imprisonment not exceeding one year, or by both said punishments . . . [at] the discretion of the Court.

Section 3. Every contract, combination in form of trust or otherwise, or conspiracy, in restraint of trade or commerce in any territory of the United States or of the District of Columbia, or in restraint of trade or commerce between any such territory and another, or between any such territory or territories and any state or states or the District of Columbia, or with foreign nations, or between the District of Columbia and any state or states or foreign nations, is hereby declared illegal. Every person who shall make any such contract or engage in any such combination or conspiracy shall be deemed guilty of a misdemeanor, and, on conviction thereof, shall be punished by fine not exceeding five thousand dollars, or by imprisonment not exceeding one year, or by both said punishments . . . [at] the discretion of the Court.

Section 4. The several circuit courts ° of the United States are hereby invested with jurisdiction [given the legal power] to prevent and restrain violations of this act; and it shall be the duty of the several district attorneys of the United States, in their respective districts, under the direction of the Attorney-General, to institute proceedings in equity ° to prevent and restrain such violations. Such proceedings may be by way of petition setting forth the case and praying that such violation shall be enjoined [forbidden] or otherwise prohibited. When the parties complained of shall have been duly notified of such petition, the courts shall proceed, as soon as may be, to the hearing and determination of the case; and pending [through the continuance of] such petition and before final decrees, the court may at any time make such temporary restraining order or prohibition as shall be deemed just in the premises [case as set forth].

Section 5. Whenever it shall appear to the court before which any proceeding under section four of this act may be pending, that the ends of justice require that other parties should be brought before the court, the court may cause them to be summoned, whether they reside in the district in which the court is held or not; and subpoenas

° The federal district courts now have the powers described in this section.
° *equity:* See note on page 119.

[writs commanding a person to appear in court] to that end may be served in any district by the marshal thereof.

Section 6. Any property owned under any contract or by any combination, or pursuant to any conspiracy (and being the subject thereof) mentioned in section one of this act, and being in the course of transportation from one state to another, or to a foreign country, shall be forfeited to the United States, and may be seized and condemned by like proceedings as those provided by law for the forfeiture, seizure, and condemnation of property imported into the United States contrary to law.

Section 7. Any person who shall be injured in his business or property by any other person or corporation by reason of anything forbidden or declared to be unlawful by this act may sue therefor in any circuit court of the United States in the district in which the defendant resides or is found, without respect to the amount in controversy, and shall recover threefold the damages by him sustained, and the costs of suit, including a reasonable attorney's fee.°

Section 8. That the word "person," or "persons," wherever used in this act shall be deemed to include corporations and associations existing under or authorized by the laws of either the United States, the laws of any of the territories, the laws of any state, or the laws of any foreign country.

The Populist Party Platform

"... we seek to restore the government of the
Republic to the hands of 'the plain people.' ..."

In the summer of 1892, delegates representing a number of farmers' organizations gathered in Omaha, Nebraska, and organized a new political party—the People's Party, or the Populist Party. The tide of discontent that finally forced the farmers to organize a third party had been swelling for a number of years. Throughout the country, and especially in the

---

° Section 7 was repealed in 1955 and superseded by a section of the Clayton Act.

Middle West and the West, farmers had been meeting in
Grange halls and schoolhouses where, in the flickering light
of oil lamps, they had expressed their bitter indignation at the
failure of either the Republicans or the Democrats to help
the farmers out of their troubles. On July 4, the 116th anniversary of the Declaration of Independence, the Populist
Party adopted a platform that came to be known as "The
Farmer's Declaration of Independence."

July 4, 1892

Assembled upon the 116th anniversary of the Declaration of Independence, the People's Party of America, in their first national
convention, invoking upon their action the blessing of Almighty God,
put forth in the name and on behalf of the people of this country,
the following preamble and declaration of principles:

The conditions which surround us best justify our co-operation;
we meet in the midst of a nation brought to the verge of moral, political, and material ruin. Corruption dominates the ballot box, the
legislatures, the Congress, and touches even the ermine of the
bench.° The people are demoralized [corrupted]; most of the states
have been compelled to isolate the voters at the polling places to
prevent universal intimidation and bribery. The newspapers are
largely subsidized [controlled by advertisers or investors] or muz-
zled, public opinion silenced, business prostrated, homes covered with
mortgages, labor impoverished, and the land concentrating [center-
ing] in the hands of capitalists. The urban workmen are denied the
right to organize for self-protection, imported pauperized labor beats
down their wages, a hireling standing army, unrecognized by our laws,
is established to shoot them down, and they are rapidly degenerating
into European conditions. The fruits of the toil of millions are
boldly stolen to build up colossal fortunes for a few, unprecedented
in the history of mankind; and the possessors of those, in turn, de-
spise the Republic and endanger liberty. From the same prolific
womb [fertile source] of governmental injustice we breed the two
great classes—tramps and millionaires.

° **ermine of the bench:** Ermine used to be a part of the robes of a judge and
it symbolized judicial impartiality. The bench refers to the courts or judiciary.

The national power to create money is appropriated to enrich bond-holders; a vast public debt payable in legal tender currency ° has been funded [converted] into gold-bearing bonds, thereby adding millions to the burdens of the people.

Silver, which has been accepted as coin since the dawn of history, has been demonetized ° to add to the purchasing power of gold by decreasing the value of all forms of property as well as human labor, and the supply of currency is purposely abridged to fatten usurers [moneylenders], bankrupt enterprise, and enslave industry. A vast conspiracy against mankind has been organized on two continents, and it is rapidly taking possession of the world. If not met and over-thrown at once, it forebodes terrible social convulsions, the destruc-tion of civilization, or the establishment of an absolute despotism.

We have witnessed for more than a quarter of a century the strug-gles of the two great political parties for power and plunder, while grievous wrongs have been inflicted upon the suffering people. We charge that the controlling influences dominating both these parties have permitted the existing dreadful conditions to develop without serious effort to prevent or restrain them. Neither do they now prom-ise us any substantial reform. They have agreed together to ignore, in the coming campaign, every issue but one. They propose to drown the outcries of a plundered people with the uproar of a sham battle over the tariff, so that capitalists, corporations, national banks, rings,° trusts, watered stock,° the demonetization of silver, and the oppres-sions of the usurers may all be lost sight of. They propose to sacri-fice our homes, lives, and children on the altar of mammon °; to destroy the multitude in order to secure corruption funds from the millionaires.

Assembled on the anniversary of the birthday of the nation, and filled with the spirit of the grand general and chief who established our independence, we seek to restore the government of the Republic

° **legal tender currency:** money which the law authorizes a debtor to offer and requires a creditor to accept in payment of debts.

° **demonetized:** deprived of its standard value as money. The reference here is to the Demonetization Act of 1873, popularly referred to as "The Crime of 1873."

° **rings:** an exclusive combination of persons for selfish, and often corrupt, pur-poses, in order to control the stock market.

° **watered stock:** stock of which the par value has been increased without a cor-responding increase in the assets represented.

° **mammon:** materialism, from an ancient god, symbol of wealth and mate-rialism.

to the hands of "the plain people," with which class it originated. We assert our purposes to be identical with the purposes of the national Constitution; to form a more perfect union and establish justice, insure domestic tranquillity, provide for the common defense, promote the general welfare, and secure the blessings of liberty for ourselves and our posterity.

We declare that this Republic can only endure as a free government while built upon the love of the people for each other and for the nation; that it cannot be pinned together by bayonets; that the Civil War is over, and that every passion and resentment which grew out of it must die with it, and that we must be in fact, as we are in name, one united brotherhood of free men.

Our country finds itself confronted by conditions for which there is no precedent in the history of the world; our annual agricultural productions amount to billions of dollars in value, which must, within a few weeks or months, be exchanged for billions of dollars' worth of commodities consumed in their production; the existing currency supply is wholly inadequate to make this exchange; the results are falling prices, the formation of combines ° and rings, the impoverishment of the producing class. We pledge ourselves that if given power we will labor to correct these evils by wise and reasonable legislation, in accordance with the terms of our platform.

We believe that the power of government—in other words, of the people—should be expanded (as in the case of the postal service) as rapidly and as far as the good sense of an intelligent people and the teachings of experience shall justify, to the end that oppression, injustice, and poverty shall eventually cease in the land.

While our sympathies as a party of reform are naturally upon the side of every proposition which will tend to make men intelligent, virtuous, and temperate, we, nevertheless, regard these questions, important as they are, as secondary to the great issues now pressing for solution, and upon which not only our individual prosperity but the very existence of free institutions depend; and we ask all men to first help us to determine whether we are to have a republic to administer [manage] before we differ as to the conditions upon which it is to be administered, believing that the forces of reform this day organized will never cease to move forward until every wrong is righted

° *combines:* combinations of persons or organizations for commercial or political advantage.

and equal rights and equal privileges securely established for all the men and women of this country.

We declare, therefore:

First: That the union of the labor forces of the United States this day consummated shall be permanent and perpetual. . . .

Second: Wealth belongs to him who creates it, and every dollar taken from industry without an equivalent is robbery. "If any will not work, neither shall he eat." The interests of rural and civic labor are the same; their enemies are identical.

Third: We believe that the time has come when the railroad corporations will either own the people or the people must own the railroads, and should the government enter upon the work of owning and managing all railroads, we should favor an amendment to the Constitution by which all persons engaged in the government service shall be placed under a civil service regulation of the most rigid character, so as to prevent the increase of the power of the national administration by the use of such additional government employees.

Finance: We demand a national currency, safe, sound, and flexible, issued by the general government only, a full legal tender for all debts, public and private, and that without the use of banking corporations, [and] a just, equitable, and efficient means of distribution direct to the people. . . .

1. We demand free and unlimited coinage of silver and gold at the present legal ratio of sixteen to one.°

2. We demand that the amount of circulating medium [money in circulation] be speedily increased to not less than fifty dollars per capita.

3. We demand a graduated [gradually increasing] income tax.

4. We believe that the money of the country should be kept as much as possible in the hands of the people, and hence we demand that all state and national revenues shall be limited to the necessary expenses of the government, economically and honestly administered.

5. We demand that postal savings banks be established by the government for the safe deposit of the earnings of the people and to facilitate exchange.

Transportation: Transportation being a means of exchange and a public necessity, the government should own and operate the railroads in the interest of the people. The telegraph and telephone, like

° *ratio of sixteen to one:* ratio of sixteen ounces of silver to one ounce of gold.

the post-office system, being a necessity for the transmission of news, should be owned and operated by the government in the interest of the people.

Land: The land, including all the natural sources of wealth, is the heritage of the people, and should not be monopolized for speculative purposes, and alien ownership of land should be prohibited. All land now held by railroads and other corporations in excess of their actual needs, and all lands now owned by aliens should be reclaimed by the government and held for actual settlers only.

Your Committee on Platform and Resolutions beg leave unanimously to report the following:

WHEREAS: Other questions have been presented for our consideration, we hereby submit the following, not as a part of the platform of the People's Party, but as resolutions expressive of the sentiment of this convention:

1. *Resolved,* That we demand a free ballot and a fair count in all elections, and pledge ourselves to secure it . . . [for] every legal voter without federal intervention, through the adoption by the states of the unperverted Australian, or secret ballot, system.

2. *Resolved,* That the revenue derived from a graduated income tax should be applied to the reduction of the burden of taxation now levied upon the domestic industries of this country.

3. *Resolved,* That we pledge our support to fair and liberal pensions to ex-Union soldiers and sailors.

4. *Resolved,* That we condemn the fallacy of protecting American labor under the present system, which opens our ports to the pauper and criminal classes of the world and crowds out our wage earners; and we denounce the present ineffective laws against contract labor, and demand the further restriction of undesirable emigration.

5. *Resolved,* That we cordially sympathize with the efforts of organized workingmen to shorten the hours of labor, and demand a rigid enforcement of the existing eight-hour law on government work, and ask that a penalty clause be added to the said law.

6. *Resolved,* That we regard the maintenance of a large standing army of mercenaries, known as the Pinkerton system,° as a menace to our liberties, and we demand its abolition; and we condemn the recent invasion of the territory of Wyoming by the hired assassins of

° **Pinkerton system:** The Pinkerton Detective Agency supplied several hundred strikebreakers to the management of the Homestead Steel Works in 1892.

plutocracy [influentially wealthy people], assisted by federal officers.

7. *Resolved,* That we commend to the favorable consideration of the people and the reform press the legislative system known as the initiative ° and referendum.°

8. *Resolved,* That we favor a constitutional provision limiting the office of President and Vice-President to one term, and providing for the election of Senators of the United States by a direct vote of the people.

9. *Resolved,* That we oppose any subsidy or national aid to any private corporation for any purpose.

10. *Resolved,* That this convention sympathizes with the Knights of Labor ° and their righteous contest with the tyrannical combine of clothing manufacturers of Rochester, and declare it to be the duty of all who hate tyranny and oppression to refuse to purchase the goods made by the said manufacturers, or to patronize any merchants who sell such goods.

William Jennings Bryan's "Cross of Gold" Speech

". . . you shall not crucify mankind upon a cross of gold."

In the summer of 1896 the Democrats gathered in Chicago to nominate their candidate for the Presidency and to draft their political platform. The delegates were split wide apart on the question of currency. Some demanded a plank in favor of the gold standard. Others, equally vehement, clamored

° *initiative:* a device enabling voters, through the use of petitions, to initiate or introduce legislation at any time.

° *referendum:* a device enabling voters, through the use of petitions, to compel the legislature to place a bill or proposal before all the voters for their approval or disapproval.

° *Knights of Labor:* one of the most important national labor organizations in our history (1869–1890).

for a plank in favor of "cheap money" and the "free and unlimited coinage of both gold and silver."

The convention was still in a tumult when, on July 8,
William Jennings Bryan, a young, thirty-six-year-old lawyer
representing the silver wing of the party, stepped forward to
address the huge audience of more than 15,000 people. "Se-
rene and self-possessed, and with a smile upon his lips," as
one observer described the scene, "he faced the roaring multitude with a splendid consciousness of power. Before a single
word had been uttered by him, the pandemonium sank to an
inarticulate murmur, and when he began to speak, even this
was hushed to the profoundest silence." In a voice that
reached to the far corners of the great hall, a voice that those
who heard him called "glorious," he delivered one of the
most moving addresses ever given from a public platform in
the United States. When he finished, the delegates broke
into a roar of applause that continued without interruption
for more than half an hour. William Jennings Bryan's "Cross
of Gold" speech won him the Democratic nomination for the
Presidency of the United States.

July 8, 1896

I would be presumptuous, indeed, to present myself against the distinguished gentlemen to whom you have listened if this were a mere
measuring of abilities; but this is not a contest between persons. The
humblest citizen in all the land, when clad in the armor of a righteous
cause, is stronger than all the hosts of error. I come to speak to you
in defense of a cause as holy as the cause of liberty—the cause of
humanity.

When this debate is concluded, a motion will be made to lay upon
the table the resolution offered in commendation of the administration, and also the resolution offered in condemnation of the administration. We object to bringing this question down to the level of persons. The individual is but an atom; he is born, he acts, he dies; but
principles are eternal; and this has been a contest over a principle.

Never before in the history of this country has there been witnessed
such a contest as that through which we have just passed. Never before in the history of American politics has a great issue been fought

out as this issue has been, by the voters of a great party. On the fourth of March 1893, a few Democrats, most of them members of Congress, issued an address to the Democrats of the nation, asserting that the money question was the paramount issue of the hour; declaring that a majority of the Democratic party had the right to control the action of the party on this paramount issue; and concluding with the request that the believers in the free coinage of silver in the Democratic party should organize, take charge of, and control the policy of the Democratic party. Three months later, at Memphis, an organization was perfected, and the silver Democrats went forth openly and courageously proclaiming their belief, and declaring that, if successful, they would crystallize into a platform the declaration which they had made. Then began the struggle. With a zeal approaching the zeal which inspired the crusaders who followed Peter the Hermit, our silver Democrats went forth from victory unto victory until they are now assembled, not to discuss, not to debate, but to enter up the judgment already rendered by the plain people of this country. In this contest brother has been arrayed against brother, father against son. The warmest ties of love, acquaintance, and association have been disregarded; old leaders have been cast aside when they have refused to give expression to the sentiments of those whom they would lead, and new leaders have sprung up to give direction to this cause of truth. Thus has the contest been waged, and we have assembled here under as binding and solemn instructions as were ever imposed upon representatives of the people. . . .

When you ° come before us and tell us that we are about to disturb your business interests, we reply that you have disturbed our business interests by your course.

We say to you that you have made the definition of a businessman too limited in its application. The man who is employed for wages is as much a businessman as his employer; the attorney in a country town is as much a businessman as the corporation counsel in a great metropolis; the merchant at the crossroads store is as much a businessman as the merchant of New York; the farmer who goes forth in the morning and toils all day—who begins in the spring and toils all summer—and who by the application of brain and muscle to the natural resources of the country creates wealth, is as much a businessman as the man who goes upon the board of trade and bets upon the

° Bryan was here addressing the gold delegates.

price of grain; the miners who go down a thousand feet into the
earth, or climb two thousand feet upon the cliffs, and bring forth
from their hiding places the precious metals to be poured into the
channels of trade are as much businessmen as the few financial mag-
nates who, in a back room, corner the money of the world. We come
to speak for this broader class of businessmen.

Ah, my friends, we say not one word against those who live upon
the Atlantic coast, but the hardy pioneers who have braved all the
dangers of the wilderness, who have made the desert to blossom as
the rose—the pioneers . . . who rear their children near to Nature's
heart, where they can mingle their voices with the voices of the
birds . . . where they have erected schoolhouses for the education of
their young, churches where they praise their Creator, and cemeteries
where rest the ashes of their dead—these people, we say, are as de-
serving of the consideration of our party as any people in this country.
It is for these that we speak. We do not come as aggressors. Our war
is not a war of conquest; we are fighting in the defense of our homes,
our families, and posterity. We have petitioned, and our petitions
have been scorned; we have entreated, and our entreaties have been
disregarded; we have begged, and they have mocked when our calamity came. We beg no longer; we entreat no more; we petition no more.
We defy them. . . .

What we need is an Andrew Jackson to stand, as Jackson stood,
against the encroachments of organized wealth.

They tell us that this platform was made to catch votes. We reply
to them that changing conditions make new issues; that the principles
upon which democracy rests are as everlasting as the hills, but that
they must be applied to new conditions as they arise. Conditions
have arisen, and we are here to meet these conditions. They tell us
that the income tax ought not to be brought in here; that it is a new
idea. They criticize us for our criticism of the Supreme Court of the
United States. My friends, we have not criticized; we have simply
called attention to what you already know. If you want criticisms,
read the dissenting opinions of the Court. There you will find criticisms. They say that we passed an unconstitutional law; ° we deny it.
The income tax law was not unconstitutional when it was passed; it

---

° *unconstitutional law:* Bryan is referring to the case of *Pollock* v. *Farmers'
Loan and Trust Company* (1894) in which the Supreme Court, in a five to four
ruling, declared the income tax law unconstitutional.

was not unconstitutional when it went before the Supreme Court for the first time; it did not become unconstitutional until one of the judges changed his mind, and we cannot be expected to know when a judge will change his mind. The income tax is just. It simply intends to put the burdens of government justly upon the backs of the people. I am in favor of an income tax. When I find a man who is not willing to bear his share of the burdens of the government which protects him, I find a man who is unworthy to enjoy the blessings of a government like ours.

They say that we are opposing national bank currency; it is true. . . . We say in our platform . . . that the right to coin and issue money is a function of government. We believe it. We believe that it is a part of sovereignty, and can no more with safety be delegated to private individuals than we could afford to delegate to private individuals the power to make penal statutes ° or levy taxes. . . . Those who are opposed to this proposition tell us that the issue of paper money is a function of the banks, and that the government ought to go out of the banking business. I stand with Jefferson . . . and tell them, as he did, that the issue of money is a function of government, and that the banks ought to go out of the governing business. . . .

And now, my friends, let me come to the paramount issue. If they ask us why it is that we say more on the money question than we say upon the tariff question, I reply that, if protection has slain its thousands, the gold standard ° has slain its tens of thousands. If they ask us why we do not embody in our platform all the things that we believe in, we reply that when we have restored the money of the Constitution, all other necessary reform will be possible; but that until this is done, there is no other reform that can be accomplished. . . .

We go forth confident that we shall win. Why? Because upon the paramount issue of this campaign there is not a spot of ground upon which the enemy will dare to challenge battle. . . . If the gold standard is a good thing, we ought to declare in favor of its retention and not in favor of abandoning it; and if the gold standard is a bad thing, why should we wait until other nations are willing to help us to let go? Here is the line of battle, and we care not upon which issue they force the fight; we are prepared to meet them on either issue or on

° *penal statutes:* laws concerning crimes and their punishment.
° *gold standard:* a monetary system under which the government supports and redeems its money with gold.

both. If they tell us that the gold standard is the standard of civilization, we reply to them that this, the most enlightened of all the nations of the earth, has never declared for a gold standard and that both the great parties this year are declaring against it. If the gold standard is the standard of civilization, why, my friends, should we not have it? If they come to meet us on that issue, we can present the history of our nation. More than that; we can tell them that they will search the pages of history in vain to find a single instance where the common people of any land have ever declared themselves in favor of the gold standard. They can find where the holders of fixed investments have declared for a gold standard, but not where the masses have. . . .

The sympathies of the Democratic party, as shown by the platform, are on the side of the struggling masses who have ever been the foundation of the Democratic party. There are two ideas of government. There are those who believe that, if you will only legislate to make the well-to-do prosperous, their prosperity will leak through on those below. The Democratic idea, however, has been that if you legislate to make the masses prosperous, their prosperity will find its way up through every class which rests upon them.

You come to us and tell us that the great cities are in favor of the gold standard; we reply that the great cities rest [ıcly] upon our broad and fertile prairies. Burn down your cities and leave our farms, and your cities will spring up again as if by magic; but destroy our farms and the grass will grow in the streets of every city in the country.

My friends, we declare that this nation is able to legislate for its own people on every question, without waiting for the aid or consent of any other nation on earth; and upon that issue we expect to carry every state in the Union. I shall not slander the inhabitants of the fair state of Massachusetts nor the inhabitants of the state of New York by saying that, when they are confronted with the proposition, they will declare that this nation is not able to attend to its own business. It is the issue of 1776 over again. Our ancestors, when but three millions in number, had the courage to declare their political independence of every other nation; shall we, their descendants, when we have grown to seventy millions, declare that we are less independent than our forefathers? No, my friends, that will never be the verdict of our people. Therefore, we care not upon what lines the battle is fought. If they say bimetallism ° is good, but that we cannot have it until other nations help us, we reply that, instead of having a gold standard because England has, we will restore bimetallism, and then let England have bimetallism because the United States has it. If they dare to come out in the open field and defend the gold standard as a good thing, we will fight them to the uttermost. Having behind us the producing masses of this nation and the world, supported by the commercial interests, the laboring interests, and the toilers everywhere, we will answer their demand for a gold standard by saying to them: You shall not press down upon the brow of labor this crown of thorns, you shall not crucify mankind upon a cross of gold.

William McKinley's War Message

"In the name of humanity . . .
the war in Cuba must stop."

In 1895, driven to the verge of desperation, the Cuban people revolted against their Spanish rulers, and the island was plunged into a bitter, bloody war. For three years, the United States maintained an official policy of neutrality, but finally, in March 1898, the government sent an ultimatum to Madrid demanding, among other things, that Spain immediately cease all fighting and grant an armistice to the Cuban revolutionists.

On April 9, the American minister to Spain sent a cable to Washington stating that the Spanish government had agreed to accept the ultimatum. "I hope," the American minister added, "that nothing will now be done to humiliate Spain. . . ."

° **bimetallism:** a monetary system under which the government supports and redeems its money with gold and silver.

Two days later, on April 11, President McKinley asked Congress to take steps to bring an end to the conflict in Cuba. "In the name of humanity, in the name of civilization, in behalf of endangered American interests which give us the right and duty to speak and to act, the war in Cuba must stop," McKinley declared.

Only at the very end of his message did the President inform Congress that Spain herself had agreed "to proclaim a suspension of hostilities. . . . This fact," he went on to say, ". . . will, I am sure, have your just and careful attention." But the war spirit had gotten out of hand, and on April 19, Congress adopted a joint resolution which plunged the United States into war on the side of the Cubans.

April 11, 1898

To the Congress of the United States:
Obedient to that precept of the Constitution which commands the President to give from time to time to the Congress information of the state of the Union and to recommend to their consideration such measures as he shall judge necessary and expedient, it becomes my duty to now address your body with regard to the grave crisis that has arisen in the relations of the United States to Spain by reason of the warfare that for more than three years has raged in the neighboring island of Cuba. . . .

The present revolution is but the successor of other similar insurrections which have occurred in Cuba against the dominion of Spain, extending over a period of nearly half a century, each of which during its progress has subjected the United States to great effort and expense in enforcing its neutrality laws, caused enormous losses to American trade and commerce, caused irritation, annoyance, and disturbance among our citizens, and, by the exercise of cruel, barbarous, and uncivilized practices of warfare, shocked the sensibilities and offended the human sympathies of our people. . . .

Our trade has suffered, the capital invested by our citizens in Cuba has been largely lost, and the temper and forbearance of our people have been so sorely tried as to beget a perilous unrest among our own citizens, which has inevitably found its expression from time to time in the national legislature. . . .

The war in Cuba is of such a nature that, short of subjugation [complete subservience] or extermination, a final military victory for either side seems impracticable. The alternative lies in the physical exhaustion of the one or the other party, or perhaps of both. . . . The prospect of such a protraction [extension] and conclusion of the present strife is a contingency hardly to be contemplated with equanimity by the civilized world, and least of all by the United States, affected and injured as we are, deeply and intimately, by its very existence. . . .

In my annual message of December last I said:

"Of the untried measures there remain only: recognition of the insurgents as belligerents; recognition of the independence of Cuba; neutral intervention to end the war by imposing a rational compromise between the contestants, and intervention in favor of one or the other party. I speak not of forcible annexation, for that cannot be thought of. That, by our code of morality, would be criminal aggression."

Thereupon I reviewed these alternatives in the light of President Grant's measured words, uttered in 1875, when, after seven years of sanguinary, destructive, and cruel hostilities in Cuba, he reached the conclusion that the recognition of the independence of Cuba was impracticable and indefensible and that the recognition of belligerence was not warranted by the facts according to the tests of public law. I commented especially upon the latter aspect of the question, pointing out the inconveniences and positive dangers of a recognition of belligerence, which, while adding to the already onerous burdens of neutrality within our own jurisdiction, could not in any way extend our influence or effective offices in the territory of hostilities.

Nothing has since occurred to change my view in this regard, and I recognize as fully now as then that the issuance of a proclamation of neutrality, by which process the so-called recognition of belligerents is published, could of itself and unattended by other action accomplish nothing toward the one end for which we labor—the instant pacification of Cuba and the cessation of the misery that afflicts the island. . . .

There remain the alternative forms of intervention to end the war, either as an impartial neutral, by imposing a rational compromise between the contestants, or as the active ally of the one party or the other.

As to the first, it is not to be forgotten that during the last few months the relation of the United States has virtually been one of friendly intervention in many ways, each not of itself conclusive, but all tending to the exertion of a potential influence toward an ultimate pacific result, just and honorable to all interests concerned. The spirit of all our acts hitherto has been an earnest, unselfish desire for peace and prosperity in Cuba, untarnished by differences between us and Spain and unstained by the blood of American citizens.

The forcible intervention of the United States as a neutral to stop the war, according to the large dictates of humanity and following many historical precedents where neighboring states have interfered to check the hopeless sacrifices of life by internecine [mutually destructive] conflicts beyond their borders, is justifiable on rational grounds. It involves, however, hostile constraint upon both the parties to the contest, as well to enforce a truce as to guide the eventual settlement.

The grounds for such intervention may be briefly summarized as follows:

First. In the cause of humanity and to put an end to the barbarities, bloodshed, starvation, and horrible miseries now existing there, and which the parties to the conflict are either unable or unwilling to stop or mitigate. It is no answer to say this is all in another country, belonging to another nation, and is, therefore, none of our business. It is specially our duty, for it is right at our door.

Second. We owe it to our citizens in Cuba to afford them that protection and indemnity [payment] for life and property which no government there can or will afford, and to that end to terminate the conditions that deprive them of legal protection.

Third. The right to intervene may be justified by the very serious injury to the commerce, trade, and business of our people and by the wanton destruction of property and devastation of the island.

Fourth, and which is of the utmost importance. The present condition of affairs in Cuba is a constant menace to our peace and entails upon this government an enormous expense. With such a conflict waged for years in an island so near us and with which our people have such trade and business relations; when the lives and liberty of our citizens are in constant danger and their property destroyed and themselves ruined; where our trading vessels are liable to seizure and are seized at our very door by warships of a foreign nation; the expeditions of filibustering ° that we are powerless to prevent altogether, and the irritating questions and entanglements thus arising— all these and others that I need not mention, with the resulting strained relations, are a constant menace to our peace and compel us to keep on a semi-war footing with a nation with which we are at peace.

These elements of danger and disorder already pointed out have been strikingly illustrated by a tragic event which has deeply and justly moved the American people. I have already transmitted to Congress the report of the naval court of inquiry on the destruction of the battleship *Maine* in the harbor of Havana during the night of the fifteenth of February. The destruction of that noble vessel has filled the national heart with inexpressible horror. Two hundred and fifty-eight brave sailors and marines and two officers of our Navy, reposing in the fancied security of a friendly harbor, have been hurled to death, grief and want brought to their homes, and sorrow to the nation.

The naval court of inquiry, which it is needless to say, commands the unqualified confidence of the government, was unanimous in its conclusion that the destruction of the *Maine* was caused by an exterior explosion—that of a submarine mine. It did not assume to place the responsibility. That remains to be fixed.

In any event, the destruction of the *Maine*, by whatever exterior cause, is a patent [obvious] and impressive proof of a state of things in Cuba that is intolerable. That condition is thus shown to be such that the Spanish government cannot assure safety and security to a vessel of the American Navy in the harbor of Havana on a mission of peace, and rightfully there. . . .

The long trial has proved that the object for which Spain has waged the war cannot be attained. The fire of insurrection may flame or may smolder with varying seasons, but it has not been and it is plain that it cannot be extinguished by present methods. The only hope of relief and repose from a condition which can no longer be endured is the enforced pacification of Cuba. In the name of humanity, in the name of civilization, in behalf of endangered American interests

° *expeditions of filibustering:* irregular, hostile military expeditions to a country with which one's own country is at peace.

which give us the right and the duty to speak and to act, the war in Cuba must stop.

In view of these facts and of these considerations I ask the Congress to authorize and empower the President to take measures to secure a full and final termination of hostilities between the government of Spain and the people of Cuba, and to secure in the island the establishment of a stable government, capable of maintaining order and observing its international obligations, ensuring peace and tranquillity and the security of its citizens as well as our own, and to use the military and naval forces of the United States as may be necessary for these purposes.

And in the interest of humanity and to aid in preserving the lives of the starving people of the island, I recommend that the distribution of food and supplies be continued and that an appropriation be made out of the public treasury to supplement the charity of our citizens.

The issue is now with the Congress. It is a solemn responsibility. I have exhausted every effort to relieve the intolerable condition of affairs which is at our doors. Prepared to execute every obligation imposed upon me by the Constitution and the law, I await your action.

Yesterday, and since the preparation of the foregoing message, official information was received by me that the latest decree of the Queen Regent of Spain directs General Blanco, in order to prepare and facilitate peace, to proclaim a suspension of hostilities, the duration and details of which have not yet been communicated to me.

This fact, with every other pertinent consideration, will, I am sure, have your just and careful attention in the solemn deliberations upon which you are about to enter. If this measure attains a successful result, then our aspirations as a Christian, peace-loving people will be realized. If it fails, it will be only another justification for our contemplated action.

The "Open-Door" Policy in China

"... to ... safeguard ... equal and impartial trade with all parts of the Chinese Empire."

During the latter half of the 1800's, the race for colonial empires gained full momentum. By the end of the century, Japan and the colonial powers of Europe had each carved out for themselves control over large areas of China, and the map of the country was beginning to resemble a huge jigsaw puzzle.

After 1898, when the United States secured the Philippine Islands, the American government became deeply concerned over developments in China. With the Philippines, the United States controlled "the crossroads of the East" and was in an excellent position to build an increasingly prosperous trade with China.

Twice, in 1898 and 1899, the British government suggested that the United States and Great Britain issue a joint declaration in favor of equal trading opportunities for all nations in China. As it had earlier done in the case of the Monroe Doctrine, the United States refused the British offer, preferring to make the declaration as a statement of American policy.

On September 6, 1899, Secretary of State John Hay sent a letter to Germany, Great Britain, and Russia urging these countries to accept the principle of the "open door" in China. Two months later, Hay sent a similar note to Japan, France, and Italy. Although Italy was the only country to give full approval to the principle, on March 20, 1900, Hay calmly announced that the "open-door" principle had been "accepted" and would be maintained.

1899–1900

Mr. Hay to Mr. White °

Department of State
Washington, September 6, 1899

Sir:

At the time when the government of the United States was informed by that of Germany that it had leased from His Majesty the Emperor of China the port of Kiao-chao and the adjacent territory in the province of Shantung, assurances were given to the ambassador of the United States at Berlin by the Imperial German minister for foreign affairs that the rights and privileges ensured by treaties from China to citizens of the United States would not thereby suffer or be in any wise impaired within the area over which Germany had thus obtained control.

More recently, however, the British government recognized by a formal agreement with Germany the exclusive right of the latter country to enjoy in said leased area and the contiguous "sphere of influence or interest" ° certain privileges, more especially those relating to railroads and mining enterprises, but, as the exact nature and extent of the rights thus recognized have not been clearly defined, it is possible that serious conflicts of interest may at any time arise, not only between British and German subjects within said area, but that the interests of our citizens may also be jeopardized thereby.

Earnestly desirous to remove any cause of irritation and to insure at the same time to the commerce of all nations in China the undoubted benefits which should accrue from a formal recognition by the various powers claiming "spheres of interest" that they shall enjoy perfect equality of treatment for their commerce and navigation within such "spheres," the government of the United States would be pleased to see His German Majesty's government give formal as-

° **Mr. White:** Andrew Dickson White, United States Ambassador to Germany.
° *sphere of influence or interest:* an area in an underdeveloped nation, in this case, China, in which a foreign power claimed the right to control a large measure of the economic activity.

surances and lend its co-operation in securing like assurances from the other interested powers that each within its respective sphere of whatever influence:

First. Will in no way interfere with any treaty port ° or any vested interest within any so-called "sphere of interest" or leased territory it may have in China.

Second. That the Chinese treaty tariff of the time being shall apply to all merchandise landed or shipped to all such ports as are within said "sphere of interest" (unless they be "free ports"), no matter to what nationality it may belong, and that duties so leviable shall be collected by the Chinese government.

Third. That it will levy no higher harbor dues on vessels of another nationality frequenting any port in such "sphere" than shall be levied on vessels of its own nationality, and no higher railroad charges over lines built, controlled, or operated within its "sphere" on merchandise belonging to citizens or subjects of other nationalities transported through such "sphere" than shall be levied on similar merchandise belonging to its own nationals transported over equal distances.

The liberal policy pursued by His Imperial German Majesty in declaring Kiao-chao a free port and in aiding the Chinese government in the establishment there of a customhouse are so clearly in line with the proposition which this government is anxious to see recognized that it entertains the strongest hope that Germany will give its acceptance and hearty support.

The recent ukase [official decree] of His Majesty the Emperor of Russia declaring the port of Talien-wan open during the whole of the lease under which it is held from China, to the merchant ships of all nations, coupled with the categorical [unqualified] assurances made to this government by His Imperial Majesty's representative at this capital at the time, and since repeated to me by the present Russian ambassador, seem to ensure the support of the Emperor to the proposed measure. Our ambassador at the Court of St. Petersburg has, in consequence, been instructed to submit it to the Russian government and to request their early consideration of it. . . .

The commercial interests of Great Britain and Japan will be so clearly served by the desired declaration of intentions, and the views of the governments of these countries as to the desirability of the

° *treaty port:* a port in China opened to European trade by treaty between China and European countries.

adoption of measures ensuring the benefits of equality of treatment of all foreign trade throughout China are so similar to those entertained by the United States, that their acceptance of the propositions herein outlined and their co-operation in advocating their adoption by the other powers can be confidently expected. . . .

In view of the present favorable conditions, you are instructed to submit the above considerations to His Imperial German Majesty's minister for foreign affairs, and to request his early consideration of the subject.

Copy of this instruction is sent to our ambassadors at London and at St. Petersburg for their information. . . .

JOHN HAY

Department of State
Washington, March 20, 1900.°

Sir:

The ____ government having accepted the declaration suggested by the United States concerning foreign trade in China, the terms of which I transmitted to you . . . and like action having been taken by all the various powers having leased territory or so-called "spheres of interest" in the Chinese Empire, as shown by the notes which I herewith transmit to you, you will please inform the government to which you are accredited, that the condition originally attached to its acceptance—that all other powers concerned should likewise accept the proposals of the United States—having been complied with, this government will therefore consider the assent given to it by ____ as final and definitive.

You will also transmit to the minister of foreign affairs copies of the present enclosures, and by the same occasion convey to him the expression of the sincere gratification which the President feels at the successful termination of these negotiations, in which he sees proof of the friendly spirit which animates the various powers interested in the untrammeled development of commerce and industry in the Chinese Empire and a source of vast benefit to the whole commercial world. . . .

JOHN HAY

° Copies of this letter were sent to the United States ambassadors at London, Paris, Berlin, St. Petersburg, and Rome and to the United States Minister at Tokyo.

Department of State
Washington, July 3, 1900 °

In this critical posture of affairs in China it is deemed appropriate to define the attitude of the United States as far as present circumstances permit this to be done. We adhere to the policy initiated by us in 1857, of peace with the Chinese nation, of furtherance of lawful commerce, and of protection of lives and property of our citizens by all means guaranteed under extraterritorial treaty rights and by the law of nations. If wrong be done to our citizens, we propose to hold the responsible authors to the uttermost accountability. We regard the condition at Pekin as one of virtual anarchy, whereby power and responsibility are practically devolved upon the local provincial authorities. So long as they are not in overt collusion with rebellion and use their power to protect foreign life and property, we regard them as representing the Chinese people, with whom we seek to remain in peace and friendship. The purpose of the President is, as it has been heretofore, to act concurrently with the other powers, first, in opening up communication with Pekin and rescuing the American officials, missionaries, and other Americans who are in danger; secondly, in according all possible protection everywhere in China to American life and property; thirdly, in guarding and protecting all legitimate American interests; and fourthly, in aiding to prevent a spread of the disorders to the other provinces of the Empire and a recurrence of such disasters. It is, of course, too early to forecast the means of attaining this last result; but the policy of the government of the United States is to seek a solution which may bring about permanent safety and peace to China, preserve Chinese territorial and administrative entity, protect all rights guaranteed to friendly powers by treaty and international law, and safeguard for the world the principle of equal and impartial trade with all parts of the Chinese Empire.

You will communicate the purport of this instruction to the minister for foreign affairs.

HAY

° This letter was sent at the time of the Boxer Rebellion—a Chinese uprising against foreigners—to the United States embassies in Berlin, Paris, London, Rome, and St. Petersburg, and to the United States missions in Vienna, Brussels, Madrid, Tokyo, The Hague, and Lisbon.

Proclamation Abolishing Peonage on the Island of Guam

*"...peonage...is, in fact, a system of slavery...
and a violation of the sacred privileges guaranteed
by the Constitution of the United States."*

In the Treaty of Paris, which marked the end of the Span-ish-American War, Spain ceded Puerto Rico, the Philippines, and Guam to the United States. Guam, with an area of only 206 square miles and a population (in 1900) of fewer than ten thousand people, was by far the smallest of the three territories. Because of its excellent anchorages and its strategic location in the Western Pacific, Guam did, however, have value as a coaling station and naval base. For this reason, the Navy was given the responsibility for administering the affairs of the island.

When naval officer Richard P. Leary assumed charge as United States Governor of Guam, many of the island's people were being held under conditions of involuntary servitude. Those who owed money were forced to work out their debts as peons on the plantations of the well-to-do landowners. Others had to work out prison sentences in the same way.

On January 1, 1900, as one of his first acts, Governor Leary issued a proclamation abolishing "human slavery or peonage in the Isle of Guam." By this proclamation, the new governor extended the "sacred privileges" of the Constitution of the United States to the people of a remote island in the Western Pacific.

January 1, 1900

PROCLAMATION!

To the inhabitants of Guam:

In issuing this decree the government desires and earnestly invokes Divine blessing and guidance in its official action and in the daily pursuits and occupations of the citizens of Guam.

By the cession of the Isle of Guam to the United States of America, all of the authority, power, and responsibilities of sovereignty were transferred to this government, and in transforming and organizing the new political power, the surest and speediest route to success, prosperity, and happiness for the inhabitants of this island is by benevolent assimilation . . . [of] the fundamental principles that constitute the basis of free American government.

Honest labor with just compensation, dignified by faithful consideration of the mutual interests and welfare of all persons concerned, should insure prosperity to this community; whereas, the existing labor-degrading system of human bondage and unjust, indefinite servitude or peonage, permitted during the late Spanish control in this island, is, in fact, a system of slavery, and as such is subversive of good government, is an obstacle to progressive civilization, a menace to popular liberty, and a violation of the sacred privileges guaranteed by the Constitution of the United States.

Now, therefore, by virtue of the authority vested in me by his Excellency, the President of the United States, I, Richard P. Leary, Captain, United States Navy, Governor of the Isle of Guam, do hereby announce and publicly proclaim absolute prohibition and total abolition of human slavery or peonage in the Isle of Guam on and after the twenty-second day of February, A.D. 1900, and all persons are hereby commanded to comply with the requirements of this proclamation.

IN WITNESS WHEREOF, I have hereunto set my hand and have caused the seal of the United States Naval Station, Isle of Guam, to be affixed.

Done at Agana, Isle of Guam, this first day of January, in the year of our Lord, one thousand nine hundred, and of the Independence of the United States of America, the one hundred and twenty-fourth.

RICHARD P. LEARY, U.S.N.
Governor

Theodore Roosevelt's
"The New Nationalism"

"I stand for the square deal."

In 1909, at the conclusion of his second term as Chief Executive, Theodore Roosevelt journeyed to Africa, where he spent several months big-game hunting, and then, after traveling through Europe, returned to the United States. Upon his return, he accepted many invitations to deliver public addresses. In a number of these speeches, collected in book form and entitled The New Nationalism, he advocated the extension of the powers of the federal government to curb unfair business practices and the political influence of powerful financiers. The following excerpt is from his speech at Osawatomie, Kansas, on August 31, 1910.

August 31, 1910

We come here today to commemorate one of the epoch-making events . . . [in] the long struggle for the rights of man, the long struggle for the uplift of humanity. Our country—this great republic—means nothing unless it means the triumph of a real democracy, the triumph of popular government, and, in the long run, of an economic system under which each man shall be guaranteed the opportunity to show the best that there is in him. That is why the history of America is now the central feature of the history of the world; for the world has set its face hopefully toward our democracy; and, oh, my fellow citizens, each one of you carries on your shoulders not only the burden of doing well for the sake of your own country, but the burden of doing well and seeing that this nation does well for the sake of mankind.

At many stages in the advance of humanity, this conflict between the men who possess more than they have earned and the men who have earned more than they possess is the central condition of progress. In our day it appears as the struggle of free men to gain and hold the right of self-government as against the special interests, who twist the methods of free government into machinery for defeating the popular will. At every stage, and under all circumstances, the essence of the struggle is to equalize opportunity, destroy privilege, and give to the life and citizenship of every individual the highest possible value. . . .

Practical equality of opportunity for all citizens, when we achieve it, will have two great results. First, every man will have a fair chance to make of himself all that in him lies, to reach the highest point to which his capacities, unassisted by special privilege of his own and unhampered by the special privilege of others, can carry him, and to get for himself and his family substantially what he has earned. Second, equality of opportunity means that the commonwealth will get from every citizen the highest service of which he is capable. . . .

I stand for the square deal. But when I say that I am for the square deal, I mean not merely that I stand for fair play under the present rules of the game, but that I stand for having those rules changed so as to work for a more substantial equality of opportunity and of reward for equally good service. One word of warning. . . . When I say I want a square deal for the poor man, I do not mean that I want a square deal for the man who remains poor because he has not got the energy to work for himself. If a man who has had a chance will not make good, then he has got to quit. . . .

Now, this means that our government, national and state, must be freed from the sinister influence or control of special interests.° Exactly as the special interests of cotton and slavery threatened our po-

---

° *special interests:* a group of individuals or corporations receiving advantages, such as favorable tax rates, because of political association.

litical integrity before the Civil War, so now the great special business interests too often control and corrupt the men and methods of government for their own profit. We must drive the special interests out of politics. That is one of our tasks today. Every special interest is entitled to justice—full, fair, and complete. . . . But not one is entitled to a vote in Congress, to a voice on the bench, or to representation in any public office. The Constitution guarantees protection to property, and we must make that promise good. But it does not give the right of suffrage to any corporation. . . .

There can be no effective control of corporations while their political activity remains. To put an end to it will be neither a short nor an easy task, but it can be done.

We must have complete and effective publicity of corporate affairs, so that the people may know beyond peradventure [doubt] whether the corporations obey the law and whether their management entitles them to the confidence of the public. It is necessary that laws should be passed to prohibit the use of corporate funds directly or indirectly for political purposes; it is still more necessary that such laws should be thoroughly enforced. Corporate expenditures for political purposes, and especially such expenditures by public service corporations,° have supplied one of the principal sources of corruption in our political affairs.

It has become entirely clear that we must have government supervision of the capitalization,° not only of public service corporations, including, particularly, railways, but of all corporations doing an interstate business. I do not wish to see the nation forced into the ownership of the railways if it can possibly be avoided, and the only alternative is thoroughgoing and effective regulation, which shall be based on a full knowledge of all the facts, including a physical valuation [dollars and cents value] of property. This physical valuation is not needed, or, at least, is very rarely needed, for fixing rates; but it is needed as the basis of honest capitalization.

We have come to recognize that franchises ° should never be granted except for a limited time, and never without proper provision for compensation to the public. It is my personal belief that the

---

° *public service corporation:* a public utility—corporations in the fields of transportation, communication, gas, electricity, water power, etc.
° *capitalization:* the face value of the stocks and bonds of a corporation.
° *franchises:* licenses or charters granted by a government.

same kind and degree of control and supervision which should be exercised over public service corporations should be extended also to combinations ° which control necessaries of life; such as meat, oil, and coal, or which deal in them on an important scale. I have no doubt that the ordinary man who has control of them is much like ourselves. I have no doubt he would like to do well, but I want to have enough supervision to help him realize that desire to do well.

I believe that the officers, and, especially, the directors, of corporations should be held personally responsible when any corporation breaks the law.

Combinations in industry are the result of an imperative [compulsory] economic law which cannot be repealed by political legislation. The effort of prohibiting all combination has substantially failed. The way out lies, not in attempting to prevent such combinations, but in completely controlling them in the interest of the public welfare. For that purpose the Federal Bureau of Corporations is an agency of first importance. Its powers, and, therefore, its efficiency, as well as that of the Interstate Commerce Commission, should be largely increased. We have a right to expect from the Bureau of Corporations and from the Interstate Commission a very high grade of public service. We should be as sure of the proper conduct of the interstate railways and the proper management of interstate business as we are now sure of the conduct and management of the national banks, and we should have as effective supervision in one case as in the other. . . .

There is a widespread belief among our people that, under the methods of making tariffs which have hitherto obtained [prevailed], the special interests are too influential. Probably this is true of both the big special interests and the little special interests. These methods have put a premium on selfishness, and, naturally, the selfish big interests have gotten more than their smaller, though equally selfish, brothers. The duty of Congress is to provide a method by which the interest of the whole people shall be all that receives consideration. To this end there must be an expert tariff commission, wholly removed from the possibility of political pressure or of improper business influence. Such a commission can find the real difference between cost of production, which is mainly the difference of labor

° **combinations:** organizations formed to monopolize any part of interstate or foreign commerce.

costs here and abroad. As fast as its recommendations are made, I believe in revising one schedule at a time. A general revision of the tariff almost inevitably leads to logrolling ° and the subordination of the general public interest to local and special interests.

The absence of effective state, and, especially, national, restraint upon unfair money-getting has tended to create a small class of enormously wealthy and economically powerful men, whose chief object is to hold and to increase their power. The prime need is to change the conditions which enable these men to accumulate power which it is not for the general welfare that they should hold or exercise. We grudge no man a fortune which represents his own power and sagacity, when exercised with entire regard to the welfare of his fellows. . . . We grudge no man a fortune in civil life if it is honorably obtained and well used. It is not even enough that it should have been gained without doing damage to the community. We should permit it to be gained only so long as the gaining represents benefit to the community. This, I know, implies a policy of a far more active governmental interference with social and economic conditions in this country than we have yet had, but I think we have got to face the fact that such an increase in governmental control is now necessary.

No man should receive a dollar unless that dollar has been fairly earned. Every dollar received should represent a dollar's worth of service rendered—not gambling in stocks, but service rendered. The really big fortune, the swollen fortune, by the mere fact of its size acquires qualities which differentiate it in kind as well as in degree from what is possessed by men of relatively small means. Therefore, I believe in a graduated income tax on big fortunes, and in another tax which is far more easily collected and far more effective—a graduated inheritance tax on big fortunes, properly safeguarded against evasion and increasing rapidly in amount with the size of the estate.

The people of the United States suffer from periodical financial panics to a degree substantially unknown among the other nations which approach us in financial strength. There is no reason why we should suffer what they escape. It is of profound importance that our financial system should be promptly investigated, and so thoroughly and effectively revised as to make it certain that hereafter our currency will no longer fail at critical times to meet our needs.

° *logrolling:* agreement among legislators to vote for each other's bills.

It is hardly necessary for me to repeat that I believe in an efficient army and a navy large enough to secure for us abroad that respect which is the surest guaranty of peace. A word of special warning to my fellow citizens who are as progressive as I hope I am. I want them to keep up their interest in our internal [domestic] affairs; and I want them also continually to remember Uncle Sam's interests abroad. Justice and fair dealing among nations rest upon principles identical with those which control justice and fair dealing among the individuals of which nations are composed, with the vital exception that each nation must do its own part in international police work. If you get into trouble here, you can call for the police; but if Uncle Sam gets into trouble, he has got to be his own policeman, and I want to see him strong enough to encourage the peaceful aspirations of other peoples in connection with us. I believe in national friendships and heartiest good will to all nations; but national friendships, like those between men, must be founded on respect as well as on liking, on forbearance as well as upon trust. I should be heartily ashamed of any American who did not try to make the American government act as justly toward the other nations in international relations as he himself would act toward any individual in private relations. I should be heartily ashamed to see us wrong a weaker power, and I should hang my head forever if we tamely suffered wrong from a stronger power.

Of conservation I shall speak more at length elsewhere. Conservation means development as much as it does protection. I recognize the right and duty of this generation to develop and use the natural resources of our land; but I do not recognize the right to waste them, or to rob, by wasteful use, the generations that come after us. I ask nothing of the nation except that it so behave as each farmer here behaves with reference to his own children. That farmer is a poor creature who skins the land and leaves it worthless to his children. The farmer is a good farmer who, having enabled the land to support himself and to provide for the education of his children, leaves it to them a little better than he found it himself. I believe the same thing of a nation.

Moreover, I believe that the natural resources must be used for the benefit of all our people, and not monopolized for the benefit of the few, and here again is another case in which I am accused of taking a revolutionary attitude. People forget now that one hundred years ago there were public men of good character who advocated the nation selling its public lands in great quantities, so that the nation could get the most money out of it, and giving it to the men who could cultivate it for their own uses. We took the proper democratic ground that the land should be granted in small sections to the men who were actually to till it and live on it. Now, with the water power, with the forests, with the mines, we are brought face to face with the fact that there are many people who will go with us in conserving the resources only if they are to be allowed to exploit them for their benefit. That is one of the fundamental reasons why the special interests should be driven out of politics. Of all the questions which can come before this nation, short of the actual preservation of its existence in a great war, there is none which compares in importance with the great central task of leaving this land even a better land for our descendants than it is for us, and training them into a better race to inhabit the land and pass it on. Conservation is a great moral issue, for it involves the patriotic duty of insuring the safety and continuance of the nation. . . .

Nothing is more true than that excess of every kind is followed by reaction; a fact which should be pondered [considered] by reformer and reactionary ° alike. We are face to face with new conceptions of the relations of property to human welfare, chiefly because certain advocates of the rights of property as against the rights of men have been pushing their claims too far. The man who wrongly holds that every human right is secondary to his profit must now give way to the advocate of human welfare, who rightly maintains that every man holds his property subject to the general right of the community to regulate its use to whatever degree the public welfare may require it.

But I think we may go still further. The right to regulate the use of wealth in the public interest is universally admitted. Let us admit also the right to regulate the terms and conditions of labor, which is the chief element of wealth, directly in the interest of the common good. The fundamental thing to do for every man is to give him a chance to reach a place in which he will make the greatest possible contribution to the public welfare. Understand what I say there. Give him a chance, not push him up if he will not be pushed. Help any man who stumbles; if he lies down, it is a poor job to try to carry him; but if he is a worthy man, try your best to see that he gets a

° *reactionary:* one who favors a return to an older order in political, economic, or social affairs.

chance to show the worth that is in him. No man can be a good citizen unless he has a wage more than sufficient to cover the bare cost of living, and hours of labor short enough so that after his day's work is done he will have time and energy to bear his share in the management of the community, to help in carrying the general load. We keep countless men from being good citizens by the conditions of life with which we surround them. We need comprehensive workmen's compensation acts, both state and national laws to regulate child labor and work for women, and, especially, we need in our common schools not merely education in book learning, but also practical training for daily life and work. We need to enforce better sanitary conditions for our workers and to extend the use of safety appliances for our workers in industry and commerce, both within and between the states. Also, friends, in the interest of the working-man himself we need to set our faces like flint against mob violence just as against corporate greed; against violence and injustice and lawlessness by wage workers just as much as against lawless cunning and greed and selfish arrogance of employers. . . .

I do not ask for overcentralization; ° but I do ask that we work in a spirit of broad and far-reaching nationalism when we work for what concerns our people as a whole. We are all Americans. Our common interests are as broad as the continent. I speak to you here in Kansas exactly as I would speak in New York or Georgia, for the most vital problems are those which affect us all alike. The national government belongs to the whole American people, and where the whole American people are interested, that interest can be guarded effectively only by the national government. The betterment which we seek must be accomplished, I believe, mainly through the national government.

The American people are right in demanding that New Nationalism, without which we cannot hope to deal with new problems. The New Nationalism puts the national need before sectional or personal advantage. It is impatient of the utter confusion that results from local legislatures attempting to treat national issues as local issues. It is still more impatient of the impotence which springs from over-division of governmental powers, the impotence which makes it possible for local selfishness or for legal cunning, hired by wealthy special

° *overcentralization:* bringing all or most government activities under a single control.

interests, to bring national activities to a deadlock. This New Nationalism regards the executive power as the steward of the public welfare. It demands of the judiciary that it shall be interested primarily in human welfare rather than in property, just as it demands that the representative body shall represent all the people. . . .

If our political institutions were perfect, they would absolutely prevent the political domination of money in any part of our affairs. We need to make our political representatives more quickly and sensitively responsive to the people whose servants they are. More direct action by the people in their own affairs under proper safeguards is vitally necessary. The direct primary ° is a step in this direction, if it is associated with a corrupt practices act effective to prevent the advantage of the man willing recklessly and unscrupulously to spend money over his more honest competitor. It is particularly important that all moneys received or expended for campaign purposes should be publicly accounted for, not only after election, but before election as well. Political action must be made simpler, easier, and freer from confusion for every citizen. I believe that the prompt removal of unfaithful or incompetent public servants should be made easy and sure in whatever way experience shall show to be most expedient in any given class of cases.

One of the fundamental necessities in a representative government such as ours is to make certain that the men to whom the people delegate their powers shall serve the people by whom they are elected, and not the special interests. I believe that every national officer, elected or appointed, should be forbidden to perform any service or receive any compensation, directly or indirectly, from interstate corporations; and a similar provision could not fail to be useful within the states.

The object of government is the welfare of the people. The material progress and prosperity of a nation are desirable chiefly so far as they lead to the moral and material welfare of all good citizens. . . . We must have—I believe we have already—a genuine and permanent moral awakening, without which no wisdom of legislation or administration really means anything; and on the other hand, we must try

---

° *direct primary:* a "nominating election" held before the regular election, at which time all registered voters have a chance to vote for the candidate of their choice. Prior to the adoption of the direct primary, all candidates for public office were nominated in political conventions.

to secure the social and economic legislation without which any improvement due to purely moral agitation is necessarily evanescent [short-lived]. . . .

Woodrow Wilson's
"The New Freedom"

*"Honest American industry has always thriven . . .
on freedom; it has never thriven on monopoly."*

Woodrow Wilson stands in the great tradition of Jefferson and Jackson in his opposition to monopoly. All three men realized that the concentration of economic power in the hands of a small group of men or corporations would destroy one of the foundation stones of the American way of life— equality of opportunity.

The 1912 campaign speeches of this scholar in politics— he had been both professor and president at Princeton University—were later published in book form. In the collection of speeches entitled The New Freedom: A Call for the Emancipation of the Generous Energies of a People, Wilson outlined a program designed to curb the power of the trusts, restore competition, and provide true industrial freedom in which American business, large and small, could grow and prosper.

In his Inaugural Address (page 252), President Wilson restated many of the principles he had developed in his campaign speeches. These principles became the basis for the antitrust, tariff, and banking legislation enacted by Congress during Wilson's first term in office.

1912

Gentlemen say ... that trusts ° are inevitable ... they say that the particular kind of combinations that are now controlling our economic development came into existence naturally and were inevitable; and that, therefore, we have to accept them as unavoidable and administer our development through them. . . .

I answer, nevertheless, that this attitude rests upon a confusion of thought. Big business is no doubt to a large extent necessary and natural. The development of business upon a great scale, upon a great scale of co-operation, is inevitable, and, let me add, is probably desirable. But that is a very different matter from the development of trusts, because the trusts have not grown. They have been artificially created; they have been put together, not by natural processes, but by the will, the deliberate planning will, of men who were more powerful than their neighbors in the business world, and who wished to make their power secure against competition. . . .

Did you ever look into the way a trust was made? It is very natural, in one sense, in the same sense in which human greed is natural. If I haven't efficiency enough to beat my rivals, then the thing I am inclined to do is to get together with my rivals and say: "Don't let's cut each other's throats; let's combine and determine prices for ourselves; determine the output, and thereby determine the prices: and dominate and control the market." That is very natural. That has been done ever since freebooting [pirating] was established. That has been done ever since power was used to establish control. The reason that the masters of combination have sought to shut out competition is that the basis of control under competition is brains and efficiency. I admit that any large corporation built up by the legitimate processes of business, by economy, by efficiency, is natural; and I am not afraid of it, no matter how big it grows. It can stay big only by doing its work more thoroughly than anybody else. And there is a point of bigness—as every businessman in this country knows, though some of them

° *trust:* used here in the sense of a group of companies centrally controlled to regulate production, reduce expenses, and eliminate competition. This is synonymous with *monopoly power*—the power to regulate production and set the prices of goods in an industry.

will not admit it—where you pass the limit of efficiency and get into the region of clumsiness and unwieldiness. You can make your combine so extensive that you can't digest it into a single system; you can get so many parts that you can't assemble them as you would an effective piece of machinery. The point of efficiency is overstepped in the natural process of development, oftentimes, and it has been overstepped many times in the artificial and deliberate formation of trusts.

A trust is formed in this way: a few gentlemen "promote" it—that is to say, they get it up—being given enormous fees for their kindness, which fees are loaded on to the undertaking in the form of securities [stocks and bonds] of one kind or another. The argument of the promoters is, not that everyone who comes into the combination can carry on his business more efficiently than he did before; the argument is: we will assign to you as your share in the pool twice, three times, four times, or five times what you could have sold your business for to an individual competitor who would have to run it on an economic and competitive basis. We can afford to buy it at such a figure because we are shutting out competition. We can afford to make the stock of the combination half a dozen times what it naturally would be and pay dividends ° on it, because there will be nobody to dispute the prices we shall fix.

Talk of that as sound business? Talk of that as inevitable? It is based upon nothing except power. It is not based upon efficiency. It is no wonder that the big trusts are not prospering in proportion to such competitors as they still have in such parts of their business as competitors have access to; they are prospering freely only in those fields to which competition has no access. Read the statistics of the Steel Trust, if you don't believe it. Read the statistics of any trust. They are constantly nervous about competition, and they are constantly buying up new competitors in order to narrow the field. The United States Steel Corporation is gaining in its supremacy in the American market only with regard to the cruder manufactures of iron and steel, but wherever, as in the field of more advanced manufactures of iron and steel, it has important competitors, its portion of the product is not increasing, but is decreasing, and its competitors, where they have a foothold, are often more efficient than it is.

Why? Why, with unlimited capital and innumerable mines and

° **dividends:** that part of the profits paid to the stockholders of a corporation.

plants everywhere in the United States, can't they beat the other fellows in the market? Partly because they are carrying too much. Partly because they are unwieldy. Their organization is imperfect. They bought up inefficient plants along with efficient, and they have got to carry what they have paid for, even if they have to shut some of the plants up in order to make any interest on their investments; or, rather, not interest on their investments, because that is an incorrect word—on their alleged capitalization.° Here we have a lot of giants staggering along under an almost intolerable weight of artificial burdens, which they have put on their own backs, and constantly looking about lest some little pigmy with a round stone in a sling may come out and slay them.

For my part, I want the pigmy to have a chance to come out. And I foresee a time when the pigmies will be so much more athletic, so much more astute, so much more active, than the giants, that it will be a case of Jack the giant-killer. Just let some of the youngsters I know have a chance and they'll give these gentlemen points. Lend them a little money. They can't get any now. See to it that when they have got a local market, they can't be squeezed out of it. . . . I am willing to let Jack come into the field with the giant, and if Jack has the brains that some Jacks that I know in America have, then I should like to see the giant get the better of him, with the load that he, the giant, has to carry—the load of water [watered stock]. For I'll undertake to put a waterlogged giant out of business any time, if you will give me a fair field and as much credit as I am entitled to, and let the law do what from time immemorial law has been expected to do —see fair play. . . .

I take my stand absolutely, where every progressive ought to take his stand, on the proposition that private monopoly is indefensible and intolerable. And there I will fight my battle. And I know how to fight it. Everybody who has even read the newspapers knows the means by which these men built up their power and created these monopolies. Any decently equipped lawyer can suggest to you statutes by which the whole business can be stopped. What these gentlemen do not want is this: they do not want to be compelled to meet all comers on equal terms. I am perfectly willing that they should beat

---

° *alleged capitalization:* Capitalization is the face value of the securities issued by a corporation. Wilson is referring to overcapitalization, or *watered stock*, that is, stock issued at a value greater than the assets of the corporation.

any competitor by fair means; but I know the foul means they have adopted, and I know that they can be stopped by law . . . there must be no squeezing out of the beginner, no crippling his credit; no discrimination against retailers who buy from a rival; no threats against concerns who sell supplies to a rival; no holding back of raw material from him; no secret arrangements against him. All the fair competition you choose, but no unfair competition of any kind.° . . . All that I ask and all I shall fight for is that they shall come into the field against merit and brains everywhere. If they can beat other American brains, then they have got the best brains.

But if you want to know how far brains go, as things now are, suppose you try to match your better wares against these gentlemen, and see them undersell you before your market is any bigger than the locality and make it absolutely impossible for you to get a fast foothold. If you want to know how brains count, originate some invention which will improve the kind of machinery they are using, and then see if you can borrow enough money to manufacture it. You may be offered something for your patent by the corporation, which will perhaps lock it up in a safe and go on using the old machinery; but you will not be allowed to manufacture. I know men who have tried it, and they could not get the money, because the great moneylenders of this country are in the arrangement with the great manufacturers of this country, and they do not propose to see their control of the market interfered with by outsiders. And who are outsiders? Why, all the rest of the people of the United States are outsiders.

They are rapidly making us outsiders with respect even of the things that come from the bosom of the earth, and which belong to us in a peculiar sense. Certain monopolies in this country have gained almost complete control of the raw material, chiefly in the mines, out of which the great body of manufactures are carried on, and they now discriminate, when they will, in the sale of that raw material between those who are rivals of the monopoly and those who submit to the monopoly. We must soon come to the point where we shall say to the men who own these essentials of industry that they have got to part with these essentials by sale to all citizens of the United States with the same readiness and upon the same terms. . . .

° Many of these ideas presented by Wilson were enacted in 1914 into the Clayton Antitrust Act and the Federal Trade Commission Act.

There is another injustice that monopoly engages in. The trust that deals in the cruder products which are to be transformed into the more elaborate manufactures often will not sell these crude products except upon the terms of monopoly—that is to say, the people that deal with them must buy exclusively from them. And so again you have the lines of development tied up and the connections of development knotted and fastened so that you cannot wrench them apart.

Again, the manufacturing monopolies are so interlaced in their personal relationships with the great shipping interests of this country, and with the great railroads, that they can often largely determine the rates of shipment.

The people of this country are being very subtly dealt with. You know, of course, that, unless our Commerce Commissions are absolutely sleepless, you can get rebates without calling them such at all.... And when you reflect that the twenty-four men who control the United States Steel Corporation, for example, are either presidents or vice-presidents or directors in fifty-five per cent of the railways of the United States, reckoning by the valuation of those railroads and the amount of their stock and bonds, you know just how close the whole thing is knitted together in our industrial system, and how great the temptation is. These twenty-four gentlemen administer that corporation as if it belonged to them. The amazing thing to me is that the people of the United States have not seen that the administration of a great business like that is not a private affair; it is a public affair.

I have been told by a great many men that the idea I have, that by restoring competition you can restore industrial freedom, is based upon a failure to observe the actual happenings of the last decades in this country; because, they say, it is just free competition that has made it possible for the big to crush the little.

I reply, it is not free competition that has done that; it is illicit competition. It is competition of the kind that the law ought to stop, and can stop—this crushing of the little man.

You know, of course, how the little man is crushed by the trusts. He gets a local market. The big concerns come in and undersell him in his local market, and that is the only market he has; if he cannot make a profit there, he is killed. They can make a profit all through the rest of the Union, while they are underselling him in his locality, and recouping themselves by what they can earn elsewhere. Thus their competitors can be put out of business, one by one, wherever they dare to show a head. Inasmuch as they rise up only one by one, these big concerns can see to it that new competitors never come into the larger field. You have to begin somewhere. You can't begin in space. You can't begin in an airship. You have got to begin in some community. Your market has got to be your neighbors first and those who know you there. But unless you have unlimited capital (which of course you wouldn't have when you were beginning) or unlimited credit (which these gentlemen can see to it that you shan't get), they can kill you out in local market any time they try, on the same basis exactly as that on which they beat organized labor; for they can sell at a loss in your market because they are selling at a profit everywhere else, and they can recoup the losses by which they beat you by the profits which they make in fields where they have beaten other fellows and put them out. If ever a competitor who by good luck has plenty of money does break into the wider market, then the trust has to buy him out, paying three or four times what the business is worth. Following such a purchase, it has got to pay the interest on the price it has paid for the business, and it has got to tax the whole people of the United States, in order to pay the interest on what it borrowed to do that, or on the stocks and bonds it issued to do it with. Therefore the big trusts, the big combinations, are the most wasteful, the most uneconomical, and, after they pass a certain size, the most inefficient, way of conducting the industries of this country.

A notable example is the way in which Mr. Carnegie was bought out of the steel business. Mr. Carnegie could build better mills and make better steel rails and make them cheaper than anybody else connected with what afterward became the United States Steel Corporation. They didn't dare leave him outside. He had so much more brains in finding out the best processes; he had so much more shrewdness in surrounding himself with the most successful assistants; he knew so well when a young man who came into his employ was fit for promotion and was ripe to put at the head of some branch of his business and was sure to make good, that he could undersell every mother's son of them in the market for steel rails. And they bought him out at a price that amounted to three or four times—I believe actually five times—the estimated value of his properties and of his business, because they couldn't beat him in competition. And then in what they charged afterward for their product—the product of his mills included—they made us pay the interest on the four or five times the difference.

That is the difference between a big business and a trust. A trust is an arrangement to get rid of competition, and a big business is a business that has survived competition by conquering in the field of intelligence and economy. A trust does not bring efficiency to the aid of business; it buys efficiency out of business. I am for big business, and I am against trusts. Any man who can survive by his brains, any man who can put the others out of the business by making the thing cheaper to the consumer at the same time that he is increasing its intrinsic [real] value and quality, I take off my hat to, and I say: "You are the man who can build up the United States, and I wish there were more of you." . . . The great monopoly in this country is the monopoly of big credits. So long as that exists, our old variety and freedom and individual energy of development are out of the question. A great industrial nation is controlled by its system of credit. Our system of credit is privately concentrated. The growth of the nation, therefore, and all our activities are in the hands of a few men who, even if their action be honest and intended for the public interest, are necessarily concentrated upon the great undertakings in which their own money is involved and who necessarily, by very reason of their own limitations, chill and check and destroy genuine economic freedom. This is the greatest question of all, and to this statesmen must address themselves with an earnest determination to serve the long future and the true liberties of men.

This money trust, or, as it should be more properly called, this credit trust, of which Congress has begun an investigation, is no myth; it is no imaginary thing. It is not an ordinary trust like another. It doesn't do business every day. It does business only when there is occasion to do business. You can sometimes do something large when it isn't watching, but when it is watching, you can't do much. And I have seen men squeezed by it; I have seen men who, as they themselves expressed it, were put "out of business by Wall Street,°" because Wall Street found them inconvenient and didn't want their competition.

° **Wall Street:** a street in New York City's financial district which is the nation's principal financial center. It is often used as a symbol of great financial interests.

Let me say again that I am not impugning the motives of the men in Wall Street. They may think that that is the best way to create prosperity for the country. When you have got the market in your hand, does honesty oblige you to turn the palm upside down and empty it? If you have got the market in your hand and believe that you understand the interest of the country better than anybody else, is it patriotic to let it go? I can imagine them using this argument to themselves.

The dominating danger in this land is not the existence of great individual combinations—that is dangerous enough in all conscience —but the combination of the combinations—of the railways, the manufacturing enterprises, the great mining projects, the great enterprises for the development of the natural water powers of the country, threaded together in the personnel of a series of boards of directors into a "community of interest" more formidable than any conceivable single combination that dare appear in the open.

The organization of business has become more centralized, vastly more centralized, than the political organization of the country itself. Corporations have come to cover greater areas than states; have come to live under a greater variety of laws than the citizen himself, have excelled states in their budgets and loomed bigger than whole commonwealths [nations] in their influence over the lives and fortunes of entire communities of men. Centralized business has built up vast structures of organization and equipment which overtop all states and seem to have no match or competitor except the federal government itself.

What we have got to do—and it is a colossal task not to be undertaken with a light head or without judgment—what we have got to do is to disentangle this colossal "community of interest." No matter how we may purpose dealing with a single combination in restraint of trade [interference with competition], you will agree with me in this, that no single avowed combination is big enough for the United States to be afraid of; but when all the combinations are combined and this final combination is not disclosed by any process of incorporation or law, but is merely an identity of personnel, or of interest, then there is something that even the government of the nation itself might come to fear—something for the law to pull apart, and gently but firmly and persistently, dissect. . . . I do not believe any one group of men has vision enough or genius enough to determine what the development of opportunity and the accomplishment by achievement shall be in this country.

The facts of the situation amount to this: that a comparatively small number of men control the raw material of this country; that a comparatively small number of men control the water powers that can be made useful for the economical production of the energy to drive our machinery; that that same number of men largely control the railroads; that by agreements handed around among themselves they control prices, and that that same group of men control the larger credits of the country.

When we undertake the strategy which is going to be necessary to overcome and destroy this far-reaching system of monopoly, we are rescuing the business of this country, we are not injuring it; and when we separate the interests from each other and dismember these communities of connection, we have in mind a greater community of interest, a vaster community of interest, the community of interest that binds the virtues of all men together, that community of mankind which is broad and catholic enough to take under the sweep of its comprehension all sorts and conditions of men; that vision which sees that no society is renewed from the top but that every society is renewed from the bottom. Limit opportunity, restrict the field of originative achievement, and you have cut out the heart and root of all prosperity.

The only thing that can ever make a free country is to keep a free and hopeful heart under every jacket in it. Honest American industry has always thriven, when it has thriven at all, on freedom; it has never thriven on monopoly. It is a great deal better to shift for yourselves than to be taken care of by a great combination of capital. I, for my part, do not want to be taken care of. I would rather starve a free man than be fed a mere thing at the caprice of those who are organizing American industry as they please to organize it. I know, and every man in his heart knows, that the only way to enrich America is to make it possible for any man who has the brains to get into the game. I am not jealous of the size of any business that has *grown* to that size. I am not jealous of any process of growth, no matter how huge the result, provided the result was indeed obtained by the processes of wholesome development, which are the processes of efficiency, of economy, of intelligence, and of invention.

Woodrow Wilson's
First Inaugural Address

"Our life contains every great thing,
and contains it in rich abundance."

On March 4, 1913, President Woodrow Wilson delivered one of the most distinguished inaugural addresses in American history. The address, with its stirring affirmation of the democratic faith, ranks in importance with Jefferson's first inaugural and Lincoln's second inaugural.

In language that was at once both eloquent and bold, Wilson summarized the principles he had outlined during the course of the political campaign, principles appropriately embodied in the general term "The New Freedom." Then, after briefly outlining the need for further regulation of trusts, tariff and currency reform, and measures designed to help labor and agriculture, he concluded with a ringing challenge to action:

"This is not a day of triumph; it is a day of dedication. . . . I summon all honest men, all patriotic, all forward-looking men, to my side. God helping me, I will not fail them, if they will but counsel and sustain me!"

March 4, 1913

My Fellow Citizens:

There has been a change of government. It began two years ago, when the House of Representatives became Democratic by a decisive majority. It has now been completed. The Senate about to assemble will also be Democratic. The offices of President and Vice President have been put into the hands of Democrats. What does the change mean? That is the question that is uppermost in our minds today.

That is the question I am going to try to answer, in order, if I may, to interpret the occasion.

It means much more than the mere success of a party. The success of a party means little except when the Nation is using that party for a large and definite purpose. No one can mistake the purpose for which the Nation now seeks to use the Democratic Party. It seeks to use it to interpret a change in its own plans and point of view. Some old things with which we had grown familiar and which had begun to creep into the very habit of our thought and of our lives, have altered their aspect as we have latterly looked critically upon them with fresh awakened eyes; have dropped their disguises and shown themselves alien and sinister. Some new things, as we look frankly upon them, willing to comprehend their real character, have come to assume the aspect of things long believed in and familiar, stuff of our own convictions. We have been refreshed by a new insight into our own life.

We see that in many things that life is very great. It is incomparably great in its material aspects, in its body of wealth, in the diversity and sweep of its energy, in the industries which have been conceived and built up by the genius of individual men and the limitless enterprise of groups of men. It is great, also, very great, in its moral force. Nowhere else in the world have noble men and women exhibited in more striking forms the beauty and the energy of sympathy and helpfulness and counsel in their efforts to rectify wrong, alleviate suffering, and ... to provide the weak ... with strength and hope. We have built up, moreover, a great system of government, which has stood through a long age as, in many respects, a model for those who seek to set liberty upon foundations that will endure against fortuitous change, against storm and accident. Our life contains every great thing, and contains it in rich abundance.

But the evil has come with the good, and much fine gold has been corroded. With riches has come inexcusable waste. We have squandered a great part of what we might have used, and have not stopped to conserve the exceeding bounty of nature, without which our genius for enterprise would have been worthless and impotent, scorning to be careful, shamefully prodigal as well as admirably efficient. We have been proud of our industrial achievements, but we have not hitherto stopped thoughtfully enough to count the human cost, the cost of lives snuffed out, of energies overtaxed and broken, the fearful physical and spiritual cost to the men and women and children upon whom the dead weight and burden of it all has fallen pitilessly the years through. The groans and agony of it all had not yet reached our ears, the solemn, moving undertone of our life, coming up out of the mines and factories and out of every home where the struggle had its intimate and familiar seat. With the great government went many deep secret things which we too long delayed to look into and scrutinize with candid, fearless eyes. The great government we loved has too often been made use of for private and selfish purposes, and those who used it had forgotten the people.

At last a vision has been vouchsafed us of our life as a whole. We see the bad with the good, the debased and decadent with the sound and vital. With this vision we approach new affairs. Our duty is to cleanse, to reconsider, to restore, to correct the evil without impairing the good, to purify and humanize every process of our common life without weakening or sentimentalizing it. There has been something crude and heartless and unfeeling in our haste to succeed and be great. Our thought has been "Let every man look out for himself, let every generation look out for itself," while we reared giant machinery which made it impossible that any but those who stood at the levers of control should have a chance to look out for themselves. We had not forgotten our morals. We remembered well enough that we had set up a policy which was meant to serve the humblest as well as the most powerful, with an eye single to the standards of justice and fair play, and remembered it with pride. But we were very heedless and in a hurry to be great.

We have come now to the sober second thought. The scales of heedlessness have fallen from our eyes. We have made up our minds to square every process of our national life again with the standards we so proudly set up at the beginning and have always carried at our hearts. Our work is a work of restoration.

We have itemized with some degree of particularity the things that ought to be altered, and here are some of the chief items: A tariff which cuts us off from our proper part in the commerce of the world, violates the just principles of taxation, and makes the government a facile instrument in the hands of private interests; a banking and currency system based upon the necessity of the government to sell its bonds 50 years ago and perfectly adapted to concentrating cash and restricting credits; an industrial system which, take it on all its sides, financial as well as administrative, holds capital . . . restricts the lib-

erties and limits the opportunities of labor, and exploits without re-
newing or conserving the natural resources of the country; a body of
agricultural activities never yet given the efficiency of great business
undertakings or served as it should be through the instrumentality
[means] of science taken directly to the farm, or afforded the facilities of credit best suited to its practical needs; watercourses undeveloped, waste places unreclaimed, forests untended, fast disappearing
without plan or prospect of renewal, unregarded waste heaps at every mine. We have studied, as perhaps no other nation has, the most
effective means of production, but we have not studied cost or economy as we should either as organizers of industry, as statesmen, or as
individuals.

Nor have we studied and perfected the means by which government
may be put at the service of humanity, in safeguarding the health of
the nation, the health of its men and its women and its children, as
well as their rights in the struggle for existence. This is no sentimen-
tal duty. The firm basis of government is justice, not pity. These are
matters of justice. There can be no equality of opportunity, the first
essential of justice in the body politic, if men and women and children be not shielded in their lives, their very vitality, from the consequences of great industrial and social processes which they cannot alter, control, or singly cope with. Society must see to it that it does not
itself crush or weaken or damage its own constituent parts. The first
duty of law is to keep sound the society it serves. Sanitary laws, pure-
food laws, and laws determining conditions of labor which individuals
are powerless to determine for themselves are intimate parts of the
very business of justice and legal efficiency.

These are some of the things we ought to do, and not leave the
others undone, the old-fashioned, never-to-be-neglected, fundamental
safeguarding of property and of individual right. This is the high enterprise of the new day: To lift everything that concerns our life as
a nation to the light that shines from the hearthfire of every man's
conscience and vision of the right. It is inconceivable that we should
do this as partisans; it is inconceivable we should do it in ignorance
of the facts as they are or in blind haste. We shall restore, not destroy.
We shall deal with our economic system as it is and as it may be
modified, not as it might be if we had a clean sheet of paper to write
upon; and step by step we shall make it what it should be, in the
spirit of those who question their own wisdom and seek counsel and

knowledge, not shallow self-satisfaction or the excitement of excursions whither they cannot tell. Justice, and only justice, shall always be our motto.

And yet it will be no cool process of mere science. The nation has been deeply stirred, stirred by a solemn passion, stirred by the knowledge of wrong, of ideals lost, of government too often debauched and made an instrument of evil. The feelings with which we face this new age of right and opportunity sweep across our heartstrings like some air out of God's own presence, where justice and mercy are reconciled and the judge and the brother are one. We know our task to be no mere task of politics but a task which shall search us through and through, whether we be able to understand our time and the need of our people, whether we be indeed their spokesmen and interpreters, whether we have the pure heart to comprehend and the rectified will to choose our high course of action.

This is not a day of triumph; it is a day of dedication. Here muster not the forces of party, but the forces of humanity. Men's hearts wait upon us; men's lives hang in the balance; men's hopes call upon us to say what we will do. Who shall live up to the great trust? Who dares fail to try? I summon all honest men, all patriotic, all forward-looking men, to my side. God helping me, I will not fail them, if they will but counsel and sustain me!

The Federal Trade Commission Act

"... unfair methods of competition in commerce are hereby declared unlawful."

According to Woodrow Wilson, the Federal Trade Commission Act was designed "to kill monopoly in the seed." Another cornerstone in the "New Freedom" program, this law, it was hoped, would bring about a better understanding between big business and the government.

In 1914, Wilson was asked at a press conference to differentiate the duties of the Department of Justice from those of the Federal Trade Commission with reference to antitrust activities. He replied: "The Commission will be smelling around for rats all the time, and when it is on the trail of one, it will call it to the attention of the Department of Justice."

The Commission has established a commendable record for itself in exposing false and misleading advertising and in opposing concentration of economic power through its investigatory activities as well as through its "cease and desist" powers.

September 26, 1914

Be it enacted by the Senate and House of Representatives of the United States of America in Congress assembled: That a commission is hereby created and established, to be known as the Federal Trade Commission (hereinafter referred to as the commission), which shall be composed of five commissioners, who shall be appointed by the President, by and with the advice and consent of the Senate. Not more than three of the commissioners shall be members of the same political party.... [They] shall be appointed for terms of seven years....

Section 5.° That unfair methods of competition in commerce are hereby declared unlawful.

The commission is hereby empowered and directed to prevent persons, partnerships, or corporations, except banks, and common carriers subject to the acts to regulate commerce, from using unfair methods of competition in commerce.

Whenever the commission shall have reason to believe that any such person, partnership, or corporation has been or is using any unfair method of competition in commerce, and if it shall appear to the commission that a proceeding by it in respect thereof would be

° Section 5: As amended by the Wheeler-Lea Act of 1938, the provision now reads: "Unfair methods of competition in commerce, and unfair or deceptive acts or practices in commerce, are hereby declared unlawful."

to the interest of the public, it shall issue and serve upon such person, partnership, or corporation a complaint stating its charges in that respect, and containing a notice of a hearing upon a day and at a place therein fixed at least thirty days after the service of said complaint. The person, partnership, or corporation so complained of shall have the right to appear at the place and time so fixed and show cause why an order should not be entered by the commission requiring such person, partnership, or corporation to cease and desist from the violation of the law so charged in said complaint. . . . If upon such hearing the commission shall be of the opinion that the method of competition in question is prohibited by this act, it shall make a report in writing in which it shall state its findings as to the facts, and shall issue and cause to be served on such person, partnership, or corporation an order requiring such person, partnership, or corporation to cease and desist from using such method of competition. . . .

Section 6. That the commission shall also have power:

(a) To gather and compile information concerning, and to investigate from time to time the organization, business, conduct, practices, and management of any corporation engaged in commerce, excepting banks and common carriers subject to the act to regulate commerce, and its relation to other corporations and to individuals, associations, and partnerships.

(b) To require . . . corporations engaged in commerce, excepting banks, and common carriers subject to the act to regulate commerce . . . to file with the commission in such form as the commission may prescribe annual or special, or both annual and special, reports or answers in writing to specific questions, furnishing to the commission such information as it may require as to the organization, business, conduct, practices, management, and relation to other corporations, partnerships, and individuals of the respective corporations, filing such reports in writing. . . .

(c) Whenever a final decree has been entered against any defendant corporation in any suit brought by the United States to prevent and restrain any violation of the antitrust acts, to make investigation . . . of the manner in which the decree has been or is being carried out . . . it shall be its duty to make such investigation. It shall transmit to the Attorney General a report embodying its findings and recommendations as a result of any such investigation, and the report shall be made public . . . [at] the discretion of the commission.

(d) Upon the direction of the President or either House of Congress to investigate and report the facts relating to any alleged violations of the antitrust acts by any corporation.

(e) Upon the application of the Attorney General to investigate and make recommendations for the readjustment of the business of any corporation alleged to be violating the antitrust acts in order that the corporation may thereafter maintain its organization, management, and conduct of business in accordance with law.

(f) To make public from time to time such portions of the information obtained by it hereunder, except trade secrets and names of customers, as it shall deem expedient in the public interest; and to make annual and special reports to the Congress and to submit therewith recommendations for additional legislation; and to provide for the publication of its reports and decisions in such form and manner as may be best adapted for public information and use.

(g) From time to time to classify corporations and to make rules and regulations for the purpose of carrying out the provisions of this act.

(h) To investigate, from time to time, trade conditions in and with foreign countries where associations, combinations, or practices of manufacturers, merchants, or traders, or other conditions, may affect the foreign trade of the United States, and to report to Congress thereon, with such recommendations as it deems advisable. . . .

The Clayton Antitrust Act

*". . . the labor of a human being is not
a commodity or article of commerce."*

The Clayton Antitrust Act, enacted by Congress in 1914, was one of the cornerstones of Wilson's "New Freedom" program. It was designed to put teeth into the Sherman Antitrust Act of 1890 which, because of its loose wording and for other reasons, had not prevented the growth of monopolies. The Clayton Act was aimed at specific business practices that substantially lessened competition or tended to create a monopoly.

Organized labor hailed the Clayton Act as its Magna Carta because of those provisions which limited the use of the antitrust laws and injunctions in labor disputes. Up to that time the federal courts had invoked the Sherman Antitrust Act of 1890 freely against organized labor. The 1914 legislation declared that strikes, peaceful picketing, and boycotts were legal under federal jurisdiction. The courts, however, continued to interpret the law in such a way that the injunction continued to be used as a major weapon against strikes.

October 15, 1914

Be it enacted by the Senate and House of Representatives of the United States of America in Congress assembled. . . .

Section 2.° That it shall be unlawful for any person engaged in commerce, in the course of such commerce, either directly or indirectly to discriminate in price between different purchasers of commodities, which commodities are sold for use, consumption, or resale within the United States or any . . . other place under the jurisdiction of the United States, where the effect of such discrimination may be to substantially lessen competition or tend to create a monopoly in any line of commerce. . . .

Section 3. That it shall be unlawful for any person engaged in commerce to lease or make a sale of goods . . . or fix a price charged therefor, or discount from, or rebate upon such price, on the condition . . . that the lessee or purchaser thereof shall not use or deal in the goods . . . or other commodities of a competitor or competitors of the lessor or seller, where the effect . . . may be to substantially lessen competition or tend to create a monopoly in any line of commerce. . . .

Section 6. That the labor of a human being is not a commodity or article of commerce. Nothing contained in the antitrust laws shall be

---

° **Section 2:** This was amended in 1936 by the Robinson-Patman Act, which was designed to protect small retailers from the use of unfair competitive methods by mass distributors, such as chain stores.

construed to forbid the existence and operation of labor, agricultural, or horticultural organizations, instituted for the purposes of mutual help ... or to forbid or restrain individual members of such organizations from lawfully carrying out the legitimate objects [purposes] thereof; nor shall such organizations, or the members thereof, be held or construed to be illegal combinations or conspiracies in restraint of trade under the antitrust laws.

Section 7.° That no corporation engaged in commerce shall acquire, directly or indirectly, the whole or any part of the stock or other share capital of another corporation engaged also in commerce, where the effect of such acquisition may be to substantially lessen competition between the corporation whose stock is so acquired and the corporation making the acquisition, or to restrain such commerce in any section or community, or tend to create a monopoly of any line of commerce. ...

This section shall not apply to corporations purchasing such stock solely for investment. ...

Section 8. That from and after two years from the date of the approval of this act no person shall at the same time be a director or other officer or employee of more than one bank, banking association or trust company, organized or operating under the laws of the United States, either of which has deposits, capital, surplus, and undivided profits aggregating more than $5,000,000. ...

That from and after two years from the date of the approval of this act no person at the same time shall be a director in any two or more corporations, any one of which has capital, surplus, and undivided profits aggregating more than $1,000,000, engaged in whole or in part in commerce, other than banks, banking associations, trust companies, and common carriers subject to the act to regulate commerce, approved February 4th, 1887, if such corporations are or shall have been theretofore, by virtue of their business and location of operation, competitors, so that the elimination of competition by agreement between them would constitute a violation of any of the provisions of any of the antitrust laws. ...

Section 10. That after two years from the approval of this act no common carrier engaged in commerce shall have any dealings in securities, supplies, or other articles of commerce ... to the amount of

° *Section 7:* This section was amended in 1950 to include mergers through purchase of assets, a device which had been used to circumvent the law.

more than $50,000, in the aggregate, in any one year, with another corporation, firm, partnership, or association when the said common carrier shall have upon its board of directors or as its president, manager, or as its purchasing or selling officer, or agent in the particular transaction, any person who is at the same time a director, manager, or purchasing or selling officer of, or who has any substantial interest in, such other corporation, firm, partnership, or association, unless and except such purchases shall be made from, or such dealings shall be with, the bidder whose bid is the most favorable to such common carrier, to be ascertained by competitive bidding under regulations to be prescribed by rule or otherwise by the Interstate Commerce Commission. . . .

Section 14. That whenever a corporation shall violate any of the penal provisions ° of the antitrust laws, such violation shall be deemed to be also that of the individual directors, officers, or agents of such corporation who shall have authorized, ordered, or done any of the acts constituting in whole or in part such violation, and such violation shall be deemed a misdemeanor, and upon conviction therefor of any such director, officer, or agent he shall be punished by a fine of not exceeding $5,000 or by imprisonment for not exceeding one year, or by both, . . . [at] the discretion of the court. . . .

Section 20. That no restraining order or injunction shall be granted by any court of the United States, or a judge or the judges thereof, in any case between an employer and employees or between employers and employees, or between employees, or between persons employed and persons seeking employment, involving, or growing out of a dispute concerning terms or conditions of employment, unless necessary to prevent irreparable injury to property, or to a property right, of the party making the application, for which injury there is no adequate remedy at law, and such property or property right must be described with a particularity in the application, which must be in writing and sworn to by the applicant or by his agent or attorney.

And no such restraining order or injunction shall prohibit any person or persons, whether singly or in concert, from terminating any relation of employment, or from ceasing to perform any work or labor, or from recommending, advising, or persuading others by peaceful means so to do; or from attending at any place where any such person or persons may lawfully be, for the purpose of peacefully ob-

---

° *penal provisions:* provisions the violation of which are subject to punishment by fine or imprisonment.

taining or communicating information, or from peacefully persuading any person to work or to abstain from working; or from ceasing to patronize or to employ any party to such dispute, or from recommending, advising, or persuading others by peaceful and lawful means so to do; or from paying or giving to, or withholding from, any person engaged in such dispute, any strike benefits or other moneys or things of value; or from peaceably assembling in a lawful manner, and for lawful purposes; or from doing any act or thing which might lawfully be done in the absence of such dispute by any party thereto; nor shall any of the acts specified in this paragraph be considered or held to be violations of any law of the United States. . . .

Woodrow Wilson's Fourteen Points

". . . we wish the right to prevail and desire a just and stable peace. . . ."

In his war message of April 2, 1917, President Wilson had declared that the United States was entering the conflict to make the world "safe for democracy." Toward the close of the year, however, the news spread that the Allies in Europe had agreed among themselves how to divide the spoils of war if they succeeded in defeating Germany and the other Central Powers. Shocked by this news and determined to do his utmost to secure "a just and stable peace," the President decided to place before the world what he considered to be "the only possible program for world peace."

On January 8, 1918, Wilson presented his fourteen-point program to Congress. The Fourteenth Point, the heart of the entire program, called for "a general association of nations" which could provide "mutual guarantees of political independence and territorial integrity to great and small states alike."

The Fourteen Points and statements explaining them were printed in the languages of the peoples of Central Europe and dropped by plane into the heart of the enemy country. Wilson's promises to work for "justice and fair dealing" for all nations, victors and vanquished alike, helped to weaken the enemy's will to fight.

January 8, 1918

Gentlemen of the Congress: . . .

We entered this war because violations of right had occurred which touched us to the quick and made the life of our own people impossible unless they were corrected and the world secured once for all against their recurrence. What we demand in this war, therefore, is nothing peculiar to ourselves. It is that the world be made fit and safe to live in; and particularly that it be made safe for every peace-loving nation which, like our own, wishes to live its own life, determine its own institutions, be assured of justice and fair dealing by the other peoples of the world as against force and selfish aggression. All the peoples of the world are in effect partners in this interest, and for our own part we see very clearly that unless justice be done to others, it will not be done to us. The program of the world's peace, therefore, is our program; and that program, the only possible program, as we see it, is this:

I. Open covenants of peace, openly arrived at, after which there shall be no private international understandings of any kind but diplomacy shall proceed always frankly and in the public view.

II. Absolute freedom of navigation upon the seas, outside territorial waters, alike in peace and in war, except as the seas may be closed in whole or in part by international action for the enforcement of international covenants.

III. The removal, so far as possible, of all economic barriers and the establishment of an equality of trade conditions among all the nations consenting to the peace and associating themselves for its maintenance.

IV. Adequate guarantees given and taken that national armaments will be reduced to the lowest point consistent with domestic safety.

V. A free, open-minded, and absolutely impartial adjustment of all colonial claims, based upon a strict observance of the principle that in determining all such questions of sovereignty the interests of the populations concerned must have equal weight with the equitable claims of the government whose title is to be determined.

VI. The evacuation of all Russian territory and such a settlement of all questions affecting Russia as will secure the best and freest co-operation of the other nations of the world in obtaining for her an unhampered and unembarrassed opportunity for the independent determination of her own political development and national policy and assure her of a sincere welcome into the society of free nations under institutions of her own choosing; and, more than a welcome, assistance also of every kind that she may need and may herself desire. The treatment accorded Russia by her sister nations in the months to come will be the acid test of their good will, of their comprehension of her needs as distinguished from their own interests, and of their intelligent and unselfish sympathy.

VII. Belgium, the whole world will agree, must be evacuated and restored, without any attempt to limit the sovereignty which she enjoys in common with all other free nations. No other single act will serve as this will serve to restore confidence among the nations in the laws which they have themselves set and determined for the government of their relations with one another. Without this healing act the whole structure and validity of international law is forever impaired.

VIII. All French territory should be freed and the invaded portions restored, and the wrong done to France by Prussia in 1871 in the matter of Alsace-Lorraine, which has unsettled the peace of the world for nearly fifty years, should be righted, in order that peace may once more be made secure in the interest of all.

IX. A readjustment of the frontiers of Italy should be effected along clearly recognizable lines of nationality.

X. The peoples of Austria-Hungary, whose place among the nations we wish to see safeguarded and assured, should be accorded the freest opportunity of autonomous development.

XI. Rumania, Serbia, and Montenegro should be evacuated; occupied territories restored; Serbia accorded free and secure access to the sea; and the relations of the several Balkan states to one another determined by friendly counsel along historically established lines of allegiance and nationality; and international guarantees of the political and economic independence and territorial integrity of the several Balkan states should be entered into.

XII. The Turkish portions of the present Ottoman Empire should be assured a secure sovereignty, but the other nationalities which are now under Turkish rule should be assured an undoubted security of life and an absolutely unmolested opportunity of autonomous development, and the Dardanelles should be permanently opened as a free passage to the ships and commerce of all nations under international guarantees.

XIII. An independent Polish state should be erected which should include the territories inhabited by indisputably Polish populations, which should be assured a free and secure access to the sea, and whose political and economic independence and territorial integrity should be guaranteed by international covenant.

XIV. A general association of nations must be formed under specific covenants for the purpose of affording mutual guarantees of political independence and territorial integrity to great and small states alike.

In regard to these essential rectifications of wrong and assertions of right we feel ourselves to be intimate partners of all the governments and peoples associated together against the Imperialists. We cannot be separated in interest or divided in purpose. We stand together until the end.

For such arrangements and covenants we are willing to fight and to continue to fight until they are achieved; but only because we wish the right to prevail and desire a just and stable peace such as can be secured only by removing the chief provocations to war, which this program does not remove. We have no jealousy of German greatness, and there is nothing in this program that impairs it. We grudge her no achievement or distinction of learning or of pacific enterprise such as have made her record very bright and very enviable. We do not wish to injure her or to block in any way her legitimate influence or power. We do not wish to fight her either with arms or with hostile arrangements of trade if she is willing to associate herself with us and the other peace-loving nations of the world in covenants of justice and law and fair dealing. We wish her only to accept a place of equality among the peoples of the world—the new world in which we now live—instead of a place of mastery.

Neither do we presume to suggest to her any alteration or modification of her institutions. But it is necessary, we must frankly say, and necessary as a preliminary to any intelligent dealings with her on our part, that we should know whom her spokesmen speak for when they speak to us, whether for the Reichstag [lower house of German Parliament] majority or for the military party and the men whose creed is imperial domination.

We have spoken now, surely, in terms too concrete to admit . . . any further doubt or question. An evident principle runs through the whole program I have outlined. It is the principle of justice to all peoples and nationalities, and their right to live on equal terms of liberty and safety with one another, whether they be strong or weak. Unless this principle be made its foundation, no part of the structure of international justice can stand. The people of the United States could act upon no other principle; and to the vindication of this principle they are ready to devote their lives, their honor, and everything that they possess. The moral climax of this, the culminating and final war for human liberty, has come, and they are ready to put their own strength, their own highest purpose, their own integrity and devotion to the test.

PART FOUR

The Nation As a World Leader

How thirteen colonies on the fringe of a vast, untamed wilderness eventually became a nation holding a position of world leadership—such is the dramatic story of the United States. This story has unfolded in less than two hundred years.

Millions of Americans living today hold vivid memories of things that have happened since the death of Theodore Roosevelt—the "Golden Twenties"; the Great Depression of the 1930's; the excitement, tragedy, and overwhelming sorrow of World War II; and the years since 1945, years filled with trouble and yet so bright with promise.

Oliver Wendell Holmes' Opinion in Schenck v. United States

*"The question ... is whether the words used ...
create a clear and present danger. ..."*

The case of Schenck v. United States, which came before
the Supreme Court in 1919, involved the extremely complex
problem of balancing the rights of the individual against the
need for maintaining an orderly society. This, the question of
individual freedom versus the general welfare, has been—and
continues to be—one of the most persistent and stubborn
issues facing the people of every democratic country.

Shortly after the United States entered World War I, Congress enacted the Espionage Act, which placed sharp limits
on the right of free speech. This act was in effect when
Schenck, General Secretary of the Socialist party, published
and circulated a leaflet opposing the draft. Schenck was convicted of violating the Espionage Act and sentenced to prison.
Upon appeal, the case was carried to the Supreme Court,
where Justice Oliver Wendell Holmes, in one of his most
celebrated opinions, formulated the famous "clear and present danger" rule for deciding cases involving freedom of
expression.

1919

This is an indictment in three counts. The first charges a conspiracy to violate the Espionage Act of June 15, 1917 ... by causing and
attempting to cause insubordination, etc., in the military and naval
forces of the United States, and to obstruct the recruiting and enlist-
ment service of the United States, when the United States was at

war with the German Empire, to wit, that the defendants willfully conspired to have printed and circulated to men who had been called and accepted for military service under the act of May 18, 1917, a document set forth and alleged to be calculated to cause such insubordination and obstruction. . . .

According to the testimony, Schenck [the defendant] said he was general secretary of the Socialist party and had charge of the Socialist headquarters from which the documents were sent. He identified a book found there as the minutes of the Executive Committee of the party. The book showed a resolution of August 13, 1917, that 15,000 leaflets should be printed on the other side of one of them in use, to be mailed to men who had passed exemption boards and for distribution. Schenck personally attended to the printing. . . . He said that he had about fifteen or sixteen thousand printed. There were files of the circular in question in the inner office which he said were printed on the other side of the one-sided circular and were there for distribution. Other copies were proved to have been sent through the mails to drafted men. Without going into confirmatory details that were proved, no reasonable man could doubt that the defendant Schenck was largely instrumental in sending the circulars. . . .

The document in question upon its first printed side recited the first section of the Thirteenth Amendment, said that the idea embodied in it was violated by the Conscription Act, and that a conscript [draftee] is little better than a convict. In impassioned language it intimated that conscription was despotism in its worst form and a monstrous wrong against humanity in the interest of Wall Street's ° chosen few. It said: "Do not submit to intimidation," but in form, at least, confined itself to peaceful measures such as a petition for the repeal of the act. The other and later-printed side of the sheet was headed: "Assert Your Rights." It stated reason for alleging that anyone violated the Constitution when he refused to recognize "your right to assert your opposition to the draft," and went on, "If you do not assert and support your rights, you are helping to deny or disparage rights which it is the solemn duty of all citizens and residents of the United States to retain." It described the arguments on the other side as coming from cunning politicians and a mercenary capitalist press, and even silent consent to the conscription law as helping to support an infamous conspiracy. It denied the power to send our citi-

° See note, page 249.

zens away to foreign shores to shoot up the people of other lands, and added that words could not express the condemnation such cold-blooded ruthlessness deserves, etc., etc., winding up, "You must do your share to maintain, support, and uphold the rights of the people of this country." Of course, the document would not have been sent unless it had been intended to have some effect, and we do not see what effect it could be expected to have upon persons subject to the draft except to influence them to obstruct the carrying of it out. The defendants do not deny that the jury might find against them on this point.

But it is said, suppose that that was the tendency of this circular, it is protected by the First Amendment to the Constitution.... We admit that in many places and in ordinary times the defendants in saying all that was said in the circular would have been within their constitutional rights. But the character of every act depends upon the circumstances in which it is done. The most stringent protection of free speech would not protect a man in falsely shouting fire in a theater and causing a panic. It does not even protect a man from an injunction [restraining order] against uttering words that may have all the effect of force. The question in every case is whether the words used are used in such circumstances and are of such a nature as to create a clear and present danger that they will bring about the substantive evils that Congress has a right to prevent. It is a question of proximity and degree. When a nation is at war, many things that might be said in time of peace are such a hindrance to its effort that their utterance will not be endured so long as men fight and that no court could regard them as protected by any constitutional right. It seems to be admitted that if an actual obstruction of the recruiting service were proved, liability for words that produced that effect might be enforced. The statute of 1917, in Section 4, punishes conspiracies to obstruct as well as actual obstruction. If the act (speaking, or circulating a paper), its tendency, and the intent with which it is done are the same, we perceive no ground for saying that success alone warrants making the act a crime. . . .

The Kellogg-Briand Peace Pact

"... the time has come when a frank renunciation of war as an instrument of national policy should be made...."

On April 6, 1927, in commemoration of America's entry into World War I ten years earlier, Aristide Briand, French Foreign Minister, gave an address to the American people. In this address, he proposed that the United States and France solemnly pledge each other to settle all future disputes between the two countries by peaceful means. The proposal caught the public imagination. Petitions bearing signatures running into the millions began to pour into the government in Washington.

Responding to this widespread enthusiasm, United States Secretary of State Frank B. Kellogg urged Briand to broaden the proposal to include other nations. France agreed, and at Paris, on August 27, 1928, representatives of fifteen nations signed the Kellogg-Briand Pact, sometimes called the Pact of Paris, renouncing "war as an instrument of national policy." Eventually, a total of sixty-two nations joined in this idealistic but—as it turned out—futile attempt to save mankind from the scourge of war.

August 27, 1928

The President of the German Reich [empire], the President of the United States of America, His Majesty the King of the Belgians, the President of the French Republic, His Majesty the King of Great Britain, Ireland, and the British Dominions beyond the Seas, Emperor of India, His Majesty the King of Italy, His Majesty the Emperor of Japan, the President of the Republic of Poland, the President of the Czechoslovak Republic,

Deeply sensible of their solemn duty to promote the welfare of mankind;

Persuaded that the time has come when a frank renunciation of war as an instrument of national policy should be made to the end that the peaceful and friendly relations now existing between their peoples may be perpetuated;

Convinced that all changes in their relations with one another should be sought only by pacific means and be the result of a peaceful and orderly process, and that any signatory power [signer of agreement] which shall hereafter seek to promote its national interests by resort[ing] to war should be denied the benefits furnished by this treaty;

Hopeful that, encouraged by their example, all the other nations of the world will join in this humane endeavor and by adhering to the present treaty as soon as it comes into force bring their peoples within the scope of its beneficent provisions, thus uniting the civilized nations of the world in a common renunciation of war as an instrument of their national policy;

Have decided to conclude a treaty and for that purpose have appointed . . . plenipotentiaries.° . . .

Who . . . have agreed upon the following articles:

Article 1. The High Contracting Parties solemnly declare in the names of their respective peoples that they condemn recourse to war for the solution of international controversies, and renounce it as an instrument of national policy in their relations with one another.

Article 2. The High Contracting Parties agree that the settlement or solution of all disputes or conflicts of whatever nature or of whatever origin they may be, which may arise among them, shall never be sought except by pacific means.

Article 3. The present treaty shall be ratified by the High Contracting Parties named in the preamble in accordance with their respective constitutional requirements, and shall take effect . . . between them as soon as all their . . . instruments of ratification shall have been deposited at Washington.

This treaty shall, when it has come into effect as prescribed in the preceding paragraph, remain open as long as may be necessary for adherence by all the other powers of the world. . . .

Done at Paris, the twenty-seventh day of August in the year one thousand nine hundred and twenty-eight.

° *plenipotentiaries:* agents invested with full power.

Herbert Hoover's "Rugged Individualism" Speech

"My conception of America is a land where men and women may walk in ordered freedom in the independent conduct of their occupations...."

During the Presidential election campaign of 1928, Herbert Hoover, the successful candidate, repeatedly expressed his firm faith in "the American system." This system, he declared in a speech delivered in New York on October 22, "is founded upon the conception that only through ordered liberty, freedom, and equal opportunity to the individual will his initiative and enterprise spur on the march of progress."

When Hoover stated his belief in the value of "rugged individualism," he was praising self-reliance, not advocating self-interest or special privilege. Scorning "a European philosophy . . . of paternalism and state socialism," he insisted that "individual initiative and enterprise" was the driving force which had carried the United States to "unparalleled greatness."

October 22, 1928

...The Republican party has ever been a party of progress. I do not need to review its seventy years of constructive history. It has always reflected the spirit of the American people. Never has it done more for the advancement of fundamental progress than during the past seven and one-half years since we took over the government amidst the ruin left by war [World War I].

It detracts nothing from the character and energy of the American people, it minimizes in no degree the quality of their accomplishments to say that the policies of the Republican party have played a large part in recuperation from the war and the building of the magnificent progress which shows upon every hand today. I say with emphasis that without the wise policies which the Republican party has brought into action during this period, no such progress would have been possible.

The first responsibility of the Republican administration was to renew the march of progress from its collapse by the war. That task involved the restoration of confidence in the future and the liberation and stimulation of the constructive energies of our people. It discharged that task. There is not a person within the sound of my voice who does not know the profound progress which our country has made in this period. Every man and woman knows that American comfort, hope, and confidence for the future are immeasurably higher this day than they were seven and one-half years ago.

It is not my purpose to enter upon a detailed recital of the great constructive measures of the past seven and one-half years by which this has been brought about. It is sufficient to remind you of the restoration of employment to the millions who walked your streets in idleness; to remind you of the creation of the budget system; the reduction of six billions of national debt which gave the powerful impulse of that vast sum returned to industry and commerce; the four sequent reductions of taxes and thereby the lift to the living of every family; the enactment of adequate protective tariff and immigration laws which have safeguarded our workers and farmers from floods of goods and labor from foreign countries; the creation of credit facilities and many other aids to agriculture; the building up of foreign trade; the care of veterans; the development of aviation, of radio, of our inland waterways, of our highways; the expansion of scientific research, of welfare activities; the making of safer highways, safer mines, better homes; the spread of outdoor recreation; the improvement in public health and the care of children; and a score of other progressive actions.

Nor do I need to remind you that government today deals with an economic and social system vastly more intricate and delicately adjusted than ever before. That system now must be kept in perfect tune if we would maintain uninterrupted employment and the high standards of living of our people. The government has come to touch this delicate web at a thousand points. Yearly the relations of government to national prosperity become more and more intimate. Only through keen vision and helpful co-operation by the government has stability in business and stability in employment been maintained during this past seven and one-half years. There always are some localities, some industries, and some individuals who do not share the prevailing prosperity. The task of government is to lessen these inequalities.

Never has there been a period when the federal government has given such aid and impulse to the progress of our people, not alone to economic progress but to the development of those agencies which make for moral and spiritual progress. . . .

But in addition to this great record of contributions of the Republican party to progress, there has been a further fundamental contribution—a contribution underlying and sustaining all the others—and that is the resistance of the Republican party to every attempt to inject the government into business in competition with its citizens.

After the war, when the Republican party assumed administration of the country, we were faced with the problem of determination of the very nature of our national life. During one hundred and fifty years we have built up a form of self-government and a social system which is peculiarly our own. It differs essentially from all others in the world. It is the American system. It is just as definite and positive a political and social system as has ever been developed on earth. It is founded upon a particular conception of self-government in which decentralized local responsibility is the very base. Further than this, it is founded upon the conception that only through ordered liberty, freedom, and equal opportunity to the individual will his initiative and enterprise spur on the march of progress. And in our insistence upon equality of opportunity has our system advanced beyond all the world.

During the war we necessarily turned to the government to solve every difficult economic problem. The government having absorbed every energy of our people for war, there was no other solution. For the preservation of the state, the federal government became a centralized despotism which undertook unprecedented responsibilities, assumed autocratic powers, and took over the business of citizens. To a large degree we regimented our whole people temporarily into a socialistic [government-controlled] state. However justified in time of war, if continued in peacetime it would destroy not only our American system but with it our progress and freedom as well.

When the war closed, the most vital of all issues both in our own country and throughout the world was whether governments should continue their wartime ownership and operation of many instrumentalities of production and distribution. We were challenged with a peacetime choice between the American system of rugged individualism ° and a European philosophy of diametrically [directly adverse] opposed doctrines—doctrines of paternalism ° and state socialism.° The acceptance of these ideas would have meant the destruction of self-government through centralization of government. It would have meant the undermining of the individual initiative and enterprise through which our people have grown to unparalleled greatness.

The Republican party from the beginning resolutely turned its face away from these ideas and these war practices. . . .

There has been revived in this campaign, however, a series of proposals which, if adopted, would be a long step toward the abandonment of our American system and a surrender to the destructive operation of governmental conduct of commercial business. Because the country is faced with difficulty and doubt over certain national problems—that is, prohibition, farm relief, and electrical power—our opponents propose that we must thrust government a long way into the businesses which give rise to these problems. In effect, they abandon the tenets of their own party and turn to state socialism as a solution for the difficulties presented by all three. It is proposed that we shall change from prohibition to the state purchase and sale of liquor. If their agricultural relief program means anything, it means that the government shall directly or indirectly buy and sell and fix prices of agricultural products. And we are to go into the hydroelectric power business. In other words, we are confronted with a huge program of government in business.

There is, therefore, submitted to the American people a question

° *rugged individualism:* individual initiative and private enterprise in business, with a minimum of government interference.

° *paternalism:* a policy in which the government assumes the role of father, or protector, toward its citizens—in this case, toward its businessmen.

° *state socialism:* a policy of government ownership and operation of the means of production and distribution.

of fundamental principle. That is, shall we depart from the principles of our American political and economic system, upon which we have advanced beyond all the rest of the world, in order to adopt methods based on principles destructive of its very foundations? And I wish to emphasize the seriousness of these proposals. I wish to make my position clear; for this goes to the very roots of American life and progress.

I should like to state to you the effect that this projection of government in business would have upon our system of self-government and our economic system. That effect would reach to the daily life of every man and woman. It would impair the very basis of liberty and freedom not only for those left outside the fold of expanded bureaucracy ° but for those embraced within it.

Let us first see the effect upon self-government. When the federal government undertakes to go into commercial business it must at once set up the organization and administration of that business, and it immediately finds itself in a labyrinth, every alley of which leads to the destruction of self-government.

Commercial business requires a concentration of responsibility. Self-government requires decentralization and many checks and balances to safeguard liberty. Our government to succeed in business would need [to] become in effect a despotism. There at once begins the destruction of self-government.

The first problem of the government about to adventure in commercial business is to determine a method of administration. It must secure leadership and direction. Shall this leadership be chosen by political agencies or shall we make it elective? The hard practical fact is that leadership in business must come through the sheer rise in ability and character. That rise can only take place in the free atmosphere of competition. Competition is closed by bureaucracy. Political agencies are feeble channels through which to select able leaders to conduct commercial business.

Government, in order to avoid the possible incompetence, corruption, and tyranny of too great authority in individuals entrusted with commercial business, inevitably turns to boards and commissions. To make sure that there are checks and balances, each member of such boards and commissions must have equal authority. Each has his separate responsibility to the public, and at once we have the conflict

° *bureaucracy:* rigid or routine procedure in administration.

of ideas and the lack of decision which would ruin any commercial business. It has contributed greatly to the demoralization of our shipping business. Moreover, these commissions must be representative of different sections and different political parties, so that at once we have an entire blight upon co-ordinated action within their ranks which destroys any possibility of effective administration.

Moreover, our legislative bodies cannot in fact delegate their full authority to commissions or to individuals for the conduct of matters vital to the American people; for if we would preserve government by the people, we must preserve the authority of our legislators in the activities of our government.

Thus every time the federal government goes into a commercial business, five hundred and thirty-one Senators and Congressmen become the actual board of directors of that business. Every time a state government goes into business, one or two hundred state senators and legislators become the actual directors of that business. Even if they were supermen and if there were no politics in the United States, no body of such numbers could competently direct commercial activities; for that requires initiative, instant decision, and action. It took Congress six years of constant discussion to even decide what the method of administration of Muscle Shoals ° should be.

When the federal government undertakes to go into business, the state governments are at once deprived of control and taxation of that business; when a state government undertakes to go into business, it at once deprives the municipalities of taxation and control of that business. Municipalities, being local and close to the people, can, at times, succeed in business where federal and state governments must fail. We have trouble enough with logrolling ° in legislative bodies today. It originates naturally from desires of citizens to advance their particular section or to secure some necessary service. It would be multiplied a thousandfold were the federal and state governments in these businesses.

The effect upon our economic progress would be even worse. Business progressiveness is dependent on competition. New methods and new ideas are the outgrowth of the spirit of adventure, of individual

° **Muscle Shoals:** an area on the Tennessee River in Alabama used during World War I to furnish power for nitrate plants. The issue of government operation of dams in this area to provide cheap electric power was debated throughout the 1920's.
° *logrolling:* see note, page 237.

initiative, and of individual enterprise. Without adventure there is no progress. . . .

The government in commercial business does not tolerate amongst its customers the freedom of competitive reprisals to which private business is subject. Bureaucracy does not tolerate the spirit of independence; it spreads the spirit of submission into our daily life and penetrates the temper of our people not with the habit of powerful resistance to wrong but with the habit of timid acceptance of irresistible might.

Bureaucracy is ever desirous of spreading its influence and its power. You cannot extend the mastery of the government over the daily working life of a people without at the same time making it the master of the people's souls and thoughts. Every expansion of government in business means that government in order to protect itself from the political consequences of its errors and wrongs is driven irresistibly without peace to greater and greater control of the nation's press and platform. Free speech does not live many hours after free industry and free commerce die.

It is a false liberalism that interprets itself into the government operation of commercial business. Every step of bureaucratizing of the business of our country poisons the very roots of liberalism—that is, political equality, free speech, free assembly, free press, and equality of opportunity. It is the road not to more liberty but to less liberty. Liberalism should be found not striving to spread bureaucracy but striving to set bounds to it. True liberalism seeks all legitimate freedom, first in the confident belief that without such freedom the pursuit of all other blessings and benefits is vain. That belief is the foundation of all American progress, political as well as economic.

Liberalism is a force truly of the spirit, a force proceeding from the deep realization that economic freedom cannot be sacrificed if political freedom is to be preserved. Even if governmental conduct of business could give us more efficiency instead of less efficiency, the fundamental objection to it would remain unaltered and unabated. It would destroy political equality. It would increase rather than decrease abuse and corruption. It would stifle initiative and invention. It would undermine the development of leadership. It would cramp and cripple the mental and spiritual energies of our people. It would extinguish equality and opportunity. It would dry up the spirit of liberty and progress. For these reasons primarily it must be resisted.

For a hundred and fifty years liberalism has found its true spirit in the American system, not in the European systems.

I do not wish to be misunderstood in this statement. I am defining a general policy. It does not mean that our government is to part with one iota of its national resources without complete protection to the public interest. I have already stated that where the government is engaged in public works for purposes of flood control, of navigation, of irrigation, of scientific research or national defense, or in pioneering a new art, it will at times necessarily produce power or commodities as a by-product. But they must be a by-product of the major purpose, not the major purpose itself.

Nor do I wish to be misinterpreted as believing that the United States is free-for-all and devil-take-the-hindmost. The very essence of equality of opportunity and of American individualism is that there shall be no domination by any group or combination in this Republic, whether it be business or political. On the contrary, it demands economic justice as well as political and social justice. It is no system of laissez-faire.

I feel deeply on this subject because during the war I had some practical experience with governmental operation and control. I have witnessed not only at home but abroad the many failures of government in business. I have seen its tyrannies, its injustices, its destructions of self-government, its undermining of the very instincts which carry our people forward to progress. I have witnessed the lack of advance, the lowered standards of living, the depressed spirits of people working under such a system. My objection is based not upon theory or upon a failure to recognize wrong or abuse, but I know the adoption of such methods would strike at the very roots of American life and would destroy the very basis of American progress.

Our people have the right to know whether we can continue to solve our great problems without abandonment of our American system. I know we can. We have demonstrated that our system is responsive enough to meet any new and intricate development in our economic and business life. We have demonstrated that we can meet any economic problem and still maintain our democracy as master in its own house and that we can at the same time preserve equality of opportunity and individual freedom. . . .

And what have been the results of our American system? Our country has become the land of opportunity to those born without inheritance, not merely because of the wealth of its resources and industry, but because of this freedom of initiative and enterprise. Russia has natural resources equal to ours. Her people are equally industrious, but she has not had the blessings of one hundred and fifty years of our form of government and of our social system.

By adherence to the principles of decentralized self-government, ordered liberty, equal opportunity, and freedom to the individual, our American experiment in human welfare has yielded a degree of well-being unparalleled in all the world. It has come nearer to the abolition of poverty, to the abolition of fear of want, than humanity has ever reached before. Progress of the past seven years is the proof of it. This alone furnishes the answer to our opponents who ask us to introduce destructive elements into the system by which this has been accomplished. . . .

In bringing this address to a conclusion I should like to restate to you some of the fundamental things I have endeavored to bring out.

The foundations of progress and prosperity are dependent as never before upon the wise policies of government, for government now touches at a thousand points the intricate web of economic and social life.

Under administration by the Republican party in the last seven and one-half years our country as a whole has made unparalleled progress and this has been in generous part reflected in this great city. Prosperity is no idle expression. It is a job for every worker; it is the safety and the safeguard of every business and every home. A continuation of the policies of the Republican party is fundamentally necessary to the further building up of this prosperity.

I have dwelt at some length on the principles of relationship between the government and business. I make no apologies for dealing with this subject. The first necessity of any nation is the smooth functioning of the vast business machinery for employment, feeding, clothing, housing, and providing luxuries and comforts to a people. Unless these basic elements are properly organized and function, there can be no progress in business, in education, literature, music, or art. There can be no advance in the fundamental ideals of a people. A people cannot make progress in poverty.

I have endeavored to present to you that the greatness of America has grown out of a political and social system and a method of control of economic forces distinctly its own—our American system—

which has carried this great experiment in human welfare further than ever before in all history. We are nearer today to the ideal of the abolition of poverty and fear from the lives of men and women than ever before in any land. And I again repeat that the departure from our American system by injecting principles destructive to it which our opponents propose will jeopardize the very liberty and freedom of our people, will destroy equality of opportunity, not alone to ourselves but to our children.

To me the foundation of American life rests upon the home and the family. I read into these great economic forces, these intricate and delicate relations of the government with business and with our political and social life, but one supreme end—that we reinforce the ties that bind together the millions of our families, that we strengthen the security, the happiness, and the independence of every home.

My conception of America is a land where men and women may walk in ordered freedom in the independent conduct of their occupations; where they may enjoy the advantages of wealth, not concentrated in the hands of the few but spread through the lives of all; where they build and safeguard their homes, and give to their children the fullest advantages and opportunities of American life; where every man shall be respected in the faith that his conscience and his heart direct him to follow; where a contented and happy people, secure in their liberties, free from poverty and fear, shall have the leisure and impulse to seek a fuller life.

Some may ask where all this may lead beyond mere material progress. It leads to a release of the energies of men and women from the dull drudgery of life to a wider vision and a higher hope. It leads to the opportunity for greater and greater service, not alone from man to man in our own land, but from our country to the whole world. It leads to an America, healthy in body, healthy in spirit, unfettered, youthful, eager—with a vision searching beyond the farthest horizons, with an open mind, sympathetic and generous. It is to these higher ideals and for these purposes that I pledge myself and the Republican party.

Franklin D. Roosevelt's First Inaugural Address

"... the only thing we have to fear is fear itself...."

At noon on March 4, 1933, Americans gathered around their radios to listen to the newly elected President, Franklin D. Roosevelt, deliver his first Inaugural Address. It was a sober, frightened audience the President prepared to address, for the country had sunk into the worst depression in its history, and the future appeared dark and grim. Then Roosevelt began to speak and, in a calm, confident voice, rallied the people with a message of faith and hope and the promise of better days.

"This great nation will endure as it has endured, will revive, and will prosper," he confidently declared. "So, first of all, let me assert my firm belief that the only thing we have to fear is fear itself—nameless, unreasoning, unjustified terror which paralyzes needed efforts to convert retreat into advance."

March 4, 1933

President Hoover, Mr. Chief Justice, my friends:

This is a day of national consecration, and I am certain that my fellow Americans expect that on my induction into the Presidency I will address them with a candor and a decision which the present situation of our nation impels.

This is pre-eminently the time to speak the truth, the whole truth, frankly and boldly. Nor need we shrink from honestly facing conditions in our country today. This great nation will endure as it has endured, will revive, and will prosper.

So, first of all, let me assert my firm belief that the only thing we have to fear is fear itself—nameless, unreasoning, unjustified terror which paralyzes needed efforts to convert retreat into advance.

In every dark hour of our national life a leadership of frankness and vigor has met with that understanding and support of the people themselves which is essential to victory. I am convinced that you will again give that support to leadership in these critical days.

In such a spirit on my part and on yours we face our common difficulties. They concern, thank God, only material things. Values have shrunken to fantastic levels; taxes have risen; our ability to pay has fallen; government of all kinds is faced by serious curtailment of income; the means of exchange are frozen in the currents of trade; the withered leaves of industrial enterprise lie on every side; farmers find no markets for their produce; the savings of many years in thousands of families are gone.

More important, a host of unemployed citizens face the grim problem of existence, and an equally great number toil with little return. Only a foolish optimist can deny the dark realities of the moment.

Yet our distress comes from no failure of substance. We are stricken by no plague of locusts. Compared with the perils which our forefathers conquered because they believed and were not afraid, we have still much to be thankful for. Nature still offers her bounty and human efforts have multiplied it. Plenty is at our doorstep, but a generous use of it languishes in the very sight of the supply.

Primarily, this is because the rulers of the exchange of mankind's goods have failed through their own stubbornness and their own incompetence, have admitted their failure and abdicated. Practices of the unscrupulous money-changers stand indicted in the court of public opinion, rejected by the hearts and minds of men.

True, they have tried, but their efforts have been cast in the pattern of an outworn tradition. Faced by failure of credit, they have proposed only the lending of more money.

Stripped of the lure of profit by which to induce our people to follow their false leadership, they have resorted to exhortations, pleading tearfully for restored confidence. They know only the rules of a generation of self-seekers.

They have no vision, and when there is no vision the people perish.

The money-changers have fled from their high seats in the temple of our civilization. We may now restore that temple to the ancient truths.

The measure of the restoration lies in the extent to which we apply social values more noble than mere monetary profit.

Happiness lies not in the mere possession of money; it lies in the joy of achievement, in the thrill of creative effort.

The joy and moral stimulation of work no longer must be forgotten in the mad chase of evanescent profits. These dark days will be worth all they cost us if they teach us that our true destiny is not to be ministered unto but to minister to ourselves and to our fellow men.

Recognition of the falsity of material wealth as the standard of success goes hand in hand with the abandonment of the false belief that public office and high political position are to be valued only by the standards of pride of place and personal profit; and there must be an end to a conduct in banking and in business which too often has given to a sacred trust the likeness of callous and selfish wrong-doing.

Small wonder that confidence languishes, for it thrives only on honesty, on honor, on the sacredness of obligations, on faithful protection, on unselfish performance. Without them it cannot live.

Restoration calls, however, not for changes in ethics alone. This nation asks for action, and action now.

Our greatest primary task is to put people to work. This is no unsolvable problem if we face it wisely and courageously.

It can be accomplished in part by direct recruiting by the government itself, treating the task as we would treat the emergency of a war, but at the same time, through this employment, accomplishing greatly needed projects to stimulate and reorganize the use of our natural resources.

Hand in hand with this, we must frankly recognize the overbalance of population in our industrial centers and, by engaging on a national scale in a redistribution, endeavor to provide a better use of the land for those best fitted for the land.

The task can be helped by definite efforts to raise the values of agricultural products and with this the power to purchase the output of our cities.

It can be helped by preventing realistically the tragedy of the growing loss, through foreclosure, of our small homes and our farms.

It can be helped by insistence that the federal, state, and local governments act forthwith on the demand that their cost be drastically reduced.

It can be helped by the unifying of relief activities which today are often scattered, uneconomical and unequal. It can be helped by national planning for and supervision of all forms of transportation and of communications and other utilities which have a definitely public character.

There are many ways in which it can be helped, but it can never be helped merely by talking about it. We must act, and act quickly.

Finally, in our progress toward a resumption of work we require two safeguards against a return of the evils of the old order; there must be a strict supervision of all banking and credits and investments; there must be an end to speculation with other people's money, and there must be provision for an adequate but sound currency.

These are the lines of attack. I shall presently urge upon a new Congress in special session detailed measures for their fulfillment, and I shall seek the immediate assistance of the several states.

Through this program of action we address ourselves to putting our own national house in order and making income balance outgo.

Our international trade relations, though vastly important, are, in point of time and necessity, secondary to the establishment of a sound national economy.

I favor as a practical policy the putting of first things first. I shall spare no effort to restore world trade by international economic readjustment, but the emergency at home cannot wait on that accomplishment.

The basic thought that guides these specific means of national recovery is not narrowly nationalistic.

It is the insistence, as a first consideration, upon the interdependence of the various elements in, and parts of, the United States—a recognition of the old and permanently important manifestation of the American spirit of the pioneer.

It is the way to recovery. It is the immediate way. It is the strongest assurance that the recovery will endure.

In the field of world policy I would dedicate this nation to the policy of the good neighbor—the neighbor who resolutely respects himself and, because he does so, respects the rights of others—the neighbor who respects his obligations and respects the sanctity of his agreements in and with a world of neighbors.

If I read the temper of our people correctly, we now realize as we have never before, our interdependence on each other; that we cannot merely take, but we must give as well; that if we are to go forward we must move as a trained and loyal army willing to sacrifice for the good of a common discipline, because, without such discipline, no progress is made, no leadership becomes effective.

We are, I know, ready and willing to submit our lives and property to such discipline because it makes possible a leadership which aims at a larger good.

This I propose to offer, pledging that the larger purposes will bind upon us all as a sacred obligation with a unity of duty hitherto evoked [summoned] only in time of armed strife.

With this pledge taken, I assume unhesitatingly the leadership of this great army of our people, dedicated to a disciplined attack upon our common problems.

Action in this image and to this end is feasible under the form of government which we have inherited from our ancestors.

Our Constitution is so simple and practical that it is possible always to meet extraordinary needs by changes in emphasis and arrangement without loss of essential form.

That is why our constitutional system has proved itself the most superbly enduring political mechanism the modern world has produced. It has met every stress of vast expansion of territory, of foreign wars, of bitter internal strife, of world relations.

It is to be hoped that the normal balance of executive and legislative authority may be wholly adequate to meet the unprecedented task before us. But it may be that an unprecedented demand and need for undelayed action may call for temporary departure from that normal balance of public procedure.

I am prepared under my constitutional duty to recommend the measures that a stricken nation in the midst of a stricken world may require.

These measures, or such other measures as the Congress may build out of its experience and wisdom, I shall seek, within my constitutional authority, to bring to speedy adoption.

But in the event that the Congress shall fail to take one of these two courses, and in the event that the national emergency is still critical, I shall not evade the clear course of duty that will then confront me.

I shall ask the Congress for the one remaining instrument to meet the crisis—broad executive power to wage a war against the emergency as great as the power that would be given me if we were in fact invaded by a foreign foe.

For the trust reposed in me I will return the courage and the devotion that befit the time. I can do no less.

We face the arduous days that lie before us in the warm courage of national unity; with the clear consciousness of seeking old and precious moral values; with the clean satisfaction that comes from the stern performance of duty by old and young alike.

We aim at the assurance of a rounded and permanent national life.

We do not distrust the future of essential democracy. The people of the United States have not failed. In their need they have registered a mandate that they want direct, vigorous action.

They have asked for discipline and direction under leadership. They have made me the present instrument of their wishes. In the spirit of the gift I take it.

In this dedication of a nation we humbly ask the blessing of God. May He protect each and every one of us! May He guide me in the days to come!

The Philippine Independence Act

*"The . . . United States shall . . . recognize
. . . the Philippine Islands as a separate
and self-governing nation. . . ."*

When, as a result of the Spanish-American war (1898), the United States acquired the Philippine Islands from Spain, President McKinley solemnly promised "not to exploit [the Filipinos], but to develop; to civilize, to educate, to train [them] in the science of self-government."

Under American rule, the Islands prospered, and as the years passed the Filipinos gained an increasingly large measure of self-government. In 1916, under President Wilson, Congress promised to give the Islands complete independence. Finally, in 1934, with the passage of the Tydings-McDuffie Act, Congress kept this promise. The Philippine Independence Act, as it was called, provided for a ten-year transitional period, at the end of which the Islands were to be completely free. Because of World War II and Japanese occupation of the Philippines, the Filipinos did not secure their independence until 1946.

March 24, 1934

An Act to provide for the complete independence of the Philippine Islands, to provide for the adoption of a constitution and a form of government for the Philippine Islands, and for other purposes. . . .

Section 1. The Philippine Legislature is hereby authorized to provide for the election of delegates to a constitutional convention, which shall . . . formulate and draft a constitution for the government of the Commonwealth of the Philippine Islands, subject to the conditions and qualifications prescribed in this act. . . .

Section 2. (a) The constitution formulated and drafted shall be republican in form, shall contain a bill of rights, and shall . . . contain provisions to the effect that, pending the final and complete withdrawal of the sovereignty of the United States over the Philippine Islands:

(1) All citizens of the Philippine Islands shall owe allegiance to the United States.

(2) Every officer of the government of the Commonwealth of the Philippine Islands shall, before entering upon the discharge of his duties, take and subscribe [sign] an oath of office, declaring, among other things, that he recognizes and accepts the supreme authority of and will maintain true faith and allegiance to the United States.

(3) Absolute toleration of religious sentiment shall be secured and no inhabitant or religious organization shall be molested in person or property on account of religious belief or mode of worship.

(4) Property owned by the United States, cemeteries, churches, and parsonages or convents appurtenant [relating] thereto, and all lands, buildings, and improvements used exclusively for religious, charitable, or educational purposes shall be exempt from taxation.

(5) Trade relations between the Philippine Islands and the United States shall be upon the basis prescribed in Section 6.

(6) The public debt of the Philippine Islands and its subordinate branches shall not exceed limits now or hereafter fixed by the Congress of the United States; and no loans shall be contracted in foreign countries without the approval of the President of the United States.

(7) The debts, liabilities, and obligations of the present Philippine government, its provinces, municipalities, and instrumentalities, valid and subsisting at the time of the adoption of the constitution, shall be assumed and paid by the new government.

(8) Provision shall be made for the establishment and maintenance of an adequate system of public schools, primarily conducted in the English language.

(9) Acts affecting currency, coinage, imports, exports, and immigration shall not become law until approved by the President of the United States.

(10) Foreign affairs shall be under the direct supervision and control of the United States.

(11) All acts passed by the legislature of the Commonwealth of the Philippine Islands shall be reported to the Congress of the United States.

(12) The Philippine Islands recognizes the right of the United States to expropriate property for public uses, to maintain military and other reservations and armed forces in the Philippines, and, upon order of the President, to call into the service of such armed forces all military forces organized by the Philippine government.

(13) The decisions of the courts of the Commonwealth of the Philippine Islands shall be subject to review by the Supreme Court of the United States as provided in paragraph 6 of Section 7.

(14) The United States may, by Presidential proclamation, exercise the right to intervene for the preservation of the government of the Commonwealth of the Philippine Islands and for the maintenance of the government as provided in the constitution thereof, and for the protection of life, property, and individual liberty and for the

discharge of government obligations under and in accordance with the provisions of the constitution.

(15) The authority of the United States High Commissioner to the government of the Commonwealth of the Philippine Islands, as provided in this act, shall be recognized.

(16) Citizens and corporations of the United States shall enjoy in the Commonwealth of the Philippine Islands all the civil rights of the citizens and corporations, respectively, thereof.

(b) The constitution shall also contain the following provisions, effective as of the date of the proclamation of the President recognizing the independence of the Philippine Islands as hereinafter provided:

(1) That the property rights of the United States and the Philippine Islands shall be promptly adjusted and settled, and that all existing property rights of citizens or corporations of the United States shall be acknowledged, respected, and safeguarded to the same extent as property rights of citizens of the Philippine Islands.

(2) That the officials elected and serving under the constitution adopted pursuant to the provisions of this act shall be constitutional officers of the free and independent government of the Philippine Islands and qualified to function in all respects as if elected directly under such government, and shall serve their full terms of office as prescribed in the constitution.

(3) That the debts and liabilities of the Philippine Islands, its provinces, cities, municipalities, and instrumentalities, which shall be valid and subsisting at the time of the final and complete withdrawal of the sovereignty of the United States, shall be assumed by the free and independent government of the Philippine Islands....

Section 7. Until the final and complete withdrawal of American sovereignty over the Philippine Islands: ...

(4) The President shall appoint, by and with the advice and consent of the Senate, a United States High Commissioner to the government of the Commonwealth of the Philippine Islands who shall hold office at the pleasure of the President and until his successor is appointed and qualified....

If the government of the Commonwealth of the Philippine Islands fails to pay any of its bonded or other indebtedness or the interest thereon when due or to fulfill any of its contracts, the United States High Commissioner shall immediately report the facts to the

President, who may thereupon direct the High Commissioner to take over the customs offices and administration of the same, administer the same, and apply such part of the revenue received therefrom as may be necessary for the payment of such overdue indebtedness or for the fulfillment of such contracts. . . .

(6) Review by the Supreme Court of the United States of cases from the Philippine Islands shall be as now provided by law; and such review shall also extend to all cases involving the constitution of the Commonwealth of the Philippine Islands. . . .

Section 10. (a) On the fourth day of July immediately following the expiration of a period of ten years from the date of the inauguration of the new government under the constitution provided for in this act the President of the United States shall by proclamation withdraw and surrender all right of possession, supervision, jurisdiction, control, or sovereignty then existing and exercised by the United States in and over the territory and people of the Philippine Islands, including all military and other reservations of the government of the United States in the Philippines (except such naval reservations and fueling stations as are reserved under Section 5), and, on behalf of the United States, shall recognize the independence of the Philippine Islands as a separate and self-governing nation and acknowledge the authority and control over the same of the government instituted by the people thereof, under the constitution then in force. . . .

The Abrogation of the Platt Amendment

"The United States ... and the Republic of Cuba ... have agreed upon the following articles. ..."

In 1901, following the Spanish-American War, Congress decided to turn Cuba over to the Cuban people. Congress did not, however, give Cuba complete freedom. The Platt Amendment, which the Cubans added to their newly adopted

constitution upon the insistence of the United States, gave
the American government, among other things, "the right to
intervene for the preservation of Cuban independence [and]
the maintenance of a government adequate for the protection
of life, property, and individual liberty."

Cubans were not happy with the Platt Amendment, which
made Cuba a protectorate of the United States, and under
which, on several occasions as the years passed, the American
government had landed troops on the island to maintain
order and protect property. Finally, in 1934, as part of its
Good Neighbor policy, the Franklin D. Roosevelt administration repealed the amendment.

May 31, 1934

The United States of America and the Republic of Cuba, being
animated by the desire to fortify the relations of friendship between
the two countries, and to modify with this purpose the relations
established between them by the Treaty of Relations signed at Havana, May 22, 1903 . . . have agreed upon the following articles:

Article I. The Treaty of Relations which was concluded between
the two contracting parties on May 22, 1903, shall cease to be in
force, and is abrogated, from the date on which the present treaty
goes into effect.

Article II. All the acts effected in Cuba by the United States of
America during its military occupation of the island, up to May 20,
1902, the date on which the Republic of Cuba was established, have
been ratified and held as valid; and all rights legally acquired by
virtue of those acts shall be maintained and protected.

Article III. Until the two contracting parties agree to the modification or abrogation of the stipulations of the agreement in regard to
the lease to the United States of America of lands in Cuba for coaling and naval stations signed by the President of the Republic of
Cuba on February 16, 1903, and by the President of the United States
of America on the twenty-third day of the same month and year,
the stipulations of that agreement with regard to the naval station
of Guantanamo shall continue in effect. The supplementary agree-

ment in regard to naval or coaling stations signed between the two governments on July 2, 1903, shall continue in effect in the same form and on the same conditions with respect to the naval station at Guantanamo. So long as the United States of America shall not abandon the said naval station of Guantanamo or the two governments shall not agree to a modification of its present limits, the station shall continue to have the territorial area that it now has, with the limits that it has on the date of the signature of the present treaty.

Article IV. If at any time in the future a situation should arise that appears to point to an outbreak of contagious disease in the territory of either of the contracting parties, either of the two governments shall, for its own protection and without its act being considered unfriendly, exercise freely and at its discretion the right to suspend communications between those of its ports that it may designate and all or part of the territory of the other party, and for the period that it may consider to be advisable.

Article V. The present treaty shall be ratified by the contracting parties in accordance with their respective constitutional methods; and shall go into effect on the date of the exchange of their ratifications, which shall take place in the city of Washington as soon as possible.

Franklin D. Roosevelt's Annual Message to Congress

". . . freedom of speech and expression . . . freedom of every person to worship God in his own way . . . freedom from want . . . freedom from fear. . . ."

Shortly after two o'clock on the afternoon of January 6, 1941, President Franklin D. Roosevelt entered the House of Representatives in the nation's Capitol and, after approaching the rostrum, opened a notebook and began to read his

State of the Union message to Congress. The House was crowded to capacity, for, although the United States was not yet involved in the war which had been raging for sixteen months on four continents, most of America's leaders realized that American entry into the conflict was almost certainly only a matter of time.

"I address you, the members of the Seventy-seventh Congress, at a moment unprecedented in the history of the Union," the President began. "I use the word 'unprecedented,' because at no previous time has American security been as seriously threatened from without as it is today. . . ."

The President then went on to discuss the crisis facing the nation, and to warn that "no realistic American" could remain indifferent to the rising tide of aggression that threatened to engulf the world. In measured words, he concluded his talk with an eloquent and deeply moving appeal to his fellow Americans to rededicate themselves to "the four essential human freedoms"—those "simple and basic things that must never be lost sight of in the turmoil and unbelievable complexity of our modern world."

January 6, 1941

I address you, the members of the Seventy-seventh Congress, at a moment unprecedented in the history of the Union. I use the word "unprecedented," because at no previous time has American security been as seriously threatened from without as it is today. . . .

Every realist knows that the democratic way of life is at this moment being directly assailed in every part of the world—assailed either by arms, or by secret spreading of poisonous propaganda by those who seek to destroy unity and promote discord in nations still at peace.

During sixteen months this assault has blotted out the whole pattern of democratic life in an appalling number of independent nations, great and small. The assailants are still on the march, threatening other nations, great and small.

Therefore, as your President, performing my constitutional duty to "give to the Congress information of the state of the Union," I find it necessary to report that the future and the safety of our country and of our democracy are overwhelmingly involved in events far beyond our borders.

Armed defense of democratic existence is now being gallantly waged in four continents. If that defense fails, all the population and all the resources of Europe, Asia, Africa, and Australasia will be dominated by the conquerors. Let us remember that the total of those populations and their resources in those four continents greatly exceeds the sum total of the population and the resources of the whole of the Western Hemisphere many times over.

In times like these it is immature—and, incidentally, untrue—for anybody to brag that an unprepared America, singlehanded, and with one hand tied behind its back, can hold off the whole world.

No realistic American can expect from a dictator's peace international generosity, or return of true independence, or world disarmament, or freedom of expression, or freedom of religion—or even good business.

Such a peace would bring no security for us or for our neighbors. "Those who would give up essential liberty to purchase a little temporary safety deserve neither liberty nor safety."

As a nation, we may take pride in the fact that we are softhearted; but we cannot afford to be softheaded.

We must always be wary of those who with sounding brass and a tinkling cymbal preach the "ism" [doctrine] of appeasement.

We must especially beware of that small group of selfish men who would clip the wings of the American eagle in order to feather their own nests. . . .

I have recently pointed out how quickly the tempo of modern warfare could bring into our very midst the physical attack which we must eventually expect if the dictator nations win this war.

There is much loose talk of our immunity from immediate and direct invasion from across the seas. Obviously, as long as the British Navy retains its power, no such danger exists. Even if there were no British Navy, it is not probable that any enemy would be stupid enough to attack us by landing troops in the United States from across thousands of miles of ocean, until it had acquired strategic bases from which to operate.

But we learn much from the lessons of the past years in Europe—

particularly the lesson of Norway, whose essential seaports were captured by treachery and surprise built up over a series of years.

The first phase of the invasion of this Hemisphere would not be the landing of regular troops. The necessary strategic points would be occupied by secret agents and their dupes and great numbers of them are already here, and in Latin America.

As long as the aggressor nations maintain the offensive, they—not we—will choose the time and the place and the method of their attack.

That is why the future of all the American republics is today in serious danger.

That is why this Annual Message to the Congress is unique in our history.

That is why every member of the executive branch of the government and every member of the Congress face great responsibility and great accountability.

The need of the moment is that our actions and our policy should be devoted primarily—almost exclusively—to meeting this foreign peril. For all our domestic problems are now a part of the great emergency.

Just as our national policy in internal affairs has been based upon a decent respect for the rights and the dignity of all our fellow men within our gates, so our national policy in foreign affairs has been based on a decent respect for the rights and dignity of all nations, large and small. And the justice of morality must and will win in the end.

Our national policy is this:

First, by an impressive expression of the public will and without regard to partisanship, we are committed to all-inclusive national defense.

Second, by an impressive expression of the public will and without regard to partisanship, we are committed to full support of all those resolute peoples, everywhere, who are resisting aggression and are thereby keeping war away from our hemisphere. By this support, we express our determination that the democratic cause shall prevail; and we strengthen the defense and the security of our own nation.

Third, by an impressive expression of the public will and without regard to partisanship, we are committed to the proposition that principles of morality and considerations for our own security will never permit us to acquiesce in a peace dictated by aggressors and sponsored by appeasers. We know that enduring peace cannot be bought at the cost of other people's freedom.

In the recent national election there was no substantial difference between the two great parties in respect to that national policy. No issue was fought out on this line before the American electorate. To-day it is abundantly evident that American citizens everywhere are demanding and supporting speedy and complete action in recognition of obvious danger.

Therefore, the immediate need is a swift and driving increase in our armament production. . . .

New circumstances are constantly begetting new needs for our safety. I shall ask this Congress for greatly increased new appropriations and authorizations to carry on what we have begun.

I also ask this Congress for authority and for funds sufficient to manufacture additional munitions and war supplies of many kinds, to be turned over to those nations which are now in actual war with aggressor nations.

Our most useful and immediate role is to act as an arsenal for them as well as for ourselves. They do not need man power. They do need billions of dollars' worth of the weapons of defense.

The time is near when they will not be able to pay for them all in ready cash. We cannot, and we will not, tell them that they must surrender, merely because of inability to pay for the weapons which we know they must have.

I do not recommend that we make them a loan of dollars with which to pay for these weapons—a loan to be repaid in dollars.

I recommend that we make it possible for those nations to continue to obtain war materials in the United States, fitting their orders into our own program. Nearly all their matériel ° would, if the time ever came, be useful for our own defense. . . .

For what we send abroad, we shall be repaid within a reasonable time following the close of hostilities, in similar materials, or, at our option, in other goods of many kinds, which they can produce and which we need.

Let us say to the democracies: "We Americans are vitally concerned in your defense of freedom. We are putting forth our energies, our resources, and our organizing powers to give you the strength

° *matériel*: equipment, apparatus, and supplies.

to regain and maintain a free world. We shall send you, in ever-increasing numbers, ships, planes, tanks, guns. This is our purpose and our pledge." . . .

The happiness of future generations of Americans may well depend upon how effective and how immediate we can make our aid felt. No one can tell the exact character of the emergency situations that we may be called upon to meet. The Nation's hands must not be tied when the Nation's life is in danger.

We must all prepare to make the sacrifices that the emergency—as serious as war itself—demands. Whatever stands in the way of speed and efficiency in defense preparations must give way to the national need.

A free nation has the right to expect full co-operation from all groups. A free nation has the right to look to the leaders of business, of labor, and of agriculture to take the lead in stimulating effort, not among other groups but within their own groups.

The best way of dealing with the few slackers or troublemakers in our midst is, first, to shame them by patriotic example, and, if that fails, to use the sovereignty of government to save government.

As men do not live by bread alone, they do not fight by armaments alone. Those who man our defenses, and those behind them who build our defenses, must have the stamina and the courage which come from an unshakeable belief in the manner of life which they are defending. The mighty action that we are calling for cannot be based on a disregard of all things worth fighting for.

The Nation takes great satisfaction and much strength from the things which have been done to make its people conscious of their individual stake in the preservation of democratic life in America. Those things have toughened the fiber of our people, have renewed their faith and strengthened their devotion to the institutions we make ready to protect.

Certainly this is no time for any of us to stop thinking about the social and economic problems which are the root cause of the social revolution which is today a supreme factor in the world.

For there is nothing mysterious about the foundations of a healthy and strong democracy. The basic things expected by our people of their political and economic systems are simple. They are:

Equality of opportunity for youth and for others.

Jobs for those who can work.

Security for those who need it.

The ending of special privilege for the few.

The preservation of civil liberties for all.

The enjoyment of the fruits of scientific progress in a wider and constantly rising standard of living.

These are the simple and basic things that must never be lost sight of in the turmoil and unbelievable complexity of our modern world. The inner and abiding strength of our economic and political systems is dependent upon the degree to which they fulfill these expectations. . . .

In the future days, which we seek to make secure, we look forward to a world founded upon four essential human freedoms.

The first is freedom of speech and expression—everywhere in the world.

The second is freedom of every person to worship God in his own way—everywhere in the world.

The third is freedom from want—which, translated into world terms, means economic understandings which will secure to every nation a healthy peacetime life for its inhabitants—everywhere in the world.

The fourth is freedom from fear—which, translated into world terms, means a world-wide reduction of armaments to such a point and in such a thorough fashion that no nation will be in a position to commit an act of physical aggression against any neighbor—anywhere in the world.

That is no vision of a distant millennium.° It is a definite basis for a kind of world attainable in our own time and generation. That kind of world is the very antithesis of the so-called new order of tyranny which the dictators seek to create with the crash of a bomb.

To that new order we oppose the greater conception—the moral order. A good society is able to face schemes of world domination and foreign revolutions alike without fear.

Since the beginning of our American history, we have been engaged in change—in a perpetual peaceful revolution—a revolution which goes on steadily, quietly adjusting itself to changing conditions—without the concentration camp or the quicklime in the ditch. The world order which we seek is the co-operation of free countries, working together in a friendly, civilized society.

  ° *millennium:* a future period characterized by happiness for all mankind.

This nation has placed its destiny in the hands and heads and hearts of its millions of free men and women; and its faith in freedom under the guidance of God. Freedom means the supremacy of human rights everywhere. Our support goes to those who struggle to gain those rights or keep them. Our strength is in our unity of purpose. To that high concept there can be no end save victory.

The Atlantic Charter

"... all of the nations of the world, for realistic as well as spiritual reasons, must come to the abandonment of the use of force."

On August 9, 1941, the sleek gray hull of a powerful British warship, bearing Prime Minister Churchill, slipped into Placentia Bay on the southeastern coast of Newfoundland. The British vessel, the Prince of Wales, moved slowly to an anchorage not far from the United States cruiser Augusta with President Franklin D. Roosevelt on board.

Great Britain had been at war for almost two years, and the United States, though still neutral in name, had already provided the British with huge supplies of war matériel, including fifty American destroyers. Now, in the summer of 1941, with the war rapidly increasing in fury, the leaders of the two great nations were meeting to plan for even closer co-operation and to agree upon a joint statement of principles to guide their conduct in the troubled years that lay before them.

On August 14, after conferences extending over several days, the two heads of state released for world-wide publication the draft of the document which has come to be known as the Atlantic Charter.

August 14, 1941

The President of the United States of America and the Prime Minister, Mr. Churchill, representing His Majesty's Government in the United Kingdom, being met together, deem it right to make known certain common principles in the national policies of their respective countries on which they base their hopes for a better future for the world.

First, their countries seek no aggrandizement, territorial or other.

Second, they desire to see no territorial changes that do not accord with the freely expressed wishes of the peoples concerned.

Third, they respect the right of all peoples to choose the form of government under which they will live; and they wish to see sovereign rights and self-government restored to those who have been forcibly deprived of them.

Fourth, they will endeavor, with due respect for their existing obligations, to further the enjoyment by all states, great or small, victor or vanquished, of access, on equal terms, to the trade and to the raw materials of the world which are needed for their economic prosperity.

Fifth, they desire to bring about the fullest collaboration between all nations in the economic field with the object of securing, for all, improved labor standards, economic advancement, and social security.

Sixth, after the final destruction of the Nazi tyranny, they hope to see established a peace which will afford to all nations the means of dwelling in safety within their own boundaries, and which will afford assurance that all the men in all the lands may live out their lives in freedom from fear and want.

Seventh, such a peace should enable all men to traverse the high seas and oceans without hindrance.

Eighth, they believe that all of the nations of the world, for realistic as well as spiritual reasons, must come to the abandonment of the use of force. Since no future peace can be maintained if land, sea, or air armaments continue to be employed by nations which threaten, or may threaten, aggression outside of their frontiers, they believe, pending the establishment of a wider and permanent system of general security, that the disarmament of such nations is essential. They will likewise aid and encourage all other practicable measures which will lighten for peace-loving peoples the crushing burden of armaments.

FRANKLIN D. ROOSEVELT

August 14, 1941   WINSTON S. CHURCHILL

The United Nations Charter

"We the peoples of the United Nations ... do hereby establish an international organization. ..."

On April 25, 1945, delegates from fifty nations and representing three-fourths of the peoples of the earth gathered in the Opera House in San Francisco. In spite of differences in language, religious beliefs, dress, and modes of living, the delegates shared a great objective—the creation of a world organization that would "save succeeding generations from the scourge of war."

Commitment to this large and noble objective held the delegates together through long, trying weeks of debate and discussion. Finally, after the delegates had agreed upon the precise wording for the United Nations Charter, the completed draft was sent to the various nations for ratification. The United States joined—with only two dissenting votes in the Senate. One by one, other nations ratified the Charter, and on October 24, now officially celebrated as United Nations Day, the new world organization was born.

October 24, 1945

We the peoples of the United Nations, determined

to save succeeding generations from the scourge of war, which twice in our lifetime has brought untold sorrow to mankind, and to reaffirm faith in fundamental human rights, in the dignity and worth of the human person, in the equal rights of men and women and of nations large and small, and

to establish conditions under which justice and respect for the obligations arising from treaties and other sources of international law can be maintained, and

to promote social progress and better standards of life in larger freedom,

And for these ends

to practice tolerance and live together in peace with one another as good neighbors, and

to unite our strength to maintain international peace and security, and

to ensure, by the acceptance of principles and the institution of methods, that armed force shall not be used, save in the common interest, and

to employ international machinery for the promotion of the economic and social advancement of all peoples,

Have resolved to combine our efforts to accomplish these aims. . . .

Accordingly, our respective Governments, through representatives assembled in the city of San Francisco, who have exhibited their full powers found to be in good and due form, have agreed to the present Charter of the United Nations and do hereby establish an international organization to be known as the United Nations.

CHAPTER I • Purposes and Principles

Article 1

The Purposes of the United Nations are:

1. To maintain international peace and security, and to that end: to take effective collective measures for the prevention and removal of threats to the peace, and for the suppression of acts of aggression or other breaches of the peace, and to bring about by peaceful means,

and in conformity with the principles of justice and international law, adjustment or settlement of international disputes or situations which might lead to a breach of the peace;

2. To develop friendly relations among nations based on respect for the principle of equal rights and self-determination of peoples, and to take other appropriate measures to strengthen universal peace;

3. To achieve international co-operation in solving international problems of an economic, social, cultural, or humanitarian character, and in promoting and encouraging respect for human rights and for fundamental freedoms for all without distinction as to race, sex, language, or religion; and

4. To be a center for harmonizing the actions of nations in the attainment of these common ends.

Article 2

1. The Organization is based on the principle of the sovereign equality of all its Members....

3. All Members shall settle their international disputes by peaceful means in such a manner that international peace and security, and justice, are not endangered.

4. All Members shall refrain in their international relations from the threat or use of force against the territorial integrity or political independence of any state, or in any other manner inconsistent with the Purposes of the United Nations.

5. All Members shall give the United Nations every assistance in any action it takes in accordance with the present Charter, and shall refrain from giving assistance to any state against which the United Nations is taking preventive or enforcement action.

6. The Organization shall ensure that states which are not Members of the United Nations act in accordance with these Principles so far as may be necessary for the maintenance of international peace and security.

7. Nothing contained in the present Charter shall authorize the United Nations to intervene in matters which are essentially within the domestic jurisdiction of any state or shall require the Members to submit such matters to settlement under the present Charter; but this principle shall not prejudice the application of enforcement measures under Chapter VII.

CHAPTER II · Membership

. . .

Article 4

1. Membership in the United Nations is open to all other peace-loving states which accept the obligations contained in the present Charter and, in the judgment of the Organization, are able and willing to carry out these obligations.

2. The admission of any such state to membership in the United Nations will be effected by a decision of the General Assembly upon the recommendation of the Security Council.

Article 5

A Member of the United Nations against which preventive or enforcement action has been taken by the Security Council may be suspended from the exercise of the rights and privileges of membership by the General Assembly upon the recommendation of the Security Council. The exercise of these rights and privileges may be restored by the Security Council.

Article 6

A Member of the United Nations which has persistently violated the Principles contained in the present Charter may be expelled from the Organization by the General Assembly upon the recommendation of the Security Council.

CHAPTER III · Organs

Article 7

1. There are established as the principal organs of the United Nations: a General Assembly, a Security Council, an Economic and Social Council, a Trusteeship Council, an International Court of Justice, and a Secretariat. . . .

Article 8

The United Nations shall place no restrictions on the eligibility of men and women to participate in any capacity and under conditions of equality in its principal and subsidiary organs.

CHAPTER IV • The General Assembly

COMPOSITION

Article 9

1. The General Assembly shall consist of all the Members of the United Nations.

2. Each Member shall have not more than five representatives in the General Assembly.

FUNCTIONS AND POWERS

Article 10

The General Assembly may discuss any questions or any matters within the scope of the present Charter or relating to the powers and functions of any organs provided for in the present Charter, and, except as provided in Article 12, may make recommendations to the Members of the United Nations or to the Security Council or to both on any such questions or matters.

Article 11

1. The General Assembly may consider the general principles of co-operation in the maintenance of international peace and security, including the principles governing disarmament and the regulation of armaments, and may make recommendations with regard to such principles to the Members or to the Security Council or to both.

2. The General Assembly may discuss any questions relating to the maintenance of international peace and security brought before it by any Member of the United Nations, or by the Security Council, or by a state which is not a Member of the United Nations.... Any such question on which action is necessary shall be referred to the Security Council by the General Assembly either before or after discussion.

3. The General Assembly may call the attention of the Security Council to situations which are likely to endanger international peace and security....

Article 12

1. While the Security Council is exercising in respect of any dispute or situation the functions assigned to it in the present Charter,

the General Assembly shall not make any recommendations with regard to that dispute or situation unless the Security Council so re-
quests. . . .

Article 13

1. The General Assembly shall initiate studies and make recommendations for the purpose of:

a. promoting international co-operation in the political field and
encouraging the progressive development of international law and
its codification;

b. promoting international co-operation in the economic, social,
cultural, educational, and health fields, and assisting in the realization of human rights and fundamental freedoms for all without distinction as to race, sex, language, or religion. . . .

Article 14

Subject to the provisions of Article 12, the General Assembly may
recommend measures for the peaceful adjustment of any situation,
regardless of origin, which it deems likely to impair the general welfare
or friendly relations among nations, including situations resulting
from a violation of the provisions of the present Charter setting forth
the Purposes and Principles of the United Nations. . . .

Article 16

The General Assembly shall perform such functions with respect to
the international trusteeship system as are assigned to it . . . including
the approval of the trusteeship agreements for areas not designated
as strategic.

Article 17

1. The General Assembly shall consider and approve the budget of
the Organization.

2. The expenses of the Organization shall be borne by the Members as apportioned by the General Assembly. . . .

VOTING

Article 18

1. Each member of the General Assembly shall have one vote.

2. Decisions of the General Assembly on important questions shall

be made by a two-thirds majority of the members present and voting. These questions shall include: recommendations with respect to the maintenance of international peace and security, the election of the non-permanent members of the Security Council, the election of the members of the Economic and Social Council, the election of members of the Trusteeship Council in accordance with paragraph 1(c) of Article 86, the admission of new Members to the United Nations, the suspension of the rights and privileges of membership, the expulsion of Members, questions relating to the operation of the trusteeship system, and budgetary questions.

3. Decisions on other questions, including the determination of additional categories of questions to be decided by a two-thirds majority, shall be made by a majority of the members present and voting. . . .

PROCEDURE

Article 20

The General Assembly shall meet in regular annual sessions and in such special sessions as occasion may require. Special sessions shall be convoked by the Secretary-General at the request of the Security Council or of a majority of the Members of the United Nations.

Article 21

The General Assembly shall adopt its own rules of procedure. It shall elect its President for each session. . . .

CHAPTER V • The Security Council

COMPOSITION

Article 23

1. The Security Council shall consist of eleven Members of the United Nations. The Republic of China, France, the Union of Soviet Socialist Republics, the United Kingdom of Great Britain and Northern Ireland, and the United States of America shall be permanent members of the Security Council. The General Assembly shall elect six other Members of the United Nations to be non-permanent members of the Security Council, due regard being specially paid, in the first instance, to the contribution of Members of the United Nations to the maintenance of international peace and security and to the

other purposes of the Organization, and also to equitable geographical distribution.

2. The non-permanent members of the Security Council shall be elected for a term of two years. . . . A retiring member shall not be eligible for immediate re-election.

3. Each member of the Security Council shall have one representative.

FUNCTIONS AND POWERS

Article 24

1. In order to ensure prompt and effective action by the United Nations, its Members confer on the Security Council primary responsibility for the maintenance of international peace and security, and agree that in carrying out its duties under this responsibility the Security Council acts on their behalf. . . .

Article 25

The Members of the United Nations agree to accept and carry out the decisions of the Security Council in accordance with the present Charter.

Article 26

In order to promote the establishment and maintenance of international peace and security . . . the Security Council shall be responsible for formulating, with the assistance of the Military Staff Committee, plans to be submitted to the Members of the United Nations for the establishment of a system for the regulation of armaments.

VOTING

Article 27

1. Each member of the Security Council shall have one vote.

2. Decisions of the Security Council on procedural matters shall be made by an affirmative vote of seven members.

3. Decisions of the Security Council on all other matters shall be made by an affirmative vote of seven members including the concurring votes of the permanent members; provided that, in decisions under Chapter VI, and under paragraph 3 of Article 52, a party to a dispute shall abstain from voting.

PROCEDURE

Article 28

1. The Security Council shall be so organized as to be able to function continuously. Each member of the Security Council shall for this purpose be represented at all times at the seat of the Organization. . . .

Article 31

Any Member of the United Nations which is not a member of the Security Council may participate, without vote, in the discussion of any question brought before the Security Council whenever the latter considers that the interests of that Member are specially affected.

Article 32

Any Member of the United Nations which is not a member of the Security Council or any state which is not a Member of the United Nations, if it is a party to a dispute under consideration by the Security Council, shall be invited to participate, without vote, in the discussion relating to the dispute. . . .

CHAPTER VI • Pacific Settlement of Disputes

Article 33

1. The parties to any dispute, the continuance of which is likely to endanger the maintenance of international peace and security, shall, first of all, seek a solution by negotiation, enquiry, mediation, conciliation, arbitration, judicial settlement, resort to regional agencies or arrangements, or other peaceful means of their own choice. . . .

Article 34

The Security Council may investigate any dispute, or any situation which might lead to international friction or give rise to a dispute, in order to determine whether the continuance of the dispute or situation is likely to endanger the maintenance of international peace and security.

Article 35

1. Any Member of the United Nations may bring any dispute, or any situation of the nature referred to in Article 34, to the attention of the Security Council or of the General Assembly.

2. A state which is not a Member of the United Nations may bring to the attention of the Security Council or of the General Assembly any dispute to which it is a party if it accepts in advance, for the purposes of the dispute, the obligations of pacific settlement provided in the present Charter. . . .

Article 36

1. The Security Council may, at any stage of a dispute . . . recommend appropriate procedures or methods of adjustment. . . .

3. In making recommendations under this Article the Security Council should also take into consideration that legal disputes should as a general rule be referred by the parties to the International Court of Justice . . .

CHAPTER VII • Action with Respect to Threats to the Peace, Breaches of the Peace, and Acts of Aggression

Article 39

The Security Council shall determine the existence of any threat to the peace, breach of the peace, or act of aggression and shall make recommendations, or decide what measures shall be taken in accordance with Articles 41 and 42, to maintain or restore international peace and security.

Article 40

In order to prevent an aggravation of the situation, the Security Council may, before making the recommendations or deciding upon the measures provided for in Article 39, call upon the parties concerned to comply with such provisional measures as it deems necessary or desirable. Such provisional measures shall be without prejudice to the rights, claims, or position of the parties concerned. The Security Council shall duly take account of failure to comply with such provisional measures.

Article 41

The Security Council may decide what measures not involving the use of armed force are to be employed to give effect to its decisions, and it may call upon the Members of the United Nations to apply such measures. These may include complete or partial interruption of economic relations and of rail, sea, air, postal, telegraphic, radio, and other means of communication, and the severance of diplomatic relations.

Article 42

Should the Security Council consider that measures provided for in Article 41 would be inadequate or have proved to be inadequate, it may take such action by air, sea, or land forces as may be necessary to maintain or restore international peace and security. Such action may include demonstrations, blockade, and other operations by air, sea, or land forces of Members of the United Nations.

Article 43

1. All Members of the United Nations, in order to contribute to the maintenance of international peace and security, undertake to make available to the Security Council, on its call and in accordance with a special agreement or agreements, armed forces, assistance, and facilities, including rights of passage, necessary for the purpose of maintaining international peace and security.

2. Such agreement or agreements shall govern the numbers and types of forces, their degree of readiness and general location, and the nature of the facilities and assistance to be provided.

3. The agreement or agreements shall be negotiated as soon as possible on the initiative of the Security Council. They shall be concluded between the Security Council and Members or between the Security Council and groups of Members and shall be subject to ratification by the signatory states in accordance with their respective constitutional processes.

Article 44

When the Security Council has decided to use force, it shall, before calling upon a Member not represented on it to provide armed forces in fulfillment of the obligations assumed under Article 43, invite that Member, if the Member so desires, to participate in the decisions of the Security Council concerning the employment of contingents of that Member's armed forces.

Article 45

In order to enable the United Nations to take urgent military measures, Members shall hold immediately available national air-force contingents for combined international enforcement action. The strength and degree of readiness of these contingents and plans for their combined action shall be determined, within the limits laid down in the special agreement or agreements referred to in Article 43, by the Security Council with the assistance of the Military Staff Committee.

Article 46

Plans for the application of armed force shall be made by the Security Council with the assistance of the Military Staff Committee.

Article 47

1. There shall be established a Military Staff Committee to advise and assist the Security Council on all questions relating to the Security Council's military requirements for the maintenance of international peace and security, the employment and command of forces placed at its disposal, the regulation of armaments, and possible disarmament.

2. The Military Staff Committee shall consist of the Chiefs of Staff of the permanent members of the Security Council or their representatives. Any Member of the United Nations not permanently represented on the Committee shall be invited by the Committee to be associated with it when the efficient discharge of the Committee's responsibilities requires the participation of that Member in its work.

3. The Military Staff Committee shall be responsible under the Security Council for the strategic direction of any armed forces placed at the disposal of the Security Council. Questions relating to the command of such forces shall be worked out subsequently.

4. The Military Staff Committee, with the authorization of the Security Council and after consultation with appropriate regional agencies, may establish regional subcommittees.

Article 48

1. The action required to carry out the decisions of the Security Council for the maintenance of international peace and security shall be taken by all the Members of the United Nations or by some of them, as the Security Council may determine. . . .

Article 51

Nothing in the present Charter shall impair the inherent right of individual or collective self-defense if an armed attack occurs against a Member of the United Nations, until the Security Council has taken measures necessary to maintain international peace and security. Measures taken by Members in the exercise of this right of self-defense shall be immediately reported to the Security Council and shall not in any way affect the authority and responsibility of the Security Council under the present Charter to take at any time such action as it deems necessary in order to maintain or restore international peace and security.

CHAPTER VIII • **Regional Arrangements**

Article 52

1. Nothing in the present Charter precludes the existence of regional arrangements or agencies for dealing with such matters relating to the maintenance of international peace and security as are appropriate for regional action, provided that such arrangements or agencies and their activities are consistent with the Purposes and Principles of the United Nations.

2. The Members of the United Nations entering into such arrangements or constituting such agencies shall make every effort to achieve pacific settlement of local disputes through such regional arrangements or by such regional agencies before referring them to the Security Council....

Article 53

1. The Security Council shall, where appropriate, utilize such regional arrangements or agencies for enforcement action under its authority....

Article 54

The Security Council shall at all times be kept fully informed of activities undertaken or in contemplation under regional arrangements or by regional agencies for the maintenance of international peace and security.

CHAPTER IX • International Economic and Social Co-operation

Article 55

With a view to the creation of conditions of stability and well-being which are necessary for peaceful and friendly relations among nations based on respect for the principle of equal rights and self-determination of peoples, the United Nations shall promote:

a. higher standards of living, full employment, and conditions of economic and social progress and development;

b. solutions of international economic, social, health, and related problems; and international cultural and educational co-operation; and

c. universal respect for, and observance of, human rights and fundamental freedoms for all without distinction as to race, sex, language, or religion. . . .

Article 58

The Organization shall make recommendations for the coordination of the policies and activities of the specialized agencies. . . .

Article 60

Responsibility for the discharge of the functions of the Organization set forth in this Chapter shall be vested in the General Assembly and, under the authority of the General Assembly, in the Economic and Social Council. . . .

CHAPTER X • The Economic and Social Council

COMPOSITION

Article 61

1. The Economic and Social Council shall consist of eighteen Members of the United Nations elected by the General Assembly.

2. . . . six members of the Economic and Social Council shall be elected each year for a term of three years. A retiring member shall be eligible for immediate re-election. . . .

4. Each member of the Economic and Social Council shall have one representative.

FUNCTIONS AND POWERS

Article 62

1. The Economic and Social Council may make or initiate studies and reports with respect to international economic, social, cultural, educational, health, and related matters and may make recommendations with respect to any such matters to the General Assembly, to the Members of the United Nations, and to the specialized agencies concerned.

2. It may make recommendations for the purpose of promoting respect for, and observance of, human rights and fundamental freedoms for all.

3. It may prepare draft conventions for submission to the General Assembly, with respect to matters falling within its competence.

4. It may call, in accordance with the rules prescribed by the United Nations, international conferences on matters falling within its competence. . . .

Article 64

1. The Economic and Social Council may take appropriate steps to obtain regular reports from the specialized agencies. It may make arrangements with the Members of the United Nations and with the specialized agencies to obtain reports on the steps taken to give effect to its own recommendations and to recommendations on matters falling within its competence made by the General Assembly.

2. It may communicate its observations on these reports to the General Assembly.

Article 65

The Economic and Social Council may furnish information to the Security Council and shall assist the Security Council upon its request. . . .

VOTING

Article 67

1. Each member of the Economic and Social Council shall have one vote.

2. Decisions of the Economic and Social Council shall be made by a majority of the members present and voting.

PROCEDURE

Article 68

The Economic and Social Council shall set up commissions in economic and social fields and for the promotion of human rights, and such other commissions as may be required for the performance of its functions.

Article 69

The Economic and Social Council shall invite any Member of the United Nations to participate, without vote, in its deliberations on any matter of particular concern to that Member. . . .

CHAPTER XI • Declaration Regarding Non-Self-governing Territories

Article 73

Members of the United Nations which have or assume responsibilities for the administration of territories whose peoples have not yet attained a full measure of self-government recognize the principle that the interests of the inhabitants of these territories are paramount, and accept as a sacred trust the obligation to promote to the utmost, within the system of international peace and security established by the present Charter, the well-being of the inhabitants of these territories, and, to this end:

a. to ensure, with due respect for the culture of the peoples concerned, their political, economic, social, and educational advancement, their just treatment, and their protection against abuses;

b. to develop self-government, to take due account of the political aspirations of the peoples, and to assist them in the progressive development of their free political institutions, according to the particular circumstances of each territory and its peoples and their varying stages of advancement;

c. to further international peace and security;

d. to promote constructive measures of development, to encourage research, and to co-operate with one another and, when and where appropriate, with specialized international bodies with a view to the practical achievement of the social, economic, and scientific purposes set forth in this Article; and

e. to transmit regularly to the Secretary-General for information purposes, subject to such limitation as security and constitutional considerations may require, statistical and other information of a technical nature relating to economic, social, and educational conditions in the territories for which they are respectively responsible other than those territories to which Chapters XII and XIII apply.

Article 74

Members of the United Nations also agree that their policy in respect of the territories to which this Chapter applics, no less than in respect of their metropolitan areas, must be based on the general principle of good-neighborliness, due account being taken of the interests and well-being of the rest of the world, in social, economic, and commercial matters.

CHAPTER XII • International Trusteeship System

Article 75

The United Nations shall establish under its authority an international trusteeship system for the administration and supervision of such territories as may be placed thereunder by subsequent individual agreements. These territories are hereinafter referred to as trust territories.

Article 76

The basic objectives of the trusteeship system, in accordance with the Purposes of the United Nations laid down in Article 1 of the present Charter, shall be:

a. to further international peace and security;

b. to promote the political, economic, social, and educational advancement of the inhabitants of the trust territories, and their progressive development toward self-government or independence as may be appropriate to the particular circumstances of each territory and its peoples and the freely expressed wishes of the peoples concerned, and as may be provided by the terms of each trusteeship agreement;

c. to encourage respect for human rights and for fundamental freedoms for all without distinction as to race, sex, language, or religion, and to encourage recognition of the interdependence of the peoples of the world; and

d. to ensure equal treatment in social, economic, and commercial matters for all Members of the United Nations and their nationals, and also equal treatment for the latter in the administration of justice, without prejudice to the attainment of the foregoing objectives. . . .

Article 77

1. The trusteeship system shall apply to such territories in the following categories as may be placed thereunder by means of trusteeship agreements:

    a. territories now held under mandate;

    b. territories which may be detached from enemy states as a result of the Second World War; and

    c. territories voluntarily placed under the system by states responsible for their administration.

2. It will be a matter for subsequent agreement as to which territories in the foregoing categories will be brought under the trusteeship system and upon what terms. . . .

Article 81

The trusteeship agreement shall in each case include the terms under which the trust territory will be administered and designate the authority which will exercise the administration of the trust territory. Such authority, hereinafter called the administering authority, may be one or more states or the Organization itself.

Article 82

There may be designated, in any trusteeship agreement, a strategic area or areas which may include part or all of the trust territory to which the agreement applies, without prejudice to any special agreement or agreements made under Article 43.

Article 83

1. All functions of the United Nations relating to strategic areas, including the approval of the terms of the trusteeship agreements and of their alteration or amendment, shall be exercised by the Security Council.

2. The basic objectives set forth in Article 76 shall be applicable to the people of each strategic area. . . .

Article 84

It shall be the duty of the administering authority to ensure that the trust territory shall play its part in the maintenance of international peace and security. To this end the administering authority may make use of volunteer forces, facilities, and assistance from the trust territory in carrying out the obligations toward the Security Council undertaken in this regard by the administering authority, as well as for local defense and the maintenance of law and order within the trust territory....

CHAPTER XIII • The Trusteeship Council

COMPOSITION

Article 86

1. The Trusteeship Council shall consist of the following Members of the United Nations:

a. those Members administering trust territories:

b. such of those Members mentioned by name in Article 23 as are not administering trust territories; and

c. as many other Members elected for three-year terms by the General Assembly as may be necessary to ensure that the total number of members of the Trusteeship Council is equally divided between those Members of the United Nations which administer trust territories and those which do not.

2. Each member of the Trusteeship Council shall designate one specially qualified person to represent it therein.

FUNCTIONS AND POWERS

Article 87

The General Assembly and, under its authority, the Trusteeship Council, in carrying out their functions, may:

a. consider reports submitted by the administering authority;

b. accept petitions and examine them in consultation with the administering authority;

c. provide for periodic visits to the respective trust territories at times agreed upon with the administering authority; and

d. take these and other actions in conformity with the terms of the trusteeship agreements.

Article 88

The Trusteeship Council shall formulate a questionnaire on the political, economic, social, and educational advancement of the inhabitants of each trust territory, and the administering authority for each trust territory within the competence of the General Assembly shall make an annual report to the General Assembly upon the basis of such questionnaire.

VOTING

Article 89

1. Each member of the Trusteeship Council shall have one vote.

2. Decisions of the Trusteeship Council shall be made by a majority of the members present and voting. . . .

CHAPTER XIV • The International Court of Justice

Article 92

The International Court of Justice shall be the principal judicial organ of the United Nations. It shall function in accordance with the annexed Statute, which is based upon the Statute of the Permanent Court of International Justice and forms an integral part of the present Charter.

Article 93

1. All Members of the United Nations are *ipso facto* parties to the Statute of the International Court of Justice.

2. A state which is not a Member of the United Nations may become a party to the Statute of the International Court of Justice on condition to be determined in each case by the General Assembly upon the recommendation of the Security Council.

Article 94

1. Each Member of the United Nations undertakes to comply with the decision of the International Court of Justice in any case to which it is a party.

2. If any party to a case fails to perform the obligations incumbent upon it under a judgment rendered by the Court, the other party may have recourse to the Security Council, which may, if it deems neces-

sary, make recommendations or decide upon measures to be taken to give effect to the judgment. . . .

Article 96

1. The General Assembly or the Security Council may request the International Court of Justice to give an advisory opinion on any legal question.

2. Other organs of the United Nations and specialized agencies, which may at any time be so authorized by the General Assembly, may also request advisory opinions of the Court on legal questions arising within the scope of their activities.

CHAPTER XV • The Secretariat

Article 97

The Secretariat shall comprise a Secretary-General and such staff as the Organization may require. The Secretary-General shall be appointed by the General Assembly upon the recommendation of the Security Council. He shall be the chief administrative officer of the Organization.

Article 98

The Secretary-General shall act in that capacity in all meetings of the General Assembly, of the Security Council, of the Economic and Social Council, and of the Trusteeship Council, and shall perform such other functions as are entrusted to him by these organs. The Secretary-General shall make an annual report to the General Assembly on the work of the Organization.

Article 99

The Secretary-General may bring to the attention of the Security Council any matter which in his opinion may threaten the maintenance of international peace and security.

Article 100

1. In the performance of their duties the Secretary-General and the staff shall not seek or receive instructions from any government or from any other authority external to the Organization. They shall refrain from any action which might reflect on their position as international officials responsible only to the Organization.

2. Each Member of the United Nations undertakes to respect the exclusively international character of the responsibilities of the Secretary-General and the staff and not to seek to influence them in the discharge of their responsibilities.

Article 101

1. The staff shall be appointed by the Secretary-General under regulations established by the General Assembly.

2. Appropriate staffs shall be permanently assigned to the Economic and Social Council, the Trusteeship Council, and, as required, to other organs of the United Nations. These staffs shall form a part of the Secretariat.

3. The paramount consideration in the employment of the staff and in the determination of the conditions of service shall be the necessity of securing the highest standards of efficiency, competence, and integrity. Due regard shall be paid to the importance of recruiting the staff on as wide a geographical basis as possible.

CHAPTER XVI • Miscellaneous Provisions

Article 102

1. Every treaty and every international agreement entered into by any Member of the United Nations after the present Charter comes into force shall as soon as possible be registered with the Secretariat and published by it. . . .

Article 103

In the event of a conflict between the obligations of the Members of the United Nations under the present Charter and their obligations under any other international agreement, their obligations under the present Charter shall prevail.

Article 104

The Organization shall enjoy in the territory of each of its Members such legal capacity as may be necessary for the exercise of its functions and the fulfillment of its purposes.

Article 105

1. The Organization shall enjoy in the territory of each of its Members such privileges and immunities as are necessary for the fulfillment of its purposes.

2. Representatives of the Members of the United Nations and officials of the Organization shall similarly enjoy such privileges and immunities as are necessary for the independent exercise of their functions in connection with the Organization. . . .

CHAPTER XVIII • Amendments

Article 108

Amendments to the present Charter shall come into force for all Members of the United Nations when they have been adopted by a vote of two-thirds of the members of the General Assembly and ratified in accordance with their respective constitutional processes by two-thirds of the Members of the United Nations, including all the permanent members of the Security Council.

Article 109

1. A General Conference of the Members of the United Nations for the purpose of reviewing the present Charter may be held at a date and place to be fixed by a two-thirds vote of the members of the General Assembly and by a vote of any seven members of the Security Council. Each Member of the United Nations shall have one vote in the conference.

2. Any alteration of the present Charter recommended by a two-thirds vote of the conference shall take effect when ratified in accordance with their respective constitutional processes by two-thirds of the Members of the United Nations including all the permanent members of the Security Council.

3. If such a conference has not been held before the tenth annual session of the General Assembly following the coming into force of the present Charter, the proposal to call such a conference shall be placed on the agenda of that session of the General Assembly, and the conference shall be held if so decided by a majority vote of the members of the General Assembly and by a vote of any seven members of the Security Council.

CHAPTER XIX • Ratification and Signature

Article 110

1. The present Charter shall be ratified by the signatory states in accordance with their respective constitutional processes.

2. The ratifications shall be deposited with the Government of the United States of America, which shall notify all the signatory states of each deposit as well as the Secretary-General of the Organization when he has been appointed.

3. The present Charter shall come into force upon the deposit of ratifications by the Republic of China, France, the Union of Soviet Socialist Republics, the United Kingdom of Great Britain and Northern Ireland, and the United States of America, and by a majority of the other signatory states. A protocol of the ratifications deposited shall thereupon be drawn up by the Government of the United States of America which shall communicate copies thereof to all the signatory states.

4. The states signatory to the present Charter which ratify it after it has come into force will become original Members of the United Nations on the date of the deposit of their respective ratifications.

Article 111

The present Charter, of which the Chinese, French, Russian, English, and Spanish texts are equally authentic, shall remain deposited in the archives of the Government of the United States of America. Duly certified copies thereof shall be transmitted by that Government to the Governments of the other signatory states.

IN FAITH WHEREOF the representatives of the Governments of the United Nations have signed the present Charter.

DONE at the city of San Francisco the twenty-sixth day of June, one thousand nine hundred and forty-five.

Proclamation Granting the Philippines Their Independence

"... I, Harry S. Truman, President of the United States ...
hereby recognize the independence of the Philippines. ..."

On July 4, 1946—as Congress had promised in the Tydings-McDuffie Act of 1934—the United States gave the Philippine Islands their independence. This was an event of great historical significance. It was the first time in modern history that a great world power had voluntarily granted independence to its most valuable colony.

During World War II, the Filipinos had fought bravely and faithfully on the side of the United States. It was fitting, therefore, that with the ending of the war, the United States should keep its promise and that the Republic of the Philippines should be one of the first new nations to appear on the world scene.

July 4, 1946

INDEPENDENCE OF THE PHILIPPINES

By the President of the United States of America

A PROCLAMATION

WHEREAS the United States of America by the Treaty of Peace with Spain of December 10, 1898, commonly known as the Treaty of Paris, and by the Treaty with Spain of November 7, 1900, did acquire sovereignty over the Philippines, and by the Convention of

January 2, 1930, with Great Britain did delimit [fix] the boundary between the Philippine Archipelago and the State of North Borneo; and

WHEREAS the United States of America has consistently and faithfully during the past forty-eight years exercised jurisdiction and control over the Philippines and its people; and

WHEREAS it has been the repeated declaration of the legislative and executive branches of the Government of the United States of America that full independence would be granted the Philippines as soon as the people of the Philippines were prepared to assume this obligation; and

WHEREAS the people of the Philippines have clearly demonstrated their capacity for self-government; and

WHEREAS the act of Congress approved March 24, 1934, known as the Philippine Independence Act, directed that, on the fourth day of July immediately following a ten-year transitional period leading to the independence of the Philippines, the President of the United States of America should by proclamation withdraw and surrender all rights of possession, supervision, jurisdiction, control, or sovereignty of the United States of America in and over the territory and people of the Philippines, except certain reservations therein or thereafter authorized to be made, and, on behalf of the United States of America, should recognize the independence of the Philippines:

Now, THEREFORE, I, HARRY S. TRUMAN, President of the United States of America, acting under and by virtue of the authority vested in me by the aforesaid act of Congress, do proclaim that, in accord with and subject to the reservations provided for in the applicable statutes of the United States.

The United States of America hereby withdraws and surrenders all rights of possession, supervision, jurisdiction, control, or sovereignty now existing and exercised by the United States of America in and over the territory and people of the Philippines; and,

In behalf of the United States of America, I do hereby recognize the independence of the Philippines as a separate and self-governing nation and acknowledge the authority and control . . . of the government instituted by the people thereof and the constitution now in force.

IN WITNESS WHEREOF, I have hereunto set my hand and caused the seal of the United States of America to be affixed.

DONE in the City of Washington this fourth day of July in the year of our Lord, nineteen hundred and forty-six, and of the Independence of the United States of America the one hundred and seventy-first.

The Truman Doctrine

"I believe that we must assist free peoples to work out their own destinies in their own way."

Faced with the threat of Communist aggression after World War II, the United States began to formulate a policy of containment. Designed to contain—or restrict—Soviet expansion and to check the spread of Communism, this policy was first applied to Greece and Turkey.

In 1947, Greek Communists, supported by the U.S.S.R., were attempting to seize control of the Greek government. At the same time the Soviets were putting political pressure on Turkey to surrender the Dardanelles and the Bosporus, the straits between European and Asiatic Turkey.

On March 12, President Truman, deeply concerned about the threatening situation, announced what has come to be called the Truman Doctrine. At the same time, he asked Congress for authority to help Greece and Turkey to resist the pressure which threatened the independence of the two countries. Congress responded with an initial appropriation of $400,000,000 for economic and military assistance.

March 12, 1947

The gravity of the situation which confronts the world today necessitates my appearance before a joint session of the Congress.

The foreign policy and the national security of this country are involved.

One aspect of the present situation, which I wish to present to you at this time for your consideration and decision, concerns Greece and Turkey.

The United States has received from the Greek government an urgent appeal for financial and economic assistance. Preliminary reports from the American Economic Mission now in Greece and reports from the American Ambassador in Greece corroborate the statement of the Greek government that assistance is imperative if Greece is to survive as a free nation. . . .

The very existence of the Greek state is today threatened by the terrorist activities of several thousand armed men, led by Communists, who defy the government's authority at a number of points, particularly along the northern boundaries. A commission appointed by the United Nations Security Council is at present investigating disturbed conditions in Northern Greece and alleged border violations along the frontiers between Greece on the one hand and Albania, Bulgaria, and Yugoslavia on the other.

Meanwhile, the Greek government is unable to cope with the situation. The Greek Army is small and poorly equipped. It needs supplies and equipment if it is to restore the authority to the government throughout Greek territory.

Greece must have assistance if it is to become a self-supporting and self-respecting democracy. The United States must supply this assistance. We have already extended to Greece certain types of relief and economic aid, but these are inadequate. There is no other country to which democratic Greece can turn. No other nation is willing and able to provide the necessary support for a democratic Greek government.

The British government, which has been helping Greece, can give no further financial or economic aid after March 31. Great Britain finds itself under the necessity of reducing or liquidating its commitments in several parts of the world, including Greece.

We have considered how the United Nations might assist in this crisis. But the situation is an urgent one requiring immediate action, and the United Nations and its related organizations are not in a position to extend help of the kind that is required.

It is important to note that the Greek government has asked for our aid in utilizing effectively the financial and other assistance we may give to Greece, and in improving its public administration. . . .

Greece's neighbor, Turkey, also deserves our attention.

The future of Turkey as an independent and economically sound state is clearly no less important to the freedom-loving peoples of the world than the future of Greece. The circumstances in which Turkey finds itself today are considerably different from those of Greece. Turkey has been spared the disasters that have beset Greece. And during the war the United States and Great Britain furnished Turkey with material aid.

Nevertheless, Turkey now needs our support.

Since the war, Turkey has sought financial assistance from Great Britain and the United States for the purpose of effecting the modernization necessary for the maintenance of its national integrity.

That integrity is essential to the preservation of order in the Middle East.

The British government has informed us that, owing to its own difficulties, it can no longer extend financial or economic aid to Turkey.

As in the case of Greece, if Turkey is to have the assistance it needs, the United States must supply it. We are the only country able to provide that help.

I am fully aware of the broad implications involved if the United States extends assistance to Greece and Turkey, and I shall discuss these implications with you at this time.

One of the primary objectives of the foreign policy of the United States is the creation of conditions in which we and other nations will be able to work out a way of life free from coercion. This was a fundamental issue in the war with Germany and Japan. Our victory was won over countries which sought to impose their will, and their way of life, upon other nations.

To ensure the peaceful development of nations, free from coercion, the United States has taken a leading part in establishing the United Nations. The United Nations is designed to make possible lasting freedom and independence for all its members. We shall not realize our objectives, however, unless we are willing to help free peoples to maintain their free institutions and their national integrity against aggressive movements that seek to impose on them totalitarian regimes.° This is no more than a frank recognition that totalitarian

° **totalitarian regimes:** governments that suppress the freedom of individual citizens and use total national resources to further the plans of a dictator or a small ruling group.

regimes imposed on free peoples, by direct or indirect aggression, undermine the foundations of international peace and hence the security of the United States.

The peoples of a number of countries of the world have recently had totalitarian regimes forced upon them against their will. The government of the United States has made frequent protests against coercion and intimidation in violation of the Yalta agreement,° in Poland, Rumania, and Bulgaria. I must also state that in a number of other countries there have been similar developments.

At the present moment in world history nearly every nation must choose between alternative ways of life. The choice is too often not a free one.

One way of life is based upon the will of the majority, and is distinguished by free institutions, representative government, free elections, guaranties of individual liberty, freedom of speech and religion, and freedom from political oppression.

The second way of life is based upon the will of a minority forcibly imposed upon the majority. It relies upon terror and oppression, a controlled press and radio, fixed elections, and the suppression of personal freedoms.

I believe that it must be the policy of the United States to support free peoples who are resisting attempted subjugation by armed minorities or by outside pressures.

I believe that we must assist free peoples to work out their own destinies in their own way.

I believe that our help should be primarily through economic and financial aid which is essential to economic stability and orderly political processes.

The world is not static, and the status quo is not sacred. But we cannot allow changes in the status quo in violation of the charter of the United Nations by such methods as coercion, or by such subterfuges as political infiltration.° In helping free and independent nations to maintain their freedom, the United States will be giving effect to the principles of the charter of the United Nations.

It is necessary only to glance at a map to realize that the survival

° **Yalta agreement:** At a Summit Conference in Yalta in the Russian Crimea in February 1945, President Roosevelt, Prime Minister Churchill, and Premier Stalin agreed, among other things, on free elections throughout Europe.

° **political infiltration:** quiet, unobtrusive joining of political parties, by Communists—singly or in small groups—for the purpose of gaining control.

and integrity of the Greek nation are of grave importance in a much wider situation. If Greece should fall under the control of an armed minority, the effect upon its neighbor, Turkey, would be immediate and serious. Confusion and disorder might well spread throughout the entire Middle East.

Moreover, the disappearance of Greece as an independent state would have a profound effect upon those countries in Europe whose peoples are struggling against great difficulties to maintain their freedoms and their independence while they repair the damages of war.

It would be an unspeakable tragedy if these countries, which have struggled so long against overwhelming odds, should lose that victory for which they sacrificed so much. Collapse of free institutions and loss of independence would be disastrous not only for them but for the world. Discouragement and possibly failure would quickly be the lot of neighboring peoples striving to maintain their freedom and independence.

Should we fail to aid Greece and Turkey in this fateful hour, the effect will be far-reaching to the West as well as to the East. We must take immediate and resolute action.

I therefore ask the Congress to provide authority for assistance to Greece and Turkey in the amount of $400,000,000 for the period ending June 30, 1948. . . .

In addition to funds, I ask the Congress to authorize the detail [assignment] of American civilian and military personnel to Greece and Turkey, at the request of those countries, to assist in the tasks of reconstruction, and for the purpose of supervising the use of such financial and material assistance as may be furnished. I recommend that authority also be provided for the instruction and training of selected Greek and Turkish personnel.

Finally, I ask that the Congress provide authority which will permit the speediest and most effective use, in terms of needed commodities, supplies, and equipment, of such funds as may be authorized. . . .

This is a serious course upon which we embark.

I would not recommend it except that the alternative is much more serious.

The United States contributed $341,000,000,000 toward winning World War II. This is an investment in world freedom and world peace.

The assistance that I am recommending for Greece and Turkey amounts to little more than one-tenth of one per cent of this investment. It is only common sense that we should safeguard this investment and make sure that it was not in vain.

The seeds of totalitarian regimes are nurtured by misery and want. They spread and grow in the evil soil of poverty and strife. They reach their full growth when the hope of a people for a better life has died.

We must keep that hope alive.

The free peoples of the world look to us for support in maintaining their freedoms.

If we falter in our leadership, we may endanger the peace of the world—and we shall surely endanger the welfare of our own Nation.

Great responsibilities have been placed upon us by the swift movement of events.

I am confident that the Congress will face these responsibilities squarely.

George C. Marshall's Address at Harvard University

"Our policy is directed ... against hunger, poverty, desperation, and chaos."

On the afternoon of June 5, 1947, Secretary of State George C. Marshall walked up to a rostrum in the famous Yard of Harvard University and, facing an audience of Harvard alumni and guests gathered before him in the open air, began to read from a prepared address. "I need not tell you, gentlemen," he began, "that the world situation is very serious." Speaking carefully and deliberately, he went on to review the desperate situation in Europe, and concluded his brief address with a proposal designed to help Europeans to recover from the ravages of the most terrible war in history.

In 1948, Congress, working closely with the leaders of Europe, adopted the European Recovery Plan, popularly known as the Marshall Plan. It was immediately hailed as one of the most significant demonstrations of international co-operation in peacetime history. The secret of its success lay in the basic conception that American aid would be meaningful only to the extent that it helped Europeans to mobilize their own resources of initiative and creative energy.

June 5, 1947

I need not tell you, gentlemen, that the world situation is very serious. That must be apparent to all intelligent people. I think one difficulty is that the problem is one of such enormous complexity that the very mass of facts presented to the public by press and radio make it exceedingly difficult for the man in the street to reach a clear appraisement of the situation. Furthermore, the people of this country are distant from the troubled areas of the earth and it is hard for them to comprehend the plight and consequent reactions of the long-suffering peoples, and the effect of those reactions on their governments in connection with our efforts to promote peace in the world.

In considering the requirements for the rehabilitation of Europe, the physical loss of life, the visible destruction of cities, factories, mines, and railroads was correctly estimated, but it has become obvious during recent months that this visible destruction was probably less serious than the dislocation of the entire fabric of European economy. For the past ten years conditions have been highly abnormal.

The feverish preparation for war and the more feverish maintenance of the war effort engulfed all aspects of national economies. Machinery has fallen into disrepair or is entirely obsolete. Under the arbitrary and destructive Nazi rule, virtually every possible enterprise was geared into the German war machine. Long-standing commercial ties, private institutions, banks, insurance companies, and shipping companies disappeared through loss of capital, absorption through nationalization, or by simple destruction.

In many countries, confidence in the local currency has been severely shaken. The breakdown of the business structure of Europe during the war was complete. Recovery has been seriously retarded by the fact that two years after the close of hostilities a peace settlement with Germany and Austria has not been agreed upon. But even given a more prompt solution of these difficult problems, the rehabilitation of the economic structure of Europe quite evidently will require a much longer time and greater effort than had been foreseen.

There is a phase of this matter which is both interesting and serious. The farmer has always produced the foodstuffs to exchange with the city dweller for the other necessities of life. This division of labor is the basis of modern civilization. At the present time it is threatened with breakdown. The town and city industries are not producing adequate goods to exchange with the food-producing farmer. Raw materials and fuel are in short supply. Machinery is lacking or worn out.

The farmer or the peasant cannot find the goods for sale which he desires to purchase. So the sale of his farm produce for money which he cannot use seems to him an unprofitable transaction. He, therefore, has withdrawn many fields from crop cultivation and is using them for grazing. He feeds more grain to stock and finds for himself and his family an ample supply of food, however short he may be on clothing and the other ordinary gadgets of civilization. Meanwhile, people in the cities are short of food and fuel. So the governments are forced to use their foreign money and credits to procure these necessities abroad. This process exhausts funds which are urgently needed for reconstruction. Thus a very serious situation is rapidly developing which bodes no good for the world. The modern system of the division of labor upon which the exchange of products is based is in danger of breaking down.

The truth of the matter is that Europe's requirements for the next three or four years of foreign food and other essential products—principally from America—are so much greater than her present ability to pay that she must have substantial additional help, or face economic, social, and political deterioration of a very grave character.

The remedy lies in breaking the vicious circle and restoring the confidence of the European people in the economic future of their own countries and of Europe as a whole. The manufacturer and the farmer throughout wide areas must be able and willing to exchange their products for currencies, the continuing value of which is not open to question.

Aside from the demoralizing effect on the world at large and the possibilities of disturbances arising as a result of the desperation of the people concerned, the consequences to the economy of the United States should be apparent to all. It is logical that the United States should do whatever it is able to do to assist in the return of normal economic health in the world, without which there can be no political stability and no assured peace.

Our policy is directed not against any country or doctrine but against hunger, poverty, desperation, and chaos. Its purpose should be the revival of a working economy in the world so as to permit the emergence of political and social conditions in which free institutions can exist. Such assistance, I am convinced, must not be on a piecemeal basis as various crises develop. Any assistance that this Government may render in the future should provide a cure rather than a mere palliative.

Any government that is willing to assist in the task of recovery will find full co-operation, I am sure, on the part of the United States government. Any government which maneuvers to block the recovery of other countries cannot expect help from us. Furthermore, governments, political parties, or groups which seek to perpetuate human misery in order to profit therefrom, politically or otherwise, will encounter the opposition of the United States.

It is already evident that, before the United States Government can proceed much further in its effort to alleviate the situation and help start the European world on its way to recovery, there must be some agreement among the countries of Europe as to the requirements of the situation and the part those countries themselves will take in order to give proper effect to whatever action might be undertaken by this government. It would be neither fitting nor efficacious for this government to undertake to draw up unilaterally a program designed to place Europe on its feet economically. This is the business of the Europeans. The initiative, I think, must come from Europe. The role of this country should consist of friendly aid in the drafting of a European program, and of later support of such a program so far as it may be practical for us to do so. The program should be a joint one, agreed to by a number, if not all European nations.

An essential part of any successful action on the part of the United

States is an understanding on the part of the people of America of the character of the problem and the remedies to be applied. Political passion and prejudice should have no part. With foresight and a willingness on the part of our people to face up to the vast responsibility which history has clearly placed upon our country, the difficulties I have outlined can and will be overcome.

Earl Warren's Opinion in Brown v. Board of Education of Topeka

"... in the field of public education the doctrine of 'separate but equal' has no place."

On May 17, 1954, in the case of Brown v. Board of Education of Topeka, the United States Supreme Court handed down one of the most momentous decisions in its long history. Reversing an earlier decision (Plessy v. Ferguson, 1896), which had declared that "separate but equal" facilities were constitutional, the Supreme Court ruled that segregated school systems violated the Fourteenth Amendment. Several months later, the Court placed upon local school authorities the responsibility for developing plans for the gradual integration of segregated schools. The Supreme Court also instructed the federal district courts to require the local school authorities to develop and carry out plans for integration "with all deliberate speed." The opinion, written by Chief Justice Warren, was unanimous.

May 17, 1954

These cases come to us from the states of Kansas, South Carolina, Virginia, and Delaware. They are premised on different facts and different local conditions, but a common legal question justifies their consideration together in this consolidated opinion.

In each of the cases, minors of the Negro race, through their legal representatives, seek the aid of the courts in obtaining admission to the public schools of their community on a nonsegregated basis. In each instance, they had been denied admission to schools attended by white children under laws requiring or permitting segregation according to race. This segregation was alleged to deprive the plaintiffs of the equal protection of the laws under the Fourteenth Amendment. In each of the cases other than the Delaware case, a three-judge Federal District Court denied relief to the plaintiffs on the so-called "separate but equal" doctrine announced by this Court in *Plessy* v. *Ferguson.* . . . Under that doctrine, equality of treatment is accorded when the races are provided substantially equal facilities, even though these facilities be separate. In the Delaware case, the Supreme Court of Delaware adhered to that doctrine, but ordered that the plaintiffs be admitted to the white schools because of their superiority to the Negro schools.

The plaintiffs contend that segregated public schools are not "equal" and cannot be made "equal" and that, hence, they are deprived of the equal protection of the laws. Because of the obvious importance of the question presented, the Court took jurisdiction. Argument was heard in the 1952 term, and reargument was heard this term on certain questions propounded by the Court. Reargument was largely devoted to the circumstances surrounding the adoption of the Fourteenth Amendment in 1868. It covered exhaustively consideration of the Amendment in Congress, ratification by the states, then existing practices in racial segregation, and the views of proponents and opponents of the Amendment. This discussion and our own investigation convince us that, although these sources cast some light, it is not enough to resolve the problem with which we are faced. At best, they are inconclusive. The most avid proponents of the postwar

Amendments ° undoubtedly intended them to remove all legal distinctions among "all persons born or naturalized in the United States." Their opponents, just as certainly, were antagonistic to both the letter and the spirit of the Amendments and wished them to have the most limited effect. What others in Congress and the state legislatures had in mind cannot be determined with any degree of certainty.

An additional reason for the inconclusive nature of the Amendment's history, with respect to segregated schools, is the status of public education at that time. In the South, the movement toward free common schools, supported by general taxation, had not yet taken hold. Education of white children was largely in the hands of private groups. Education of Negroes was almost nonexistent, and practically all of the race were illiterate. In fact, any education of Negroes was forbidden by law in some states. Today, in contrast, many Negroes have achieved outstanding success in the arts and sciences as well as in the business and professional world. It is true that public school education ... had advanced further in the North, but the effect of the Amendment on Northern states was generally ignored in the Congressional debates. Even in the North, the conditions of public education did not approximate those existing today. The curriculum was usually rudimentary; ungraded schools were common in rural areas; the school term was but three months a year in many states; and compulsory school attendance was virtually unknown. As a consequence, it is not surprising that there should be so little in the history of the Fourteenth Amendment relating to its intended effect on public education.

In the first cases in this Court construing the Fourteenth Amendment, decided shortly after its adoption, the Court interpreted it as proscribing all state-imposed discriminations against the Negro race. The doctrine of "separate but equal" did not make its appearance in this Court until 1896 in the case of *Plessy* v. *Ferguson, supra,* involving not education but transportation. American courts have since labored with the doctrine for over half a century. In this Court, there have been six cases involving the "separate but equal" doctrine in the field of public education. ... In more recent cases, all on the graduate school level, inequality was found in that specific benefits enjoyed by

° *postwar Amendments:* Amendments Thirteen, Fourteen, and Fifteen to the United States Constitution.

white students were denied to Negro students of the same educational qualifications.... In none of these cases was it necessary to re-examine the doctrine to grant relief to the Negro plaintiff....

In the instant cases, that question is directly presented. Here... there are findings below ° that the Negro and white schools involved have been equalized, or are being equalized, with respect to buildings, curricula, qualifications and salaries of teachers, and other "tangible" factors. Our decision, therefore, cannot turn on merely a comparison of these tangible factors in the Negro and white schools involved in each of the cases. We must look instead to the effect of segregation itself on public education.

In approaching this problem, we cannot turn the clock back to 1868, when the Amendment was adopted, or even to 1896, when *Plessy* v. *Ferguson* was written. We must consider public education in the light of its full development and its present place in American life throughout the nation. Only in this way can it be determined if segregation in public schools deprives these plaintiffs of the equal protection of the laws.

Today, education is perhaps the most important function of state and local governments. Compulsory school attendance laws and the great expenditures for education both demonstrate our recognition of the importance of education to our democratic society. It is required in the performance of our most basic public responsibilities, even service in the armed forces. It is the very foundation of good citizenship. Today, it is a principal instrument in awakening the child to cultural values, in preparing him for later professional training, and in helping him to adjust normally to his environment. In these days, it is doubtful that any child may reasonably be expected to succeed in life if he is denied the opportunity of an education. Such an opportunity, where the state has undertaken to provide it, is a right which must be made available to all on equal terms.

We come then to the question presented: Does segregation of children in public schools solely on the basis of race, even though the physical facilities and other "tangible" factors may be equal, deprive the children of the minority group of equal educational opportunities? We believe that it does.

In *Sweatt* v. *Painter, supra* ... in finding that a segregated law school for Negroes could not provide them equal educational oppor-

° *below*: refers to lower courts.

tunities, this Court relied in large part on "those qualities which are incapable of objective measurement but which make for greatness in a law school." In *McLaurin* v. *Oklahoma State Regents, supra,* the Court, in requiring that a Negro admitted to a white graduate school be treated like all other students, again resorted to intangible considerations: "... his ability to study, to engage in discussions and exchange views with other students, and, in general, to learn his profession." Such considerations apply with added force to children in grade and high schools. To separate them from others of similar age and qualifications solely because of their race generates a feeling of inferiority as to their status in the community that may affect their hearts and minds in a way unlikely ever to be undone. The effect of this separation on their educational opportunities was well stated by a finding in the Kansas case by a court which nevertheless felt compelled to rule against the Negro plaintiffs:

> "Segregation of white and colored children in public schools has a detrimental effect upon the colored children. The impact is greater when it has the sanction of the law; for the policy of separating the races is usually interpreted as denoting the inferiority of the Negro group. . . . A sense of inferiority affects the motivation of a child to learn. Segregation with the sanction of law, therefore, has a tendency to [retard] the educational and mental development of Negro children and to deprive them of some of the benefits they would receive in a racial[ly] integrated school system."

Whatever may have been the extent of psychological knowledge at the time of *Plessy* v. *Ferguson,* this finding is amply supported by modern authority. Any language in *Plessy* v. *Ferguson* contrary to this finding is rejected.

We conclude that in the field of public education the doctrine of "separate but equal" has no place. Separate educational facilities are inherently unequal. Therefore, we hold that the plaintiffs and others similarly situated for whom the actions have been brought are, by reason of the segregation complained of, deprived of the equal protection of the laws guaranteed by the Fourteenth Amendment. This disposition makes unnecessary any discussion whether such segregation also violates the Due Process Clause of the Fourteenth Amendment.

Because these are class actions, because of the wide applicability of this decision, and because of the great variety of local conditions, the formulation of decrees in these cases presents problems of considerable complexity. On reargument, the consideration of appropriate relief was necessarily subordinated to the primary question—the constitutionality of segregation in public education. We have now announced that such segregation is a denial of the equal protection of the laws. In order that we may have the full assistance of the parties in formulating decrees, the cases will be restored to the docket,° and the parties are requested to present further argument. . . .

The Attorney General of the United States is again invited to participate. The Attorneys General of the states requiring or permitting segregation in public education will also be permitted to appear . . . upon request to do so. . . .

It is so ordered.°

The Disarmament Proposals of the United States

"I propose . . . that we . . . give each other a complete blueprint of our military establishments. . . ."

On July 21, 1955, President Dwight D. Eisenhower seized an opportunity to make a bold proposal for bringing an end to the armaments race. At a Big Four "summit conference" held in Geneva, Switzerland, and attended by the heads of state of Great Britain, France, the Soviet Union, and the United States, Eisenhower proposed that the Soviet Union and the United States exchange plans of their military installations and open their skies for aerial observation. Although a spirit of cordiality prevailed throughout the conference, the Soviet Union rejected President Eisenhower's daring proposal.

° **docket:** record of cases to be tried.
° In 1955 the Court unanimously ordered the states to begin desegregation with "all deliberate speed."

July 21, 1955

Disarmament is one of the most important subjects on our agenda. It is also extremely difficult. In recent years the scientists have discovered methods of making weapons many, many times more destructive of opposing armed forces—but also of homes, and industries, and lives—than ever known or imagined before. These same scientific discoveries have made much more complex the problem of limitation and control and reduction of armament.

After our victory as allies in World War II, my country rapidly disarmed. Within a few years our disarmament was at a very low level. Then events occurred which caused us to realize that we had disarmed too much. For our own security and to safeguard peace, we needed greater strength. Therefore we proceeded to rearm and to associate with others in a partnership for peace and for mutual security.

But we know that a mutually dependable system for less armament on the part of all nations would be a better way to safeguard peace and to maintain our security.

It would ease the fears of war in the anxious hearts of people everywhere. It would lighten the burdens upon the backs of the people. It would make it possible for every nation, great and small, developed and less developed, to advance the standards of living of its people, to attain better food, and clothing, and shelter, more of education and larger enjoyment of life.

Therefore the United States government is prepared to enter into a sound and reliable agreement making possible the reduction of armament....

No sound and reliable agreement can be made unless it is completely covered by an inspection and reporting system adequate to support every portion of the agreement.

The lessons of history teach us that disarmament agreements without adequate reciprocal inspection increase the danger of war and do not brighten the prospect of peace....

We have not as yet been able to discover any scientific or other inspection method which would make certain of the elimination of nuclear weapons. So far as we are aware, no other nation has made such a discovery. Our study of this problem is continuing....

Gentlemen, since I have been working on this memorandum to present to this conference, I have been searching my heart and mind for something that I could say here that could convince everyone of the great sincerity of the United States in approaching this problem of disarmament.

I should address myself for a moment principally to the delegates from the Soviet Union, because our two great countries admittedly possess new and terrible weapons in quantities which do give rise in other parts of the world, or reciprocally, to the fear and danger of surprise attack.

I propose, therefore, that we take a practical step, that we begin an arrangement very quickly; as between ourselves—immediately. These steps would include:

To give each other a complete blueprint of our military establishments, from beginning to end, from one end of our countries to the other. . . .

Next, to provide within our countries facilities for aerial photography to the other country—we to provide you the facilities within our country, ample facilities for aerial reconnaissance, where you can make all the pictures you choose and take them to your own country to study, you to provide exactly the same facilities for us and we to make these examinations, and by this step to convince the world that we are providing as between ourselves against the possibility of great surprise attack, thus lessening danger and relaxing tension.

Likewise we will make more easily attainable a comprehensive and effective system of inspection and disarmament, because what I propose, I assure you, would be but a beginning.

Now from my statements I believe you will anticipate my suggestion. It is that we instruct our representatives . . . to give priority effort to the study of inspection and reporting. . . .

The United States is ready to proceed in the study and testing of a reliable system of inspections and reporting. And when that system is proved, then to reduce armaments with all others to the extent that the system will provide assured results.

The successful working out of such a system would do much to develop the mutual confidence which will open wide the avenues of progress for all our people.

The quest for peace is the statesman's most exacting duty. Security of the nation entrusted to his care is his greatest responsibility. Practical progress in lasting peace is his fondest hope. Yet in pursuit of his hope he must not betray the trust placed in him as guardian of the people's security. A sound peace—with security, justice, well-being, and freedom for the people of the world—can be achieved, but only by patiently and thoughtfully following a hard and sure tested road.

John F. Kennedy's Inaugural Address

"Ask not what your country can do for you—
ask what you can do for your country."

At noon on January 20, 1961, John F. Kennedy prepared to take the oath of office and become, at the age of 43, the youngest President ever elected in the nation's history. The crowd gathered in a great semicircle in front of the Capitol waited expectantly, for during the hotly contested political campaign Kennedy had promised, if elected, to lead the American people out upon a "new frontier," and soon, in his Inaugural Address, he would for the first time speak as the Chief Executive.

With the swearing-in ceremony behind him, President Kennedy, facing his audience and the batteries of television cameras, opened his speech and began to read. Before he had finished the first few sentences, everyone in his audience, those gathered on the benches before him and the millions seated before television receivers across the land, realized that they were listening to an historic address. His voice ringing with sincerity, the youthful President challenged his fellow Americans to join in "a struggle against the common enemies of man: tyranny, poverty, disease, and war itself." "The energy, the faith, the devotion which we bring to this endeavor," he declared, "will light our country and all who serve it—and the glow from that fire can truly light the world."

January 20, 1961

My Fellow Citizens:

We observe today not a victory of party but a celebration of freedom—symbolizing an end as well as a beginning—signifying renewal as well as change. For I have sworn before you and Almighty God the same solemn oath our forebears prescribed nearly a century and three-quarters ago.

The world is very different now. For man holds in his mortal hands the power to abolish all forms of human poverty and all forms of human life. And yet the same revolutionary beliefs for which our forebears fought are still at issue around the globe—the belief that the rights of man come not from the generosity of the state but from the hand of God.

We dare not forget today that we are the heirs of that first revolution. Let the word go forth from this time and place, to friend and foe alike, that the torch has been passed to a new generation of Americans—born in this century, tempered by war, disciplined by a hard and bitter peace, proud of our ancient heritage—and unwilling to witness or permit the slow undoing of those human rights to which this nation has always been committed, and to which we are committed today at home and around the world.

Let every nation know, whether it wishes us well or ill, that we shall pay any price, bear any burden, meet any hardship, support any friend, oppose any foe to assure the survival and the success of liberty.

This much we pledge—and more.

To those old allies whose cultural and spiritual origins we share, we pledge the loyalty of faithful friends. United, there is little we cannot do in a host of co-operative ventures. Divided, there is little we can do—for we dare not meet a powerful challenge at odds and split asunder.

To those new states whom we welcome to the ranks of the free, we pledge our word that one form of colonial control shall not have passed away merely to be replaced by a far more iron tyranny. We shall not always expect to find them supporting our view. But we shall always hope to find them strongly supporting their own freedom—

and to remember that, in the past, those who foolishly sought power by riding the back of the tiger ended up inside.

To those peoples in the huts and villages of half the globe struggling to break the bonds of mass misery, we pledge our best efforts to help them help themselves, for whatever period is required—not because the Communists may be doing it, not because we seek their votes, but because it is right. If a free society cannot help the many who are poor, it cannot save the few who are rich.

To our sister republics south of our border, we offer a special pledge —to convert our good words into good deeds—in a new alliance for progress—to assist free men and free governments in casting off the chains of poverty. But this peaceful revolution of hope cannot become the prey of hostile powers. Let all our neighbors know that we shall join with them to oppose aggression or subversion anywhere in the Americas. And let every other power know that this hemisphere intends to remain the master of its own house.

To that world assembly of sovereign states, the United Nations, our last best hope in an age where the instruments of war have far outpaced the instruments of peace, we renew our pledge of support—to prevent it from becoming merely a forum for invective—to strengthen its shield of the new and the weak—and to enlarge the area in which its writ may run.

Finally, to those nations who would make themselves our adversary, we offer not a pledge but a request: that both sides begin anew the quest for peace, before the dark powers of destruction unleashed by science engulf all humanity in planned or accidental self-destruction.

We dare not tempt them with weakness. For only when our arms are sufficient beyond doubt can we be certain beyond doubt that they will never be employed.

But neither can two great and powerful groups of nations take comfort from our present course—both sides overburdened by the cost of modern weapons, both rightly alarmed by the steady spread of the deadly atom, yet both racing to alter that uncertain balance of terror that stays the hand of mankind's final war.

So let us begin anew—remembering on both sides that civility is not a sign of weakness, and sincerity is always subject to proof. Let us never negotiate out of fear. But let us never fear to negotiate.

Let both sides explore what problems unite us instead of belaboring those problems which divide us.

Let both sides, for the first time, formulate serious and precise proposals for the inspection and control of arms—and bring the absolute power to destroy other nations under the absolute control of all nations.

Let both sides seek to invoke the wonders of science instead of its terrors. Together let us explore the stars, conquer the deserts, eradicate disease, tap the ocean depths, and encourage the arts and commerce.

Let both sides unite to heed in all corners of the earth the command of Isaiah—to "undo the heavy burdens ... (and) let the oppressed go free."

And if a beachhead of co-operation may push back the jungles of suspicion, let both sides join in creating a new endeavor—not a new balance of power, but a new world of law, where the strong are just and the weak secure and the peace preserved.

All this will not be finished in the first one hundred days. Nor will it be finished in the first one thousand days, nor in the life of this Administration, nor even perhaps in our lifetime on this planet. But let us begin.

In your hands, my fellow citizens, more than mine, will rest the final success or failure of our course. Since this country was founded, each generation of Americans has been summoned to give testimony to its national loyalty. The graves of young Americans who answered the call to service surround the globe.

Now the trumpet summons us again—not as a call to bear arms, though arms we need—not as a call to battle, though embattled we are—but a call to bear the burden of a long twilight struggle, year in and year out, "rejoicing in hope, patient in tribulation"—a struggle against the common enemies of man: tyranny, poverty, disease, and war itself.

Can we forge against these enemies a grand and global alliance, north and south, east and west, that can assure a more fruitful life for all mankind? Will you join in that historic effort?

In the long history of the world, only a few generations have been granted the role of defending freedom in its hour of maximum danger. I do not shrink from this responsibility—I welcome it. I do not believe that any of us would exchange places with any other people or any other generation. The energy, the faith, the devotion which we bring to this endeavor will light our country and all who serve it— and the glow from that fire can truly light the world.

And so, my fellow Americans: Ask not what your country can do for you—ask what you can do for your country.

My fellow citizens of the world: Ask not what America will do for you, but what together we can do for the freedom of man.

Finally, whether you are citizens of America or citizens of the world, ask of us here the same high standards of strength and sacrifice which we ask of you. With a good conscience our only sure reward, with history the final judge of our deeds, let us go forth to lead the land we love, asking His blessing and His help, but knowing that here on earth God's work must truly be our own.

FOR FURTHER READING

The books listed below contain additional documents related to the history of the United States. These books were designed for use by scholars and college students and therefore contain many more documents than high school students would ordinarily find useful. Interested students, however, will find these books helpful in developing special projects and exploring the background of historical events.

Biesele, Rudolph L., et al., eds., Readings in American History, 2nd ed. Boston: Houghton Mifflin, 1957. Two volumes: 371 pp. and 403 pp.

Billington, R. A., B. J. Loewenberg, and S. H. Brokunier, The Making of American Democracy, Readings and Documents. New York: Holt, Rinehart & Winston, 1950. Two volumes: 393 pp. and 547 pp.

Bishop, H. M., and S. Hendel, eds., Basic Issues of American Democracy, 3rd ed. New York: Appleton-Century-Crofts, 1956. 484 pp.

Commager, H. S., ed., Documents of American History, 6th ed. New York: Appleton-Century-Crofts, 1958. Two volumes: 450 pp. and 842 pp.

Commager, H. S., ed., Living Ideas in America. New York: Harper & Brothers, 1951. 766 pp.

Craven, Avery Odelle, et al., eds., Documentary History of the American People. Boston: Ginn & Company, 1951. 871 pp.

Curti, Merle, Willard Thorp, and Carlos Baker, American Issues: The Social Record, 2nd ed. Philadelphia: J. B. Lippincott, 1961. 1200 pp.

Cushman, R. E., Leading Constitutional Decisions, 11th ed. New York: Appleton-Century-Crofts, 1958. 453 pp.

Hacker, L. M., Shaping of the American Tradition. New York: Columbia University Press, 1947. 1247 pp.

Handlin, Oscar, ed., Readings in American Democracy. New York: Alfred A. Knopf, 1957. 715 pp.

Monaghan, Frank, Heritage of Freedom. Princeton: Princeton University Press, 1947. 150 pp. (facsimiles).

The People Shall Judge: Readings in the Formation of American Policy (edited by Social Sciences Staff, University of Chicago). Chicago: University of Chicago Press, 1949. Two volumes.

Perry, Richard L., ed., Sources of Our Liberties. New York: Associated College Presses, 1959. 456 pp.

Sheehan, Donald H., The Making of American History, 2nd ed. New York: Holt, Rinehart & Winston, 1954. Two volumes: 462 pp. and 450 pp.

Smith, Bernard, et al., eds., Democratic Spirit. New York: Alfred A. Knopf, 1941. 927 pp.

Smith, J. M., and P. L. Murphy, eds., Liberty and Justice. New York: Alfred A. Knopf, 1958. 566 pp.

INDEX

In the Index each document is listed alphabetically for easy reference. In addition, documents related to certain important principles and ideas, such as Education, Federalism, and Rights of Individuals, have been grouped chronologically under specific headings. This arrangement makes it possible for students to trace the progress of important movements in American history over short or long periods of time.